COMPUTERS
EXPLORING CONCEPTS

FLOYD FULLER

Appalachian State University

EMCParadigm

D1402739

Todd Wehr
Memorial Library

Senior Developmental Editor: Sonja M. Brown
Special Projects Coordinator: Joan D'Onofrio
Proofreader: Joy McComb
Copy Editor: Sharon O'Donnell

Senior Designer: Jennifer Wreisner
Illustrator: Colin Hayes
Photo Researchers: Desiree Faulkner, Courtney Kost
Indexer: Terri Hudoba

Publishing Team: George Provol, Publisher; Janice Johnson, Director of Product Development; Lori Landwer, Marketing Manager; Shelley Clubb, Electronic Design and Production Manager

---

DEDICATION TO SONJA BROWN

An author, whose name appears on a book's cover, typically receives credit for the work. In truth, many individuals are essential to every successful book. This work, like other successful works, represents the diligent and professional efforts and talents of many individuals. One person in particular, Sonja Brown, far exceeded those expectations.

Throughout this work—our first collaboration—it has been my good fortune to work closely with Ms. Brown, and it is she who deserves more credit than I. Her friendly and professional demeanor, attention to accuracy and detail, helpful recommendations, text revisions, and content contributions are reflected throughout this work.

For her untiring efforts in seeing this work through to completion and for her many valuable contributions, I consider it an honor to dedicate this work to her, my editor and my friend, Sonja Brown.

—*Floyd Fuller*
Author

Library of Congress Cataloging-in-Publication Data

    Fuller, Floyd.
        Computers : exploring concepts / Floyd Fuller.
           p.cm.
        Includes index.
        ISBN 0-7638-1295-1
        1. Computer science. 2. Computers. I. Title.

QA76 .F813 2002
004—dc21
                                         2001016025

Care has been taken to verify the accuracy of information presented in this book. However, the author, editor, and publisher cannot accept any responsibility for Web, e-mail, newsgroup, or chat room subject matter or content, or for consequences from application of the information in this book, and make no warranty, expressed or implied, with respect to its content.

Trademarks: Some of the product names and company names included in this book have been used for identification purposes only and may be trademarks or registered trademarks of their respective manufacturers and sellers. The author, editor, and publisher disclaim any affiliation, association, or connection with, or sponsorship or endorsement by, such owners. Copyrights are found at the end of the book on pages I–15, 16, which constitute an extension of the copyright page.

Text: ISBN 0-7638-1295-1   Order Number: 01527

© 2002 by Paradigm Publishing Inc.
    Published by **EMC**Paradigm
    875 Montreal Way
    St. Paul, MN 55102
    (800) 535-6865
    E-mail: educate@emcp.com
    Web site: www.emcp.com

All rights reserved. No part of this book may be reproduced, stored in a retrieval system, or transmitted, in any form or by any means, electronic, mechanical, photocopying, recording, or otherwise, without prior written permission of Paradigm Publishing Inc.

Printed in the United States of America   10 9 8 7 6 5 4 3 2

CONTENTS

Preface   vii

CHAPTER 1

MANAGING INFORMATION AND CHANGE IN A CONNECTED WORLD   A-1

Cyber Scenario   A-3
The Global Community of the Internet   A-4
The Internet and the World Wide Web   A-4
  Size of the Internet   A-5
  Navigating the Internet: A Survival Skill   A-7
  What Is the Internet?   A-7
  A Brief History of the Internet and the World Wide Web   A-7
  The World Wide Web within the Internet   A-9
How Information Travels over the Internet   A-10
  Ways to Use the Internet   A-11
Networks: Skeletal Framework of the Internet   A-12
Computers: Keys to the Internet   A-12
  The Role of the Computer   A-13
Computers and Computer Systems   A-14
  Computer Hardware and Software: An Overview   A-15
Categories of Computers   A-16
  Personal Computers   A-16
  Minicomputers   A-18
  Mainframe Computers   A-18
  Supercomputers   A-19
How Computers Work   A-19
  Data Representation: Bits and Bytes   A-19
  ASCII and EBCDIC Coding Schemes   A-19
  The Central Processing Unit (CPU)   A-20
Computer Storage   A-24
  Internal Storage   A-24
  Secondary (External) Storage   A-26
On the Horizon   A-28
  Computer Chips: Denser, Faster, and More Powerful   A-28
  Computers: Shrinking Size and Growing Capabilities   A-28
  Molecular Data Storage   A-28
  Embedded Computers Everywhere   A-28
  Expanding Use of Artificial Intelligence   A-28
  Faster Communication and a Shrinking Global Community   A-29
Chapter Summary   A-30
Timeline   A-30
Key Terms   A-31
Internet Tutorial: Browsing the Web Using Web Addresses   A-32
Communicating Clearly   A-36
  Technology Terms   A-36
  Techno Literacy   A-36
Connecting with Concepts   A-37
  Technology Processes   A-37

Key Principles	A-38
Mining Data	A-39
Things That Think	A-40
Predicting Next Steps	A-40
Solving Problems	A-40
Examining Ethical Issues	A-41
Answers to Technology Terms and Key Principles Questions	A-41

Special Features

Computers in Your Future?	A-5
Drivers: Tim Berners-Lee	A-6
Hot Wired: Teledesic: Internet in the Sky	A-12
E-thics: Opening the New World to Disabled Persons	A-15
Globe Trotting: Will the Internet Crack the Great Wall?	A-17
Hot Wired: Coming Soon—Organ Gardens	A-23
Globe Trotting: Uniting Africa Online	A-26
E-thics: A Tower as Lovely as a Tree	A-26
Upstarts: Girl Tech	A-27
Hot Wired: Are You My Mother?	A-29

CHAPTER 2

HARDWARE: ENABLING INFORMATION PROCESSING

HARDWARE: ENABLING INFORMATION PROCESSING	B-1
Cyber Scenario	B-3
Embedded Computers in Your Future	B-4
What Is Hardware?	B-4
Personal Computer Hardware	B-4
Types of Hardware Devices	B-4
System Unit Hardware	B-5
Motherboards	B-5
Microprocessors	B-6
RAM Chips	B-7
Cache Memory	B-8
ROM Chips	B-8
Ports	B-9
Expansion Slots	B-9
PC Cards	B-10
Buses	B-10
Input Hardware	B-10
Keyboards	B-11
Special-Function Keyboards	B-11
The Mouse and Other Point-and-Click Devices	B-13
Trackballs	B-14
Touch Pads and Touch Screens	B-14
Joysticks	B-15
Pens and Tablets	B-16
Graphics Tablets	B-16
Optical Scanners	B-16
Bar Code Readers	B-18
Audio Input	B-18
Video Input	B-19
Applications for Video Input	B-20
Digital Cameras	B-20
Output Hardware	B-22
Monitors	B-22
Printers	B-23
Plotters	B-27
Speakers	B-29
Storage Devices	B-29
Magnetic Storage Devices	B-29
Types of Magnetic Storage Media	B-29
Floppy Disks and Disk Drives	B-30
Hard Disks and Disk Drives	B-33
Optical Disks and Disk Drives	B-34
Large Computer Hardware	B-37
Storage Devices	B-37
WORM Disks	B-39
On the Horizon	B-40
Wireless, Wireless, and More Wireless	B-40
Increased Magnetic Data Storage Capacities	B-40
Improved Monitors	B-40
More Smart Cards	B-40
Biometric Authentication Devices as Security Measures	B-41
Internet Tutorial 2: Conducting a Simple Search	B-42
Chapter Summary	B-46
Timeline	B-46
Key Terms	B-47
Communicating Clearly	B-48
Technology Terms	B-48
Techno Literacy	B-48
Connecting with Concepts	B-50
Technology Processes	B-50
Key Principles	B-50
Mining Data	B-51
Things That Think	B-52
Predicting Next Steps	B-52
Solving Problems	B-53
Examining Ethical Issues	B-53
Answers to Technology Terms and Key Principles Questions	B-53

Special Features

Hot Wired: Is There a Pocket for my Cell Phone?	B-7
Globe Trotting: Reaching Mongolia	B-9
E-thics: Votes for Sale?	B-10
Drivers: Michael Dell	B-12
Hot Wired: Subzero Meteor Hunting	B-15
Drivers: Jack S. Kilby	B-24

Drivers: Steven Jobs — B-28
Computers in Your Future: The Online Job
  Search — B-39
Hot Wired: Leading by a Nose — B-41

CHAPTER 3

SOFTWARE: OPERATING SYSTEMS AND
PRODUCTIVITY APPLICATIONS — C-1

Cyber Scenario — C-3
Software for a Soft Job? — C-4
What Is Computer Software? — C-4
System Software — C-4
  Operating Systems — C-4
Software User Interfaces — C-8
  Command-Line Interfaces — C-8
  Graphical User Interfaces (GUIs) — C-9
  Features of a Graphical User Interface — C-10
  Icons That Represent Common Commands — C-13
  On-screen Desktop — C-14
  Display Windows — C-14
  Dialog Boxes — C-14
  Online Help — C-18
Commonly Used Operating Systems
  Platforms — C-19
  Windows 3.x — C-19
  Windows 95 — C-20
  Windows 98 — C-20
  Windows NT — C-22
  Windows 2000 Professional — C-23
  Windows 2000 Server — C-25
  Windows Me — C-25
  Windows CE — C-26
  Palm OS — C-26
  Macintosh Operating System (Mac OS) — C-26
  OS/2 — C-27
  UNIX — C-27
  Linux — C-28
  Java™ — C-29
Utilities and Translators — C-29
  Utility Programs — C-29
  Language Translators — C-31
Productivity (Application) Software — C-32
Categories of Productivity Software — C-33
  Word Processors — C-33
  Spreadsheets — C-37
  Database Management Software — C-38
  Presentation Graphics Software — C-42
  Communications Software — C-44
  Desktop Publishing Software — C-45
  Software Suites — C-46
  Proprietary Software vs. Freeware/Shareware — C-47
On the Horizon — C-48

Speech Recognition Software — C-48
Pattern Recognition Software — C-48
Enhanced Artificial Intelligence — C-49
Rentable Productivity Applications — C-49
Chapter Summary — C-50
Timeline — C-50
Key Terms — C-51
Internet Tutorial 3: Conducting an
  Advanced Search — C-52
Communicating Clearly — C-56
  Technology Terms — C-56
  Techno Literacy — C-56
Connecting with Concepts — C-57
  Technology Processes — C-57
  Key Principles — C-58
Mining Data — C-59
Things That Think — C-60
Predicting Next Steps — C-60
Solving Problems — C-60
Examining Ethical Issues — C-61
Answers to Technology Terms and Key
  Principles Questions — C-61

Special Features
Hot Wired: A Dog with a Byte — C-4
Drivers: Bill Gates — C-12
Hot Wired: Keep 'Em Moving — C-19
Globe Trotting: India's Silicon Valley — C-22
Drivers: Bill Atkinson — C-24
Hot Wired: Bluetooth — C-45
E-thics: Onward Cyber Soldiers — C-46
Computers in Your Future: Computer
  Security Engineer — C-47

CHAPTER 4

CONNECTIVITY: TELECOMMUNICATIONS,
NETWORKS, AND THE INTERNET — D-1

Cyber Scenario — D-3
Networking over the Net — D-4
Telecommunications: Connecting Networks
  to the Internet — D-4
Networking Components — D-4
Characteristics of Data Transmission — D-5
  Bandwidth — D-5
  Analog versus Digital Transmission — D-6
  Serial versus Parallel Transmission
Communications Media — D-8
  Wire versus Wireless Media — D-8
  Types of Wire Media — D-9
  Internet Services Digital Network (ISDN) — D-11
  T Lines — D-11
Wireless Communications Media — D-11

Microwave Systems — D-11
Satellite Systems — D-13
Cellular Technology — D-14
Infrared Technology — D-16
Network Classifications — D-16
    Networks Classified by Architecture — D-17
    Networks Classified by Coverage — D-18
    Networks Classified by Users — D-20
Network Topologies (Layouts) — D-23
    Bus Topologies — D-23
    Star Topologies — D-25
    Ring Topologies — D-25
    Hybrid Topologies — D-26
Networking and Communications Hardware — D-27
    Hubs — D-27
    Repeaters — D-27
    Routers — D-27
    Bridges — D-28
    Gateways — D-28
    Multiplexers — D-29
    Concentrators — D-20
Communications Software and Protocols — D-29
    Features of Communications Utilities — D-30
    Communications Protocols — D-30
    Protocols for Local Area Networks (LANs) — D-33
    Protocols for Wide Area Networks (WANs) — D-33
    Internet and Web Protocols — D-33
    Electronic Mail Protocols — D-34
    Wireless Application Protocols — D-34
The Internet: A Worldwide Network — D-34
    Electronic Mail (E-Mail) — D-37
    Information Retrieval — D-38
    File Transfer — D-38
    Chat Rooms — D-38
    Entertainment — D-38
    Online Shopping — D-38
    Distance Learning — D-39
    Electronic Commerce (E-Commerce) — D-40
    Electronic Bulletin Boards — D-40
    Telecommuting — D-41
Connecting to the Internet — D-41
    Types of Internet Connections — D-41
    Alternatives to the Telephone/Modem
        Connection — D-42
    Using a Browser — D-43
    Using Search Engines — D-46

Networking and Internet Concerns — D-47
    Standard Protocols and Adequate
        Bandwidths — D-47
    Privacy Issues — D-47
    Security Protections — D-47
    Copyright Infringement — D-48
    Viruses — D-49
On the Horizon — D-50
    Optical Networks: Shining Light of the
        Future — D-50
    Another Internet? — D-50
Chapter Summary — D-52
Timeline — D-52
Key Terms — D-55
Internet Tutorial 4: Creating a Web Page in
    Word — D-56
Communicating Clearly — D-60
    Technology Terms — D-60
    Techno Literacy — D-61
Connecting with Concepts — D-61
    Technology Processes — D-61
    Key Principles — D-62
Mining Data — D-63
Things That Think — D-64
Predicting Next Steps — D-64
Solving Problems — D-65
Examining Ethical Issues — D-65
Answers to Technology Terms and Key
    Principles Exercises — D-65

Special Features
Hot Wired: All Together Now — D-6
E-thics: Crossing the Digital Divide — D-9
Drivers: Larry Ellison — D-12
E-thics: The Internet Is the Water Cooler — D-13
Computers in Your Future: Webmaster — D-15
Globe Trotting: Connecting Native
    Americans — D-19
Hot Wired: Wearable PCs — D-23
Upstarts: David Versus Goliath — D-24
Computers in Your Future: Computer
    Network Technician — D-49

GLOSSARY — G-1
INDEX — I-1

PREFACE

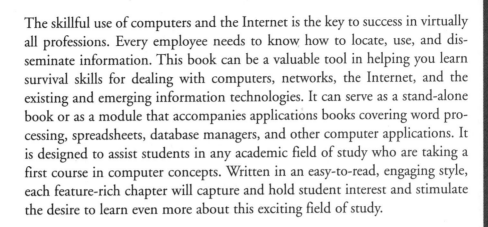

The skillful use of computers and the Internet is the key to success in virtually all professions. Every employee needs to know how to locate, use, and disseminate information. This book can be a valuable tool in helping you learn survival skills for dealing with computers, networks, the Internet, and the existing and emerging information technologies. It can serve as a stand-alone book or as a module that accompanies applications books covering word processing, spreadsheets, database managers, and other computer applications. It is designed to assist students in any academic field of study who are taking a first course in computer concepts. Written in an easy-to-read, engaging style, each feature-rich chapter will capture and hold student interest and stimulate the desire to learn even more about this exciting field of study.

Guiding Philosophy

Two important themes serve as the intellectual foundation of this book:

- *Understanding information technology is critical to productivity.*
  In today's competitive environment, businesses use computers to become more efficient, competitive, and profitable. To compete in the job market, individuals must be productive. A knowledge and understanding of computer concepts, including the functions of the Internet and Web, will help students become more productive in school and in their careers.
- *Your personal success as a student will serve both you and society.*
  Knowing how computers work and how they are used will help you get a good job. A career that supports your financial and creative needs also will contribute to the well being of the economy and the communities in which you live. This book is written in the hope that the ideas and insights gained from reading it will contribute greatly to your success.

Acknowledgments

Writing a book is a team project and I am fortunate in having had this opportunity to work with a group of dedicated, highly skilled professionals at EMC/Paradigm Publishing. From the outset of our collaboration, it was apparent that the entire staff is committed to producing state-of-the-art books of exceptional quality. Words cannot adequately express my appreciation to each individual who put forth every effort to make this book the best of its kind. I want to acknowledge some individuals whose contributions merit special recognition.

Vice President and Publisher George Provol ensured that the necessary resources were in place to create a high-quality product in every respect.

Senior Editor Sonja Brown shepherded this project from beginning to end and worked diligently on the organization and content of the chapters. As developmental editor, she proved to be a continuing inspiration and made many valuable contributions throughout the development of this work. She is a professional in every sense of the word and deserves much credit for the success of this book. Thank you, Sonja.

Director of Product Development Janice Johnson was instrumental in the planning of the text and is a well of creative ideas.

Senior Designer Jennifer Wreisner and other members of the Electronic Design and Production Department are responsible for the colorful, exciting look of the text.

Thank you also to the many other professionals who worked behind the scenes.

My family deserves recognition. To my wife, Edith, I offer a special word of thanks for her steadfast love, support, and encouragement throughout this project. To others in my family, I extend my heartfelt appreciation for their love and support.

I am indebted to those who reviewed the manuscript for this book. Many of their suggestions and recommendations were incorporated into the final manuscript. Their experience as instructors who teach introductory computer concepts courses brought a real-world perspective to the project:

Patty Anderson
Lake City Community College
Lake City, FL

David Laxton
Southern Ohio College
Cincinnati, OH

Charles N. Calvin
Computer Learning Centers
Somerville, MA

Bernard Levite
Jefferson Community College
Steubenville, OH

Dale Craig
Fullerton College
Fullerton, CA

Janet Sheppard
Collin County Community College
Plano, TX

Meredith Flynn
Bowling Green State University
Bowling Green, OH

Mary Kelly Weaver
St. Johns River Community College
Palatka, FL

Stoney Gaddy
Independence Community College
Independence, KS

James Webb
Austin Community College
Austin, TX

—Floyd Fuller

CHAPTER 1

MANAGING INFORMATION AND CHANGE IN A CONNECTED WORLD

learning objectives

- Define the Internet and distinguish between the Internet and the World Wide Web

- Explain how the Internet works and identify some popular uses of the Internet

- Define information processing and explain how a computer works

- Identify the four major computer classifications and give examples of each

- Identify the main components of a central processing unit (CPU) and their functions

- Explain how data is represented inside a computer and how it is stored

- Browse the Web using Web addresses

OUR CONNECTED WORLD

CYBER SCENARIO

It's 10:45 A.M. and Jason's flight has just taken off from St. Louis, heading for Chicago's O'Hare International Airport. After the Boeing 747 reaches its cruising altitude, the flight attendant announces that passengers are now permitted to use personal electronic devices, including their computers.

Jason reaches under his seat, retrieves his notebook computer, and plugs it into the telephone slot on the rear of the seat in front of him. With a few keystrokes, his computer is activated and he is ready to begin his business day.

His first task is to review his busy schedule. Ramona Ramirez will meet him upon his arrival at 11:50 A.M. Then, there's lunch with Mirax Corporation's purchasing agents, during which time he will present his company's marketing suggestions. His busy day will end with dinner at the Lough Bispo Restaurant on Chicago's north side.

Jason quickly accesses the Internet. He sends an e-mail message to his company letting his supervisor know he is en route to Chicago, followed by an e-mail to Mark Reminger at Teledex Company in Chicago confirming their meeting at 3 P.M. Four more messages are sent during the next few minutes to branch offices across the country.

Accessing his broker's Web site, he carefully reviews his investment portfolio. IBM is down $3.25, Dell Computer is up $2.75, Microsoft Corporation is up $2.25, and Alcoa is up $1.13. All in all, not bad! With the press of a button, a graphical summary of his portfolio appears on the screen.

Quickly accessing *USA Today's* Web site, Jason scans the latest headlines. One article grabs his attention. The article announces that his company's union has agreed to a settlement. Next, Jason accesses Acme Auto Rental's Web site and arranges for a rental car for the following day. His business tasks taken care of in 20 minutes, Jason leans back and relaxes for the rest of the flight. Shortly, he arrives at O'Hare and calls Ramona on his cell phone. She tells him she will be waiting curbside at the entrance to United Airlines.

Jason Edmiston's six or so e-mails are among the 4 billion e-mail messages sent daily throughout North America. The Web sites he accessed are part of the 17 million Web sites on the Internet in the year 2000, a stunning expansion from the 130 Web sites available in 1993. During the one hour it takes Jason to fly from St. Louis to Chicago, he has, with his notebook computer connected to the Internet, accomplished the following tasks:

- communicated with at least six different people at diverse locations
- reviewed the day's trading prices of his stock investments
- read the latest news
- arranged for a car rental in Chicago

Shortly, perhaps by the year 2002, Jason will be able to accomplish all of these tasks—and more—on a handheld device that he controls with his voice and carries in his pocket.

THE GLOBAL COMMUNITY OF THE INTERNET

Like Jason, we live in a world where the activities of our daily lives and the business of the workplace are increasingly being driven by the Internet and the information connections it makes possible. Layers of networks making up the Internet are linked together by means of telephone lines, microwave systems, satellites, and other modern systems, including wireless infrared and radio wave systems. Computers linked to networks and, in turn, networks linked to communications media provide us with access to millions of locations worldwide. With the click of a mouse, vast information resources around the globe are available almost instantly. And day by day, more people are joining the connected world in which communications and information are readily available 24/7/365—the global community of the twenty-first century.

THE INTERNET AND THE WORLD WIDE WEB

Even if you do not have regular Internet access, you likely have heard about this worldwide computer network. The development of the **Internet (the Net)** over the past two decades has proved to be among the most important, useful, and amazing developments in history. Almost daily, we hear of yet another new economic or social change brought about by the instant communication power of the Net. Individuals use it to send and receive e-mail messages, purchase products and services, play games, listen to music, and find and retrieve information. Businesses use the Net to sell products and services to the public, purchase product inventories and raw materials, recruit new employees, send required information to the government, and to maintain a competitive edge by keeping current with industry developments. The Internet, along with ever-improving computer technology, has also spawned new industries and more jobs—for example, the manufacturing of new hardware devices, including handheld computers and mobile communication devices; the production of telecommunications equipment and services; software development; and the creation of biotechnology companies.

KEY TERMS

Infrared a type of radiation similar to light with a wavelength outside the visible spectrum; used in TV remote controls and in wireless handheld computers to send data

network a group of two or more computers plus software and other devices connected by communications media

e-mail (electronic mail) a text, voice, or video message sent or received remotely, over a computer network

biotechnology the application of computer processing or technical processes to the science of living organisms

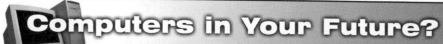

Computers in Your Future?

The Northwest Center for Emerging Technologies has identified eight career clusters for the information technology industry. Visit their careers Web page at http://www.nwcet.org/educators/careerit.htm to explore one or more of the following technical career areas:

Database development and administration	Enterprise systems analysis and integration	Programming/software engineering
Digital media	Network design and administration	Technical support
		Technical writing
		Web development and administration

SIZE OF THE INTERNET

Because of the Internet's huge size, it is difficult for industry observers to determine the exact number of Internet users here and in other countries. The best estimates, however, suggest that by early 2000, the United States had some 130 million Internet users; worldwide, the figure was more than 170 million. Figure 1-1 shows selected countries and the estimated number of online users in early 2000. Figures 1-2 and 1-3 show the projected growth in the number of Internet users by the years 2003–2004.

WWW infolinks

global Internet use:
www.internettraffic
report.com
www.mediametrix.com

FIGURE 1-1: Online Users in Selected Countries in the Year 2000

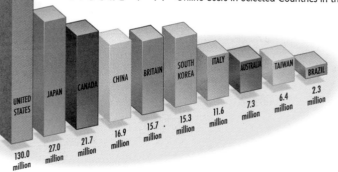

UNITED STATES 130.0 million
JAPAN 27.0 million
CANADA 21.7 million
CHINA 16.9 million
BRITAIN 15.7 million
SOUTH KOREA 15.3 million
ITALY 11.6 million
AUSTRALIA 7.3 million
TAIWAN 6.4 million
BRAZIL 2.3 million

D R I V E R S

Tim Berners-Lee, the father of the World Wide Web, gradu-
ated from Queen's College, Oxford, in 1976. While working
as an independent consultant for the Centre Européen pour la
Recherche Nucléaire (CERN) in Geneva, Switzerland, he conceived of a program for storing information based on the
associations between ideas. This program, which Berners-Lee
called Enquire, later became the basis for the World Wide
Web. In 1984, Berners-Lee began a fellowship at CERN,
where he worked on computer systems for scientific data
acquisition. While a fellow at CERN, he proposed a hypertext
system, based on his Enquire program, to be known as the

World Wide Web. This system would allow computer users around the world to
exchange information using linked hypertext documents. Berners-Lee introduced URLs,
HTTP, and HTML; wrote the first World Wide Web server-and-client software; and created
a WYSIWYG ("what you see is what you get") hypertext browser for the NeXT Step
operating system. The World Wide Web made its debut on the Internet in the summer
of 1991. Since then, the Web has grown to become one of the primary modes of communication in the contemporary world. In 1994, Berners-Lee took a staff position at
the Laboratory for Computer Science at the Massachusetts Institute of Technology,
where he works as director of the W3 Consortium, an organization that sets standards
and helps to bring coherence to global Web development.

Berners-Lee's efforts have earned him numerous awards. In 1995, he received
the Kilby Foundation's Young Innovator of the Year award and was co-recipient of
the ACM Software Systems award. He has honorary degrees from the Parsons School
of Design, New York, and Southampton University and is a Distinguished Fellow of
the British Computer Society.

Source: <http://www.w3.org/People/Berners-Lee>.

Navigating the Internet: A Survival Skill

For many individuals and businesses, an understanding of the Internet and how to use it effectively is considered a survival skill, a skill that enables a higher quality of life and makes a person more marketable in the workplace. Increasingly, employers are asking job applicants about their knowledge of the Internet because so many routine business activities are being performed using this technology. In addition, the growth of computer- and Internet-related businesses has created an unprecedented demand for highly skilled technology workers, particularly computer programmers, systems analysts, and software engineers. According to the U.S. Department of Labor, the number of systems analyst jobs added to the economy will grow by 94 percent between the years 1998 and 2008. Similarly, the number of computer engineer and computer support specialist jobs will grow by 108 percent and 102 percent, respectively. In the year 2000 alone, some 300,000 high-tech jobs remained unfilled. In response to this high demand and the lack of enough workers to fill the positions, Congress passed a bill in the fall of 2000 to increase the number of annual visas for skilled foreign workers from 115,000 to 195,000. (In 1998, a similar resolution had upped the total from 65,000 to 115,000.) The bill also continues a program to train U.S. workers for high-tech jobs and teach information technology skills to children.

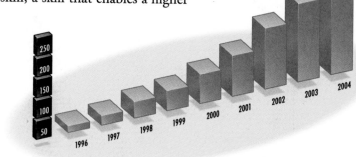

FIGURE 1-2: Projected Number (in Millions) of Internet Users in the United States

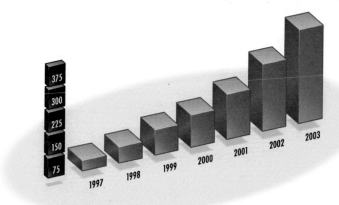

FIGURE 1-3: Projected Number (in Millions) of Internet Users Worldwide

What Is the Internet?

The Internet is a worldwide network of computer networks linked together via communications software and media, such as telephone lines, for the purpose of sharing information. Any properly equipped computer can be connected to the Internet. Your personal computer (PC), your neighbor's Macintosh, your school's mainframe computer system, and NASA's supercomputers can all be connected to the Internet at the same time. Figure 1-4 illustrates the layered structure of the Internet.

A Brief History of the Internet and the World Wide Web

Although the Internet is a fairly recent phenomenon, it did not develop overnight. Like so many other inventions, its evolution took shape from several different technologies that piggybacked on each other as scientists, government leaders, and technology wizards worked to meet large-scale communication needs.

The Internet grew out of a defense-related computer network known as **ARPANet.** The launch of the *Sputnik* satellite by the Soviet Union in 1955 set off

KEYTERMS

computer programmer
person whose profession is to write sets of coded instructions that direct a computer's operations

systems analyst
person whose profession is to study and evaluate computer operations and procedures used to accomplish specific goals

software engineer
person whose profession is to design and build computer programs

personal computer
a single-user computer capable of performing its own input, processing, output, and storage

mainframe computer
a large, powerful, expensive computer system capable of accommodating hundreds of users doing different computing tasks

supercomputer
fastest, most powerful, and most expensive type of computer designed for multiple users

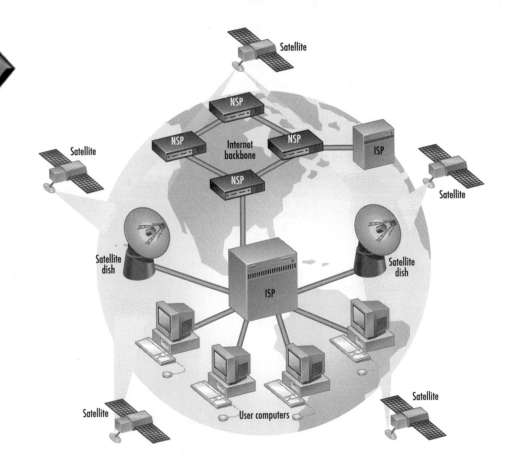

FIGURE 1-4: The Internet

The Internet is a worldwide network of networks linked together by communications media.

alarms in Western governments. Fearing that the United States was losing its scientific superiority to the Soviets, in 1957 President Dwight D. Eisenhower created the **Advanced Research Projects Agency (ARPA)** to fund and coordinate defense-related scientific research. In 1969, supercomputers at four sites—the University of California at Los Angeles (UCLA), the Stanford Research Institute, the University of California at Santa Barbara, and the University of Utah in Salt Lake City—were linked by telephone connections, and the ARPANet was born. ARPANet allowed scientists to communicate with each other and to share data files and research findings via computers. Later, the technology was adopted to create a backup communications system in case of war or natural disasters.

In 1986 the National Science Foundation developed and implemented a similar network, called the **National Science Foundation Network**, or **NSFnet**, that connected various supercomputers located throughout the United States, thereby providing users with greater computing power and expanded communications capabilities. NSFnet soon became the "backbone" of what we now know as the Internet. Although only members could use the NSFnet during its first few years, the National Science Foundation lifted the restriction on commercial use in 1991, clearing the way for public and private use. The term "internet" was coined to represent the interlinking of computer networks around the world as more and more networks were linked together. By the early 1990s, more than 100,000 computers were connected via the Internet.

THE WORLD WIDE WEB WITHIN THE INTERNET

During its early years, the Internet was difficult to use because it was slow and required some technical know-how. For this reason, Internet access was limited primarily to users in academic settings. The situation changed in 1989 when a European researcher named Tim Berners-Lee proposed the creation of a worldwide communication system based on hypertext documents. A **hypertext** document is one that contains one or more links, which contain special codes in **Hypertext Markup Language (HTML)** represented on the computer screen by highlighted or underlined text or pictures. When selected (clicked) with a mouse, a link automatically sends the user to a related, linked document called a **Web page** (see Figure 1-5). This system of organizing and coding information in HTML allowed documents on computers all over the world to be connected to one another.

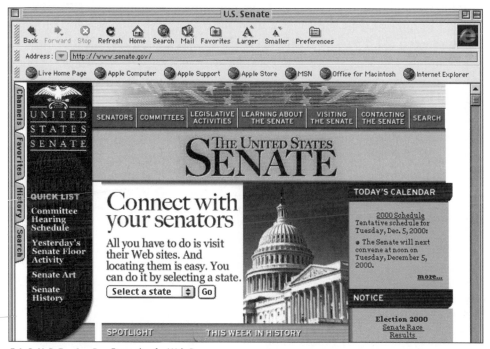

F I G U R E 1 - 5 : Example of a Web Page

A Web page is created using a special coding called Hypertext Markup Language (HTML). Clicking on the underlined words or highlighted text, called links, "jumps" the user to another linked Web page.

Additional progress toward easy universal access to the Web was realized with the development of operating systems that incorporated **graphical user interfaces (GUIs)** such as Apple Computer's Macintosh and Microsoft's Windows. As the use of Windows 3.0 and later versions spread widely, programmers designed special Internet navigation software called **browsers** to work smoothly with Windows, making moving from site to site on the Internet both fun and easy. Within a few years, Berners-Lee's vision had become a reality that he named the **World Wide Web (the Web)**. By 1995, the Internet was widely available to the public, and private individuals, businesses, organizations, and governmental units soon represented the bulk of Internet traffic. The Internet celebrated its 25th anniversary in 1996. Today, with more than 175 million users worldwide, the Web has become the fastest-growing and the most interesting and useful part of the Internet. The **virtual age** has arrived.

KEYTERMS

HTML (Hypertext Markup Language) a set of codes used to create pages for the World Wide Web; codes specify typefaces, images, and links within text

operating system a type of software that creates a user interface and supports the workings of computer devices and software programs that perform specific jobs

GUI (graphical user interface) a computer interface that enables a user to control the computer and launch commands by pointing and clicking at graphical objects such as windows, icons, and menu items

browser a software application that enables a person to access sites on the World Wide Web and that may include an e-mail or newsgroup program

virtual age a term applied to the present era in which computers and their ability to simulate reality are the dominant economic force

URL (Uniform Resource Locator)
an Internet address

HTTP (Hypertext Transfer Protocol)
the communications standard used to transfer documents on the World Wide Web

HOW INFORMATION TRAVELS OVER THE INTERNET

In concept, the transmission of information across the Internet seems like a simple, essentially linear, process. In reality, the process is actually quite complex.

To understand how information travels across the Internet, assume that you are writing a research paper on the Electoral College and need some historical data from the U.S. Senate Historian's office. Having put off the research work until the last minute, you need the information sent to you by priority mail. However, the post office and parcel delivery services no longer accept large packages for overnight delivery. To ensure that you receive the data in time to meet the report deadline, you ask the U.S. Senate Historian's researcher to divide the huge stack of printed pages into small groups (for example, five pages in each group), insert each group into an envelope, and then mail all of the envelopes at the same time, along with instructions about the order in which the groups of pages should be combined. When the pages arrive, you will quickly reassemble the data.

Information travels over the Internet in a similar way, although much faster (see Figure 1-6). An electronic data file sent from one computer to another is first broken into small parts called **packets**. Each packet includes the Internet addresses of the sender and the recipient, as well as the placement order needed to reassemble the original file at its destination. Special communications instructions called **Transmission Control Protocol/Internet Protocol (TCP/IP)** direct the travel of the packets over the Internet. The packets may take quite different paths to reach the recipient, depending on which routes are available and which are faster. However, all of this activity occurs within a few seconds. Thus, a request for information sent by

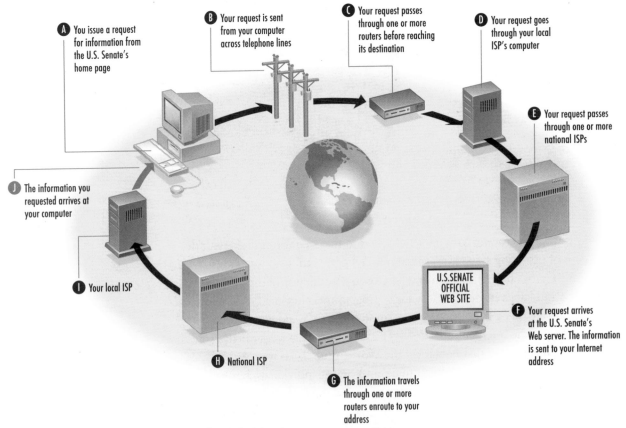

FIGURE 1-6: How Information Travels over the Internet

A file of information traveling over the Internet is broken into parts called packets and routed to its destination by the most efficient means.

electronic mail (e-mail) over the Internet to the U.S. Senate's Web site could produce your research data almost instantly versus the twenty-four hours required for an express courier service.

WAYS TO USE THE INTERNET

In addition to electronic mail for sending and receiving messages and attached files, the Internet provides users with numerous other applications, which can be grouped into these categories:

- **Information retrieval:** A vast storehouse of information is accessible over the Internet. Information retrieval is an especially important application for students and others needing to research a particular topic.
- **Online discussion:** Using a service called a chat room, a user can communicate back and forth with other users. Some chat rooms are dedicated to specific topics.
- **Entertainment:** Thousands of computer games and music pieces are available for downloading to the user's computer. A user can play an individual game or participate with other users in multi-player games.
- **Online shopping:** Thousands of retail businesses sell their products and services over the Internet. From the convenience of a home or office, a user can buy almost any product that can be found in a typical store.
- **Distance learning:** Numerous publishers and academic institutions offer electronic courses and programs over the Internet. A user can enroll in a specific course and retrieve complete course information and materials over the Internet. Grading and regular communication also are accomplished online.
- **Electronic commerce:** Thousands of businesses now use the Internet to buy and sell products and services, purchase supplies and inventories, advertise, and recruit new employees.

KEY TERMS

online connected to a network such as the Internet

chat room an online area, provided by an online service or an Internet host, where people can meet, exchange ideas and information, and interact socially

download to transmit data, such as a digitized text file, sound, or picture, from a remote site to one's own computer via a network

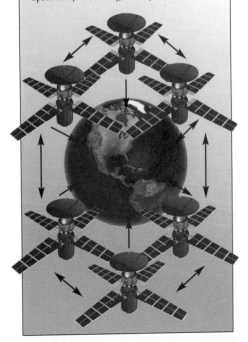

Teledesic: Internet in the Sky

An ambitious new venture called Teledesic is capturing the attention of Internet users throughout the world. Co-owned by telecommunications expert Craig McCaw and Microsoft's Bill Gates, this revolutionary telecommunications system, if successful, may alter the Internet as we now know it.

Using a constellation of several hundred low-orbiting satellites, Teledesic will create the world's first satellite network to provide affordable, worldwide, high-speed access. Low-orbiting satellites eliminate the long signal delay inherent in high-orbiting satellite communications. Users simply install small, low-power terminals and antennas, about the size of today's direct broadcast satellite (DBS) dishes.

Boeing Company will be the prime contractor for the company's network for an estimated contract value of $9 billion. Service partners in worldwide host countries will supply communications from the large urban centers to the most remote villages, with service targeted to begin in 2002.

Source: Maney, Kevin. "Power Players Join in Space Race," *USA Today,* January 26, 1999.

NETWORKS: SKELETAL FRAMEWORK OF THE INTERNET

The Internet is comprised of layers of linked networks in a structure similar to a pyramid, as shown in Figure 1-7. Beginning with the base and moving upward, each layer of the pyramid consists of a smaller group of computer sites, but each of those sites represents a greater number of users because networks are connecting groups of other networks. Note that there is no single agency or computer site in control of the entire Internet.

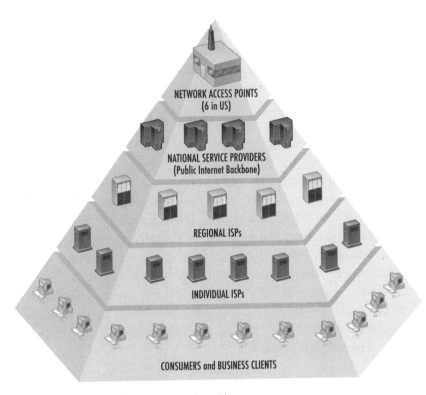

FIGURE 1-7: The Internet as a Pyramid

Think of the Internet as a layered pyramid built on a base of individual users who connect to networks, which then connect to larger and larger networks.

A **network** consists of two or more computers, devices, and software connected by means of one or more communications media, such as telephone lines (see Figure 1-8). Some networks are relatively small, consisting of only a few computers and devices. Others are large and complex, accommodating hundreds of computers and devices. Thus, a network may consist of any number of computers, terminals, and other equipment that uses software and communications media to share data, information, hardware devices, and software. It allows users convenient access to programs, data, and other information stored on another computer. It also allows users to communicate with each other.

COMPUTERS: KEYS TO THE INTERNET

The Internet is made up of networks, and networks are made up of linked computers. All network and Internet activities begin with

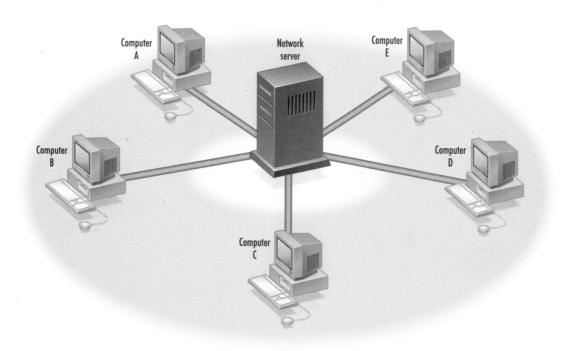

FIGURE 1-8: Structure of a Simple Network

Networks form the skeletal framework of the Internet. A network consists of two or more computers, devices, and software connected by communications media such as cables or telephone lines.

individual computers. The information that drives our economy resides and/or originates at the computer level. Without computers, neither networks nor the Internet would exist.

THE ROLE OF THE COMPUTER

Turning data into usable information is the essential job of the computer. This process is called the **information processing cycle**. The term **"data"** refers to a collection of raw, unorganized content in the form of words, numbers, sounds, or images. **Information** is data that is organized to be meaningful and potentially useful. Information processed by a computer can take a variety of forms:

- written, or textual form, as in research reports and letters
- numerical form, as in a spreadsheet analysis of a company's finances
- verbal or audio form, as in recorded voice and music
- visual form, such as photos, drawings, and videos

Steps in the Information Processing Cycle

Data entered into a computer is called **input**, which is the first step of the information processing cycle. Once entered through an input device such as a keyboard or mouse, the data is manipulated, or processed, according to a set of instructions called a **program**. Processing occurs in the electrical circuits of the microprocessor chip and results in the creation of information called **output** that can either be sent to an output device, such as a printer, or kept for future use on **storage** media. Figure 1-9 illustrates the steps in the information processing cycle.

technology news:
www.businessweek.com
/technology

spreadsheet an application program used primarily for financial analyses and record keeping, resembling on the screen the paper with rows and columns used by accountants

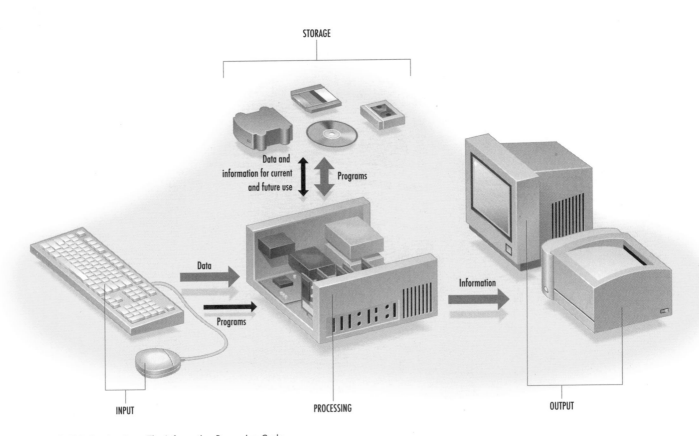

STORAGE

Data and information for current and future use

Programs

Data

Programs

Information

INPUT

PROCESSING

OUTPUT

FIGURE 1-9: The Information Processing Cycle

During an information processing cycle, data is entered into a computer, processed, output, and stored (if required for future use).

COMPUTERS AND COMPUTER SYSTEMS

In some ways any counting device, such as an electronic calculator, may be called a computer in that it "computes." But today, the term **"computer"** commonly refers to an electronic device that accepts input (programs and data), processes data into information, stores programs and information, and delivers output (information) to the user.

Technically, the term "computer" identifies only the system unit, the part of a computer system that processes data into information. A personal computer system, however, includes the computer itself along with input devices, output devices, and storage devices. For example, a buyer shopping for a new computer would expect to purchase an entire system, including a keyboard, mouse, monitor, storage devices, and perhaps a printer. The number and kinds of devices included are a matter of individual need or preference. A buyer wanting to use the Internet would need a **modem**. Figure 1-10 shows the components of a typical personal computer system.

KEYTERMS

modem a hardware device that translates signals from digital to analog and from analog to digital, making it possible for digital computers to communicate over analog telephone lines

FIGURE 1-10: A Typical Personal Computer System

A personal computer system includes a system unit, one or more input devices, one or more output devices, and one or more storage devices.

COMPUTER HARDWARE AND SOFTWARE: AN OVERVIEW

A computer system consists of two broad categories of components—hardware and software. **Hardware** includes all of the physical components that comprise the system unit and other devices connected to it, such as a keyboard or monitor. Collectively, these connected devices are referred to as **peripheral devices** because they are outside of, or peripheral to, the system unit. Nevertheless, peripheral devices are essential components of a computer system.

Software consists of programs containing instructions that direct the operation of the computer system. Two main classifications of software are system software and application software.

System software tells the computer how to operate itself. Two types of system software are the operating system and utility programs. The **operating system** is the most important piece of software in a personal computer system. It contains instructions for starting the computer and coordinates the activities of all hardware devices. **Utility software** consists of programs that perform administrative tasks, such as managing disk drives and printers and checking for computer viruses.

Application software consists of programs that perform specific tasks, such as word processing and spreadsheet preparation. More than 20,000 commercially prepared application programs are available for purchase. With these programs, people can manage personal and age personal and

business activities, create and produce impressive graphics, prepare and submit tax documents, access and use the Internet, and more.

KEYTERMS

disk drive a storage device that houses a secondary storage medium such as a floppy or hard disk

computer virus a bit of programming code, created as a prank or as a malicious action, that secretly affects other programs and causes unintended consequences

graphics still or moving images, including photos, illustrations, and symbols

ethics

Opening the New World to Disabled Persons

Five percent of all Americans have some sort of disability, a number that is sure to grow as our population ages. The Americans with Disabilities Act was passed in 1990 to ensure the accessibility of the physical world to all people. Now that law is being used to knock down the barriers to the new frontier of the Internet. When the National Federation of the Blind sued America Online in 1999 because its software was not compatible with screen readers, the Justice Department reached the decision that because they are "public accommodations," Web sites must offer access. A separate law has determined that all federal sites created after August 2000 must be accessible.

Making the Internet accessible to disabled persons does not necessarily have to be costly. New authoring tools are being designed that would automatically create accessible pages. In addition, technology is moving in the direction of mobile use. The same technology that provides large print for Palm Pilots, or Internet access over the telephone, can be used to make Web sites more navigable for persons who are deaf and blind.

Source: Heim, Judy. "Locking Out the Disabled," *PC World,* September 2000.

CATEGORIES OF COMPUTERS

Computers are typically categorized according to differences in size, speed, processing capabilities, and price. Four main categories are **personal computers, minicomputers, mainframe computers,** and **supercomputers** (see Table 1-1). However, rapidly changing technology often blurs the distinction between categories. For example, technological improvements to personal computers may soon render them as fast and powerful as today's minicomputers.

	SIZE	INSTRUCTIONS EXECUTED PER SECOND	NUMBER OF ACCOMMODATED USERS	APPROX PRICE RANGE
PERSONAL COMPUTER	Fits in hand or on desktop	500 million or more	A single user, or a part of a network	A few hundred to thousands of dollars
MINICOMPUTER	About the size of a 4-drawer file cabinet	Millions of instructions	Hundreds of users concurrently	Up to thousands of dollars
MAINFRAME COMPUTER	With needed equipment, occupies a full or partial room	Millions of instructions	Hundreds of users concurrently	Up to millions of dollars
SUPERCOMPUTER	With equipment, occupies a full room	Billions of instructions	Thousands of users concurrently	Several million dollars

TABLE 1-1: Categories of Computers

Computers are often categorized on the basis of processing speed and cost.

PERSONAL COMPUTERS

A **personal computer** is a self-contained computer capable of performing its own input, processing, output, and storage. A personal computer must have at least one input device, one storage device, one output device, a **processor**, and **memory.** The processor (also called **microprocessor**) is contained on a single **chip,** or thin piece of silicon containing electrical circuitry, and serves as the computer's central processing unit.

PCs and Apple Macintosh computers are the most popular personal computer types. These two types use different processors and different operating systems. Almost all PCs use the Windows operating system and the Apple Macintosh computers use the Macintosh operating system. Although both types use different processors and operating systems, both types are referred to as PCs.

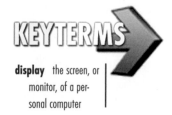

KEYTERMS

display the screen, or monitor, of a personal computer

Two major groups of PCs are desktop computers and portable computers. A **desktop computer** is a PC designed to allow the system unit, input devices, output devices, and other connected devices to fit on top of, or under, a user's desk or table, as shown in Figure 1-11.

A **portable computer** is a personal computer that is small enough to be carried around by the user. Laptop computers and handheld computers are specially designed portable computers. A **laptop computer**, also called **notebook computer**, can fit comfortably on one's lap (see Figure 1-12).

FIGURE 1-11:
Desktop Computer

A desktop, as the name suggests, is a personal computer designed to fit on top of the user's work area, although if the system unit is a tower type, many people place that component on the floor.

FIGURE 1-12: Laptop Computer

A laptop, or notebook, computer is a portable computer designed for mobile users, people who frequently move about in their work.

Even smaller personal computers called **handhelds** and **palmtops** can fit into one's hand (see Figure 1-13). One problem with computers of this size is that their displays and keyboards are quite small. Instead of having disk drives, several kinds of handheld computers contain chips in which both programs and data are stored.

Handheld computers are popular among business travelers. Once back in the office, the user can connect her handheld computer to a larger computer, such as a company's central mainframe, for exchanging information. In recent years a type of handheld computer called a **personal digital assistant (PDA)** has become widely used. With a

FIGURE 1-13: Handheld Computer

A handheld computer is small enough to fit in the palm of a user's hand.

GLOBE TROTTING

Will the Internet Crack the Great Wall?

The People's Republic of China has always counted on its ability to control information as a means of controlling its people. Yet, the Chinese government's ability to censor information is rapidly being challenged by the exploding use of the Internet. The number of Chinese using the Internet quadrupled from 2.1 million in 1998 to almost 9 million a year later. With one billion people and counting, a virtual stampede toward Internet use is well under way.

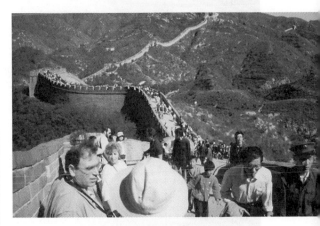

How is the Chinese government trying to stem the free flow of information via the Web? By imposing rigid regulations and blocking unauthorized sites. Chinese Internet sites are allowed to use only government-controlled news sources. What's more, Internet sites, chat rooms, e-mail messages, and news groups are forbidden from discussing anything that is not "government approved." The government has even gone so far as to block the Web sites of many top international news organizations, such as the BBC and The New York Times.

Nonetheless, the task of controlling the more than 2,400 Internet sites that are now operating in China has become an almost insurmountable hurdle for the government. It simply can't keep up with blocking smaller news sites and other sources of information. As a result, in the same way that television played a role in bringing down the Berlin Wall, the technology of the Internet may start chipping away at the ability of the Great Wall to insulate China from the influences of the outside world.

Source: "Chinese Internet use explodes," *Windows User News,* August 2000.

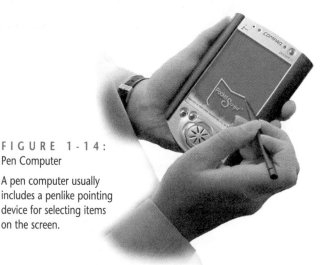

FIGURE 1-14:
Pen Computer

A pen computer usually includes a penlike pointing device for selecting items on the screen.

PDA, a user can perform calculations, keep track of schedules and appointments, and write memos. Some use wireless transmitting technology (in the form of radio waves) that provides Internet access from almost any physical location.

Because of their small keyboards and displays, many models of PDAs use a pen or stylus for inputting data. Thus, they are called **pen computers** (see Figure 1-14). Pen computers use a special kind of software that allows the computers to recognize human handwriting. Utility meter readers, package delivery persons, and other workers who need to continually move about on their jobs use pen computers.

KEYTERMS

digital representing information using ones and zeros

stylus a sharp, pointed instrument used for writing or marking

monitor the screen, or display, on which computer output appears

server a computer and its associated storage devices that are accessed remotely over a network by users

MINICOMPUTERS

A **minicomputer** is a large and powerful computer capable of accommodating hundreds of users at the same time. Users can access a minicomputer through a terminal or a personal computer. A **terminal** contains only a monitor and keyboard, but no processing capability of its own. Because it has no processing power and must rely on the processing power of a minicomputer, this terminal is often referred to as a **dumb terminal**. Minicomputers, such as the one shown in Figure 1-15, are widely used for scientific, engineering, and research applications. A minicomputer can also function as a server in a network environment.

FIGURE 1-15:
Minicomputer

A minicomputer can accommodate multiple users and often functions as a network server.

MAINFRAME COMPUTERS

Larger, more powerful, and more expensive than minicomputers, a **mainframe computer** (see Figure 1-16) is capable of accommodating hundreds of users doing different computing tasks. A mainframe's internal storage can handle hundreds of millions of characters. Mainframe applications are often large and complex. These computers are useful for dealing with large, ever-changing collections of data that can be accessed by many users simultaneously. Like minicomputers, a mainframe computer can also function as a network server. Government agencies, banks, universities, and insurance companies use mainframes to handle millions of transactions each day.

FIGURE 1-16: Mainframe Computer

A mainframe computer is a large and expensive computer system that can accommodate multiple users at the same time. Mainframes and minicomputers are differentiated by their processing capabilities.

SUPERCOMPUTERS

Supercomputers are the Goliaths of the computer industry. A **supercomputer** (see Figure 1-17) is the fastest, most powerful, and most expensive of all computers. Many are so powerful they are capable of performing trillions of calculations in a single second. By comparison, it would take a person two million years to perform the same number of calculations using a handheld calculator.

A particular supercomputer may contain hundreds of separate microprocessors and provide enough disk storage capacity for hundreds of terabytes of data. (One **terabyte** is the equivalent of one trillion alphabet letters, numbers, or special characters.) Primary applications include weather forecasting, comparing DNA sequences, creating artificially intelligent robots, and managing air and telecommunications traffic.

HOW COMPUTERS WORK

All computers are **electronic devices**, which means they operate on electricity, and their programs and data are in electronic form. Computer components contain electronic circuitry that allows electrical currents to move about very quickly inside the computer and between components.

DATA REPRESENTATION: BITS AND BYTES

To fully understand how a computer works and processes data, you need to know how data is represented inside the computer. In a computer, all information is represented by numbers. The first large computers made use of the decimal number system in which numbers are indicated by the symbols 0 through 9. Soon, however, engineers hit upon a much simpler system that used **binary** numbers ("bi" means two), which are constructed solely of the symbols 0 and 1. The beauty of binary numbers was that they could be represented by simple electrical switches that were either off (0) or on (1). Since electricity has only two states, "off" or "on," the binary number system for representing data was an ideal design. To picture the concept, consider an electric light switch. Flipping the switch to one position turns the light "on," while flipping the switch to the opposite position turns the light "off" (see Figure 1-18).

ASCII AND EBCDIC CODING SCHEMES

Each of these "0" and "1" digits is called a **bit** (an abbreviation for **bi**nary digi**t**), which represents the

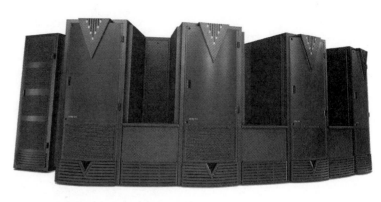

FIGURE 1-17: Supercomputer

Supercomputers are the world's fastest, most powerful, and most expensive computers, capable of processing huge amounts of data quickly and accommodating thousands of users at the same time.

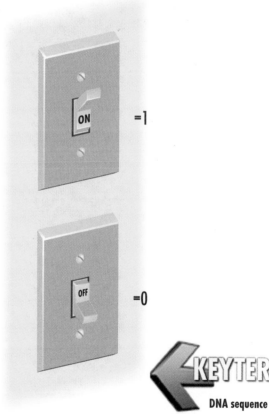

FIGURE 1-18:
Binary Number System as "Off" and "On" States

In the binary number system, a zero (0) represents an "off" state in which there is no electronic charge, and a one (1) represents an "on" state in which there is an electronic charge. This condition is similar to what happens when an electrical switch is turned on, causing current to flow.

KEYTERMS

DNA sequence
an arrangement of DNA (deoxyribonucleic acid) molecules that make up the human cell

artificial intelligence
the science of using computers to simulate intelligent mental activities or physical behaviors such as problem solving, learning, and natural language processing

ASCII AND EBCDIC CODING SCHEMES

SYMBOL	ASCII	EBCDIC
0	01100000	11110000
1	01100001	11110001
2	01100010	11110010
3	01100011	11110011
4	01100100	11110100
5	01100101	11110101
6	01100110	11110110
7	01100111	11110111
8	01101000	11111000
9	01101001	11111001
A	01000001	11000001
B	01000010	11000010
C	01000011	11000011
D	01000100	11000100
E	01000101	11000101
F	01000110	11000110
G	01000111	11000111
H	01001000	11001000
I	01001001	11001001
J	01001010	11010001
K	01001011	11010010
L	01001100	11010011
M	01001101	11010100
N	01001110	11010101
O	01001111	11010110
P	01010000	11010111
Q	01010001	11011000
R	01010010	11011001
S	01010011	11100010
T	01010100	11100011
U	01010101	11100100
V	01010110	11100101
W	01010111	11100110
X	01011000	11100111
Y	01011001	11101000
Z	01011010	11101001
!	00100001	01011010
"	00100010	01111111
#	00100011	01111011
$	00100100	01011011
%	00100101	01101100
&	00100110	01010000
(	00101000	01001101
)	00101001	01011101
*	00101010	01011100
+	00101011	01001110

FIGURE 1-19: ASCII and EBCDIC Coding Schemes

ASCII is a coding scheme used on many computers, including personal computers. The EBCDIC coding scheme is used mainly on large computers such as IBM mainframe computers.

smallest unit of data in the **binary system.** By itself, a bit is not very meaningful. However, a group of eight bits, called a **byte**, is meaningful because, in a byte, there are enough possible combinations of 0's and 1's to represent 256 (2^8) separate characters, including letters of the alphabet, numbers, and special symbols (such as dollar signs, question marks, and pound signs).

The specific combinations of 0's and 1's that are used to represent alphabet letters, numbers, and special characters are determined by the particular coding scheme being used by the computer. Two widely used coding schemes are the **ASCII** (**A**merican **S**tandard **C**ode for **I**nformation **I**nterchange) and **EBCDIC** (**E**xtended **B**inary **C**oded **D**ecimal **I**nterchange **C**ode) schemes. The ASCII scheme is used on many personal computers and minicomputers. The EBCDIC scheme is used mainly on mainframe computers. Figure 1-19 illustrates these two coding schemes and the combinations that represent specific characters.

Coding schemes such as ASCII and EBCDIC make it possible for a user to interact with a computer. For example, pressing a specific key on a keyboard, such as the letter "J," generates an electronic signal. The generated signal is converted into a binary form (a byte) and is stored in memory. The computer then processes the signal and quickly displays an image (in this case, a "J") on the monitor screen, as shown in Figure 1-20.

THE CENTRAL PROCESSING UNIT (CPU)

The computer component containing the electrical circuits where data processing occurs is called the **central processing unit (CPU),** as illustrated in Figure 1-21. Often referred to as the *brains* of a computer system, the CPU has five main functions:

- receives input
- interprets instructions provided by programs
- processes data
- directs other components of the system to act
- controls output

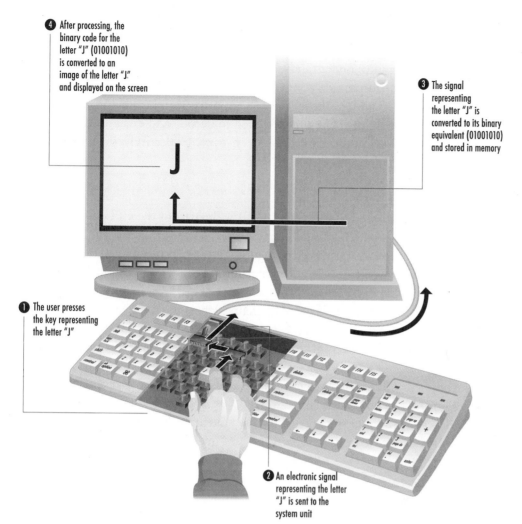

4 After processing, the binary code for the letter "J" (01001010) is converted to an image of the letter "J" and displayed on the screen

3 The signal representing the letter "J" is converted to its binary equivalent (01001010) and stored in memory

1 The user presses the key representing the letter "J"

2 An electronic signal representing the letter "J" is sent to the system unit

FIGURE 1-20: Keyboard Entry Processed and Output on Computer Monitor

Pressing a specific key generates an electronic signal that is converted into a binary form (a byte) and is stored in memory. The computer then processes the signal and quickly displays the character on the screen.

The work of the CPU is performed by four subcomponents:

- control unit
- arithmetic/logic unit
- registers
- system clock

Control Unit

The **control unit** directs and coordinates the overall operation of the computer system. It acts as a traffic officer, signaling to other parts of the computer system what they are to do. It interprets each instruction in a program, and then initiates the action needed to carry out the instruction. For each instruction, the control unit performs four basic operations. These operations, collectively called a **machine cycle**, include *fetching* an instruction, *decoding* the instruction, *executing* the instruction, and *storing* the result (see Figure 1-22).

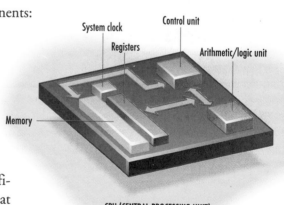

System clock   Registers   Control unit   Arithmetic/logic unit   Memory

CPU (CENTRAL PROCESSING UNIT)

FIGURE 1-21: Central Processing Unit (CPU)

Every computer contains a central processing unit (CPU) that processes data into information. In a small computer, such as a personal computer, the CPU is housed on a single small chip, the microprocessor chip.

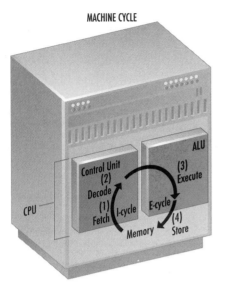

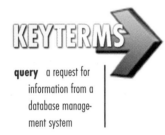

Fetching means retrieving an instruction or data from memory. **Decoding** means interpreting or translating the instruction into a form the computer understands. **Executing** means carrying out the instruction. **Storing** means writing or recording the result to memory.

The time required to fetch an instruction is called **instruction time**, or **I-time**. The time required to decode and execute an instruction is called **execution time**, or **E-time**. Collectively, these two times make up a machine cycle.

Arithmetic/Logic Unit

The **arithmetic/logic unit (ALU)** is the part of the CPU that carries out the instructions and performs the actual arithmetic and logical operations on the data (see Figure 1-23). Arithmetic operations the ALU can perform are addition, subtraction, multiplication, and division. The ALU can also compare data items with each other. For example, the ALU can determine if one data item, such as the number of hours an employee has worked, is less than, equal to, or exceeds the number of hours in a standard 40-hour workweek. If the number of hours worked is less than or equal to 40, the employee's pay is calculated using a particular formula. If the hours worked exceeds 40, a different formula is used for calculating overtime pay. Logical operations use specific operators such as AND, OR, and NOT. These operators can be used in statements that are true or false, depending on the truth or falsehood of their constituent parts. Logical operators are also used to query databases and to search the Internet. For example, if you are searching for information about brown bears, you can limit your search specifically to brown bears by typing "brown bears NOT black bears" in the search box.

Registers

To speed up processing, the ALU uses temporary storage locations, called **registers** (see Figure 1-23), to hold instructions and data. Registers are accessed much faster than memory locations outside the CPU. Various kinds of registers are used, each serving a specific purpose. Once processing begins, **instruction registers** hold

FIGURE 1-22:
Machine Cycle

A machine cycle includes four steps for reading and carrying out an instruction: fetching, decoding, executing, and storing.

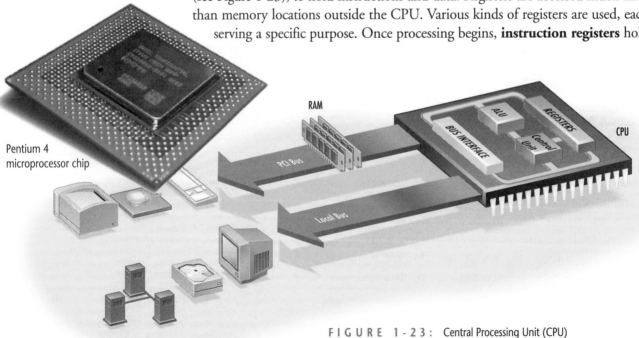

Pentium 4 microprocessor chip

FIGURE 1-23: Central Processing Unit (CPU)
The control unit, ALU, and registers carry out the work of the CPU.

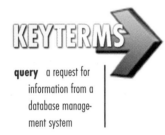

query a request for information from a database management system

instructions currently being executed. **Data registers** hold the data items being acted upon. **Storage registers** hold the intermediate and final results of processing.

System Clock

A computer contains a **system clock** in the form of a small electronic chip that synchronizes or controls the timing of all computer operations. The clock generates evenly spaced electrical pulses that synchronize the flow of information through the computer's internal communication channels.

Instructions are executed or "triggered" by pulses of the clock. Since an instruction may direct the execution of other events either internal or external to the CPU, the clock pulse provides a way for these events to occur in harmony. Pulse speed is measured according to the number of clock pulses, called **hertz**, per second. One hertz is equal to one pulse per second.

One **clock cycle** is equal to two ticks of the clock. Speeds of most modern computers are rated in **megahertz** (one million hertz) or **gigahertz** (one billion hertz). A CPU uses a fixed number of clock cycles to execute each instruction. The faster the clock ticks, the faster the CPU can execute instructions. Personal computers today operate at clock speeds of hundreds of megahertz, and some operate faster than one gigahertz. The speed of the clock affects only the speed of the CPU. It has no effect on the operation of peripheral devices, such as a printer. The faster the clock cycle, the faster a CPU processes information. Table 1-2 compares the processing speed of several microprocessors.

Coming Soon – Organ Gardens

A critical shortage of organ donors in the United States is one more source of anxiety for patients waiting for a transplant. If organs could magically grow on trees, the medical community wouldn't be so dependent upon recruiting donors. Now, tissue engineers at the Draper Laboratory in Cambridge, Massachusetts, are working to make an organ-growing laboratory a viable alternative.

Although cells of complex organs have been successfully grown in the lab, until now science has been unable to provide the circulatory system to support that organ's growth. An organ needs the network of capillaries, arteries, and veins to deliver nutrients vital for growth and to remove wastes.

The team at the Draper Lab uses photolithography to etch a tiny mosaic of blood vessels onto a 4-inch-wide silicon wafer. The chip is then implanted with lung cells from a rat. As the cells grow, they coat the etching, eventually forming the plumbing that could support an organ. The master plan is to develop a biodegradable chip that could be implanted into a patient. As the chip biodegrades, it would leave behind a network of new tissue that could grow into a functioning organ. The researchers at the Draper Lab hope to generate a complete liver within a decade. Their success could mean a new lease on life for many awaiting a new organ.

Source: Alexander, Brian. "The Organ Chip," *Wired,* August 2000.

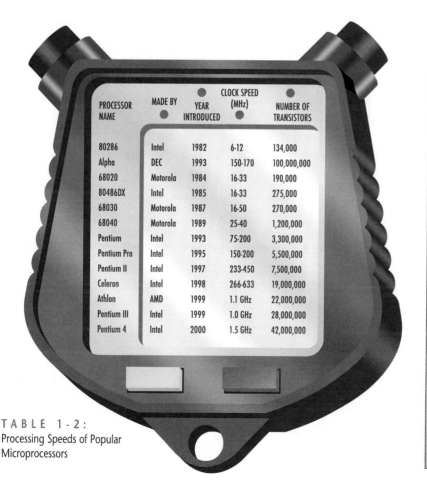

PROCESSOR NAME	MADE BY	YEAR INTRODUCED	CLOCK SPEED (MHz)	NUMBER OF TRANSISTORS
80286	Intel	1982	6-12	134,000
Alpha	DEC	1993	150-170	100,000,000
68020	Motorola	1984	16-33	190,000
80486DX	Intel	1985	16-33	275,000
68030	Motorola	1987	16-50	270,000
68040	Motorola	1989	25-40	1,200,000
Pentium	Intel	1993	75-200	3,300,000
Pentium Pro	Intel	1995	150-200	5,500,000
Pentium II	Intel	1997	233-450	7,500,000
Celeron	Intel	1998	266-633	19,000,000
Athlon	AMD	1999	1.1 GHz	22,000,000
Pentium III	Intel	1999	1.0 GHz	28,000,000
Pentium 4	Intel	2000	1.5 GHz	42,000,000

TABLE 1-2:
Processing Speeds of Popular Microprocessors

COMPUTER STORAGE

All computers have the capability for storing programs, data, and information, both internally and externally. Special components inside the CPU case store programs and data internally so that program instructions can be read and executed and data processed. Storage is also classified as temporary or permanent. Some storage chips allow programs and data to be stored temporarily while the programs are being executed and the data processed. Other internal chips allow for permanent storage of instructions that manage a computer's components, devices, and operations.

External peripheral devices, called **secondary storage**, allow programs, data, and information to be stored permanently, so they can be used again and again. Examples of permanent storage devices include **hard disk drives** and **floppy disk drives**. These devices use media, such as hard disks and floppy disks, on which programs, data, and information are permanently recorded.

INTERNAL STORAGE

Computers contain various types of internal storage components, called **memory**. Two types of memory typically found in personal computers are read-only memory (ROM) and random access memory (RAM) (see Figure 1-24). Random access memory is also referred to as **main memory**, or just memory.

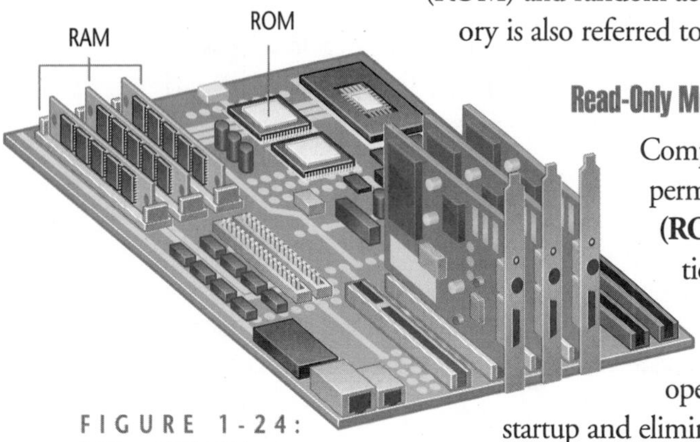

Read-Only Memory (ROM)

Computers contain memory chips on which special instructions are permanently stored. These chips are called **read-only memory (ROM)** chips because the computer can read predefined instructions from the chips, but cannot store (write) instructions on them. ROM is **nonvolatile** memory. If power is interrupted, the content of ROM is not lost. In some computers, the operating system is stored on ROM chips to facilitate faster startup and eliminate the need to load the system from floppy disk or hard disk every time the computer is started.

A computer may have several ROM chips containing permanent instructions that direct the operations of peripheral devices, including the keyboard, monitor, and disk drives. Without these ROM chips, a user would need to enter complex instructions each time the devices are used.

Random-Access Memory (RAM)

Random-access memory (RAM) is the temporary, or **volatile**, memory in which programs and data are stored while the computer is in use. Before programs are executed or data is processed, they must first be entered, or input, into RAM. The CPU then moves information from RAM into its registers for processing. RAM performs the following functions:

- accepts and holds program instructions and data
- acts as the CPU's source for data and instructions and as a destination for operation results
- holds the final processed information until it can be sent to the desired output or storage devices, such as a printer or disk drive

RAM   ROM

FIGURE 1-24:
RAM and ROM Chips

ROM chips contain permanent instructions for managing peripheral devices such as a keyboard. RAM chips temporarily store programs and data during the processing stage of the information processing cycle.

Once programs and data are stored in RAM, the CPU must be able to find them. Program instructions and data reside in memory locations known as **addresses**. Each location has its own unique address, just as each person is given a single mailbox at a post office (see Figure 1-25). When the CPU needs an instruction or data from RAM, an electronic message is sent to the instruction's address and the instruction is transferred to the appropriate register in the CPU.

Random access means that because each RAM location has an individual address, the computer can go directly to the instructions and data it wants, using that address, rather than searching each individual location one after another (sequentially). RAM memory is both **readable** and **writable,** meaning that the contents of any RAM location can be changed and/or read at any time.

RAM memory is also **volatile,** meaning that it requires a constant charge to keep its contents intact. If a computer loses power, the contents of its memory are lost. Therefore, it is important to frequently save any valuable work to secondary disk storage.

The temporary nature of RAM is its most important characteristic. When the computer is finished with one set of instructions and data, it can store another set in the first set's place. RAM works similarly to a chalkboard, chalk, and eraser. You can write any instructions and data on the chalkboard, and then erase and write new instructions and data in the same space. Like a chalkboard, RAM can be used over and over again.

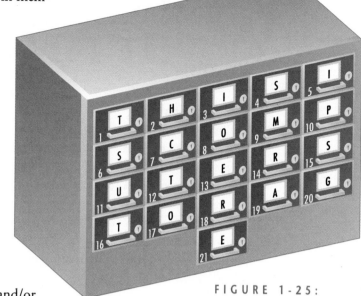

FIGURE 1-25:
Addresses for Program Instructions and Data

Each memory location has its own unique address, just as each person is given a single mailbox at a post office. When the CPU needs an instruction or data from memory, an electronic message is sent to the appropriate address and the instruction or data is transferred to the appropriate register in the CPU.

Measuring RAM Storage Capacities

RAM storage capacities are measured in bytes. One **byte** is one alphabet letter, a number, or a special character. Since most personal computers have enough memory to store thousands or millions of bytes, it is common to refer to storage capacity in terms of **kilobytes** (one thousand bytes), **megabytes** (one million bytes), and even **gigabytes** (one billion bytes). Storage capacities of personal computers are typically quoted as 32 megabytes, 64 megabytes, or 128 megabytes. By contrast, today's mainframe computer storage is often measured in **terabytes,** or trillions of bytes. (The prefix *tera-* is derived from the Greek word for monster or freak.) Table 1-3 displays the various measurements of storage.

ABBREVIATION	UNIT OF STORAGE	EQUIVALENT AMOUNT
Bit	Binary storage	Takes value of 0 or 1
Byte	8 Bits	1 byte usually represents one keystroke
K	Kilobyte	1,024 bytes or 2^{10}
MB	Megabyte	1,024,000 bytes or about one million bytes
GB	Gigabyte	1,024,000,000 bytes or about 1,000 MB
TB	Terabyte	1,024,000,000,000 bytes or about one million MB

TABLE 1-3: Measures of Data Storage

SECONDARY (EXTERNAL) STORAGE

Secondary storage devices and media provide for the permanent storage of programs, data, and information. Recall from the earlier discussion of RAM that information stored in RAM is lost when the computer is turned off. Reentering a program, data, or information each time a computer is used would waste considerable time. Programs and data stored on a secondary storage medium can be loaded into a computer much faster. Popular types of secondary storage include the floppy disk, hard disk, Zip disk, and a variety of optical disks, including CD-ROM, CD-R, CD-RW, and CD-DVD, all of which are discussed in Chapter 2.

Computers and the Internet, including the World Wide Web, are unquestionably among the most important technological developments in history. Cell phones, wireless personal digital assistants, and the use of the Internet for communications of all kinds are becoming almost commonplace. But what about the future? Where is computing technology heading? Futurists and computer experts may not agree on specific predictions, but their thoughts tend to converge in the area of technology trends, or directions, we can expect to occur in the first decade of the twenty-first century, as discussed in the next section.

Uniting Africa Online

There are fewer phone lines on the entire African continent than there are in Manhattan alone, but the growth in data traffic between Africa and the rest of the world is growing exponentially. Africa desperately needs a communication system that it can count on to give it access to the e-mail, e-commerce, and e-business that are fueling the world's economic boom. Africa has high hopes for Africa ONE, a project to bring all African nations together and link them into one network.

The system will use 32,000 kilometers of undersea fiber-optic cable to link Africa to 25 countries and 200 cities globally by 2002. Global Crossing will manage the cable and Lucent Technologies will provide the equipment software, but Africa ONE will be privately owned and operated. Africa ONE has the support of African and international carriers as well as African regional organizations.

Backers of Africa ONE hope that the reliability and security offered by the proposed new network will provide Africa with something it has never had before—dependable global communication.

Sources: "Africa jumps into ebiz race with undersea cable and proposed links to 200 world cities," *Ebiz Chronicle*, February 2, 2000. October 2000 <http://www.ebizchronicle.com>; "Africa.com, Continental Shift," *Wired*, July 2000.

A Tower as Lovely as a Tree

Progress often comes at a cost. The technological developments that have dramatically changed and improved our world have also cluttered it with an endless number of electrical lines, wires, cables, towers, and poles. More than 100,000 cell phone sites are scattered across the country, and an endless number of radio receivers are springing up on top of roofs, street lamps, and traffic lights. Obtrusive and unsightly, they can also cause property values to fall. As the demand for wireless data and voice transmissions grows, this techno-blight could reach epic proportions.

A groundswell is forming to combat these technological eyesores, in the same way litter and billboards were battled in decades past. People are forming citizen groups and lobbying their local governments to regulate the location of telecommunications equipment. Lawsuits have been filed. City planners are belatedly working with utility and media companies to come up with solutions to appease all parties. Newer housing developments routinely have their cables and wires buried or hidden on rooftops. A number of communities have moved all their wires to alleys or camouflaged them behind shrubs or trees. And some really creative sorts have developed cell phone towers that look like pine trees or even large Saguaro cactuses!

Source: Guernsey, Lisa. "A Spreading Techno-blight of Wires," *The New York Times*, September 7, 2000.

Upstarts

According to the Bureau of Labor Statistics, the top three occupations with the fastest employment growth from 1996 to 2006 will be computer scientist, computer engineer, and systems analyst. Yet females make up fewer than 20 percent of those taking the High School Advanced Placement Computer Science Test, and fewer than 30 percent of those earning degrees in computer science.

Janese Swanson aims to change that. Swanson is the founder and CEO of Girl Tech, a company dedicated to making technology more interesting for girls. The company's mission is to encourage technology use, provide role models, and boost self-esteem through the products it offers. Girl Tech gadgets include a diary that only opens with the sound of the owner's voice uttering the secret password, a voice-activated door monitor, and a safe-deposit box that opens with infrared light instead of a key. Girl Tech also offers a magazine, an Internet site, and books.

Ironically, the 39-year-old Swanson has a history of traditional female occupations: model, flight attendant, and teacher. She moved on to obtain six academic degrees, and wrote one doctoral dissertation on gender issues in product design. Swanson credits her 9-year-old daughter with helping her invent toys and keeping her in touch with what girls want and need.

Sources: Wolfson, Jill. "An Interview with Janese Swanson," *San Jose Mercury News,* http://www.thetech.org/revolutionaires/swanson; "Getting Girls Interested in Computers," http://www.math.rice.edu/~lanius/club/girls.

ON THE HORIZON

COMPUTER CHIPS: DENSER, FASTER, AND MORE POWERFUL

Microprocessors and memory chips in computers consist of electronic circuitry containing tiny transistors that allow programs and data to be stored on them. As scientists and engineers discover ways to pack more and more transistors onto chips, computers become faster and more powerful. This tendency is called **Moore's Law,** named after Gordon Moore, cofounder of Intel, who in 1965 observed that the number of transistors per square inch on integrated circuits had doubled every year since the integrated circuit was invented. Moore predicted this trend would continue for the foreseeable future. However, density has actually doubled every eighteen months. Most experts, including Moore himself, expect Moore's Law to be valid for at least the next two decades.

COMPUTERS: SHRINKING SIZE AND GROWING CAPABILITIES

Computers will also become smaller and with far greater capabilities. Already technologies exist that allow users to operate computers using voice commands. Picture telling your computer to write a letter and send it to a friend and your computer doing exactly as instructed. Also, try to imagine looking into a computer monitor having the same detailed clarity and resolution as a professionally prepared photograph. This, too, will soon become a reality.

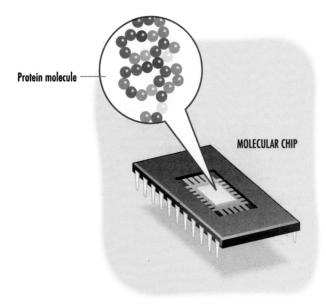

Protein molecule

MOLECULAR CHIP

MOLECULAR DATA STORAGE

Tremendous strides will be made in developing new storage technologies. **Molecular storage,** in which programs and data will be stored on chips consisting of billions of atomic particles, may become available within a few years. Chip manufacturers will be able to mass reproduce these particles, resulting in greater storage capacity at less expense.

EMBEDDED COMPUTERS EVERYWHERE

In the future, expect embedded computers in all areas of personal and work life. Consumers will be able to scan foods and other types of products embedded with special chips to get information on product content, age, and freshness. Soon, we can expect to use small plastic cards with tiny microchips containing our complete medical, credit, military, and driving records. And "smart highways" embedded with millions of tiny sensors may alleviate any driving-record worries because they will guide our cars speeding along at 120 mph, all the time aware of surrounding traffic.

EXPANDING USE OF ARTIFICIAL INTELLIGENCE

During the next decade, the use of robots will expand beyond the factory to the home and into the hospital. Computerized "workers" will perform common household chores plus lawn tasks, including planting flowers and shrubs, raking leaves, and mowing grass. Miniaturized nanorobots, less than 1/25,000th of an inch in size, may be injected into the bloodstream of a hospital patient to remove cancer cells, blood vessel obstructions, or invading germs.

FASTER COMMUNICATION AND A SHRINKING GLOBAL COMMUNITY

In the future, the Internet will grow dramatically in user numbers and in the ways this information-sharing medium is used. Consider these comparisons. Radio took 38 years to reach 50 million listeners. Television took 13 years to reach 50 million viewers. Amazingly, the Internet took only 5 years to reach 50 million users and is reaching millions more each year. Within the present decade, increased bandwidths of communications media will provide instant access to the Internet and Web, allowing information to be accessed in fractions of a second. By the year 2010, say the experts, the dollar amount of online shopping will represent more than 40 percent of all sales. Eventually, almost everyone in the world will have a personal Web site, and distance learning will become common for people of all ages.

For the twenty-first century, it is safe to say that *virtually* anything is possible.

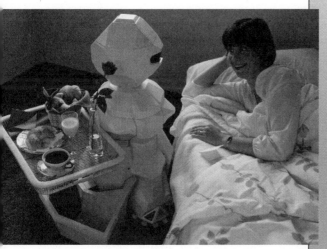

Are You My Mother?

The ability to reproduce is one of the definitions of a living creature. Now scientists at Brandeis University have developed a robot that can design and build other robots virtually on its own.

The robot off-spring are a mere 8 inches long and can only crawl slowly on the floor—but they were engineered and manufactured by a robot. The "mother" computer was given a list of parts to work with, the physical laws of gravity and friction, and the goal: movement on a horizontal surface. It was also shown 200 randomly constructed, nonworking designs.

Using the available parts and following the guidelines, the computer tinkered with the designs and ran simulations, gradually improving upon itself. After 600 evolutions, the computer sent a design to a prototyping machine to build the robot. The baby computer pushes itself along like a caterpillar. When given a different parts list, the computer gave birth to a second robot that moved something like a crab.

Although this is a primitive example of what may come, it is considered a major milestone by many. A robot designed by human engineers can cost up to millions of dollars. The development of robots that can design and replicate other intelligent devices could possibly lead to the inexpensive production of durable, adaptive robots.

The Brandeis scientists do not believe robots will displace humans anytime soon. Present-day robots do not have the power supply, intellect, or the autonomy to take over the world. But others worry that self-replicating research could take us down a path leading to the evolution of robots as artificial life, able to eventually overtake or even supplant human life.

Sources: Chang, Kenneth. "Aping Biology, Computer Guides Automated Evolution of a Robot," *The New York Times,* August 31, 2000.

infolinks

a look at the future:
www.time.com/v21

quantum computing:
www.cpsc.ucalgary.ca

global demographics:
www.internetstats.com

1946
Mauchly and Eckert complete the ENIAC, a vacuum-tube computer.

1950
The UNIVAC 1, built by Remington Rand, is delivered to the U.S. Census Bureau.

1958-59
The integrated circuit is invented by Robert Noyce and Jack Kilby.

1960
DEC introduces the minicomputer.

1964
IBM announces its System/360 series of computers, which will sweep the industry in the U.S.

1971
Intel introduces the first microprocessor.

1972
The Intel 8008 microprocessor ushers in the era of personal computing.

1976
Steven Jobs and Steve Wozniak create the Apple I. The Cray I supercomputer is introduced.

1981
IBM introduces its personal computer.

1986
IBM introduces its first laptop computer.

1990
Pocket computers are introduced.

1993
Intel releases the Pentium microprocessor. Apple introduces the first PDA, the Message Pad.

1999
Palm Computing launches their wireless Palm VII, providing access to the Internet with a single device.

2000
Intel develops the Pentium 4 chip.

1950
1960
1970
1980
1990
2000

CHAPTER SUMMARY

- **Our Connected World.** We live in a connected world that enables us to communicate globally and to access enormous quantities of information. Computers linked to networks and networks, in turn, linked to communications media provide us with access to businesses, libraries, universities, and individuals worldwide through the Internet. Our economy is driven by information.

- **The Internet and World Wide Web.** The development of the Internet has proved to be among the most important developments in history. Knowledge about the Internet and how to use it effectively is considered a basic survival skill.

  The **Internet** (or **Net**) is a worldwide network of computer networks linked together via communications software and media for the purpose of sharing information. Internet applications include information retrieval, online discussion, entertainment, online shopping, distance learning, electronic commerce, and more.

  The **World Wide Web** (or **Web**) is a part of the Internet that uses HTML (Hypertext Markup Language) to allow users to jump from one Web site to another, and from one Web page to another.

- **Networks.** Networks form the skeletal framework of the Internet. A **network** consists of two or more computers, devices, and software, and is connected by means of one or more communications media. It allows users access to programs and data stored on another computer and allows users to communicate with each other.

- **Computers.** All network and Internet activities begin with computers, which are the source of information processing. Data (words, numbers, sounds, and images) is converted into information during the **information processing cycle** of input, processing, output, and storage.

  The term **computer** refers to an electronic device that accepts input (programs and data), processes data into information, stores programs and information, and delivers output (information) to the user.

  A computer system consists of two broad categories of components—hardware and software. **Hardware** includes all of the physical components that comprise the system unit and other devices connected to it. Collectively, these connected devices are referred to as **peripheral devices. Software** consists of sets of instructions that direct the operation of the computer system. Two main classifi-

cations of software are system software (operating systems and utility programs) and application software (task-oriented programs such as spreadsheets).

- **Categories of Computers.** Computers are typically categorized according to differences in size, speed, processing capability, and price. Four main categories are **personal computers** (which include laptop, notebook, handheld, and palmtop computers)**, minicomputers, mainframe computers,** and **supercomputers**.

- **How Computers Work.** All computers are **digital** devices that use the *binary number system*. They are capable of recognizing only "off" and "on" ("0" and "1") states. Each of these "0" and "1" digits is called a bit. A **bit** represents the smallest unit of data in the binary system. A group of bits is called a **byte.** Combinations of 0s and 1s are used to represent alphabetic letters, numbers, and special characters in coding schemes such as ASCII and EBCDIC. The **central processing unit (CPU)** interprets and carries out instructions that operate the computer and manages the computer's devices and resources. The CPU consists of the **control unit**, the **arithmetic/logic unit (ALU)**, **registers**, and the **system clock.**

- **Computer Storage.** Computers store programs, data, and information. They contain various types of internal storage components, called **memory**. Two types of memory typically found in personal computers are **random access memory (RAM)** and **read-only memory (ROM)**. External peripheral devices, called **secondary storage**, allow programs, data, and information to be stored permanently.

- **Future of Computing in a Virtual Age**. Computers will continue to be smaller, faster, and more powerful. The number of Internet users will continually expand, as will the possibilities for using the Internet. Artificial intelligence will improve to the point where robots will perform much of the hands-on work in factories, homes, hospitals, and other areas that involve manual labor of varying complexity.

KEY TERMS

Page numbers indicate where key terms are first cited in the chapter. A complete list of key terms with definitions can be found in the Glossary at the end of the book.

address, 25
Advanced Research Projects Agency (ARPA), 8
American Standard Code for Information Interchange (ASCII), 20
application software, 15
arithmetic/logic unit (ALU), 22
ARPANet, 7
binary system, 20
bit (binary digit), 19
browser, 9
byte, 20
central processing unit (CPU), 20
chat room (chat group), 11
chip, 16
clock cycle, 23
computer, 14
control unit, 21
data, 13
data register, 23
decoding, 22
desktop computer, 17
digital, 18
distance learning, 11
dumb terminal, 18
electronic commerce, 11
electronic mail (e-mail), 5
executing, 22
execution time (E-time), 22
Extended Binary Coded Decimal Interchange Code (EBCDIC), 20
fetching, 22
floppy disk drive, 24
gigabyte, 25
gigahertz, 23
graphical user interface (GUI), 9
handheld computer, 17
hard disk drive, 24
hardware, 15
hertz, 23
Hypertext Markup Language (HTML), 9
information, 13
information processing cycle, 13
input, 13
instruction register, 22

instruction time (I-time), 22
Internet (the Net), 4
kilobyte, 25
laptop computer, 17
machine cycle, 21
main memory, 24
mainframe computer, 8
megabyte, 25
megahertz, 23
memory, 16
minicomputer, 16
modem, 14
molecular storage, 28
Moore's Law, 28
National Science Foundation Network (NSFnet), 8
network, 5
nonvolatile memory, 24
notebook computer, 17
operating system, 9
output, 13
packet, 10
palmtop computer, 17
pen computer, 18
peripheral device, 15
personal computer, 7
personal digital assistant (PDA), 17
processor, 16
program, 13
random-access memory (RAM), 24
read-only memory (ROM), 24
register, 22
secondary storage, 24
software, 15
storage, 13
storage register, 23
supercomputer, 8
system clock, 23
system software, 15
terabyte, 19
terminal, 18
Transmission Control Protocol/Internet Protocol (TCP/IP), 10
utility software, 15
virtual age, 9
volatile memory, 24
Web page, 9
World Wide Web (the Web), 9

INTERNET

TUTORIAL 1

BROWSING THE WEB USING WEB ADDRESSES

The Internet is a collection of computers around the world connected together through telephone lines, cables, satellites, and other telecommunications media. The World Wide Web, called the Web, is a part of the Internet that contains Web pages consisting of text, sounds, video, and graphics that link to other related Web pages. These links are called hyperlinks. Web pages are stored in a common language called HTML (Hypertext Markup Language) which can be viewed on any computer regardless of the operating system platform (Macintosh, Windows, UNIX, and so on).

CONNECTING TO THE WEB

To connect to the Internet and view Web pages, you will need the following resources:

1. A computer with a modem or a network connection to a server with Internet access.
2. Browser software, such as Internet Explorer or Netscape, that provides the interface for viewing Web pages.
3. An account with an ISP (Internet Service Provider) if you are using a computer that is not connected to a network server. An ISP sells Internet access usually by charging a monthly fee for a set time period. The ISP has the computers, network equipment, and modems to allow multiple users to connect at the same time.

In the steps that follow you will explore Web sites on the Internet using Web addresses and Microsoft's Internet Explorer version 5.5. If you are using another browser or a different version of Internet Explorer, you may need to alter these instructions slightly.

Steps

1. Click the Launch Internet Explorer Browser button on the QuickLaunch toolbar, or click the *Internet Explorer* icon on the desktop. If there are no icons on your desktop, click the Start button, point to <u>P</u>rograms, and then click *Internet Explorer.*

Step 1

QuickLaunch Toolbar

Title bar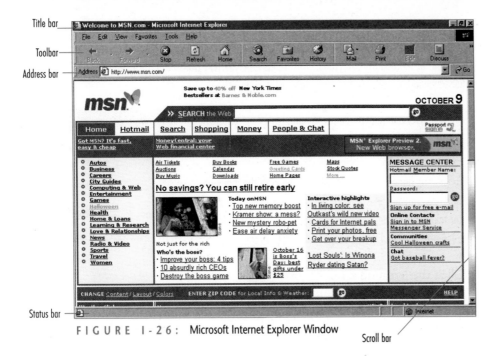

Toolbar

Address bar

Status bar

FIGURE 1-26: Microsoft Internet Explorer Window

Scroll bar

If you are completing this tutorial using your computer at home, you may need to enter your password and then click OK to connect through a dial-up connection to your ISP.

The Microsoft Internet Explorer window will appear with a Web page displayed in the window as shown in Figure 1-26. (The Web page shown in your window may vary.)

2. Move the mouse pointer over the current entry in the A̲ddress text box, and then click the left mouse button.

Clicking the left mouse button selects the entire address and changes the white arrow pointer to an I-beam, which indicates you can key text and/or move the insertion point using the arrow keys on the keyboard.

3. Key (type) **www.usatoday.com**, and then press Enter.

The USA Today home page will appear in the window. Watch the status bar for messages displaying the status of loading the page. When the page has finished displaying all of its text, graphics, and other components, the status bar will display the word "Done."

A feature called *AutoComplete* is invoked as soon as you begin keying an address. AutoComplete displays addresses visited by you in the past that match with the text as you key it. If one of the addresses offered is the correct address, click the mouse over it.

The entry in the A<u>d</u>dress text box is called a URL (Uniform Resource Locator). URLs are the addressing method used to identify Web pages. After pressing Enter, notice the browser automatically inserted *http://* in front of the address you typed: *http* stands for Hypertext Transfer Protocol, which is the communications standard used for transferring data within the Web.

Home
News
Main Categories
<u>News briefs</u>
<u>Washington</u>
<u>Editorial/Opinion</u>
<u>States</u>
<u>World</u>
More News
<u>Health</u>
<u>Science</u>
<u>Politics</u>
<u>Offbeat news</u>
<u>Columnists</u>
<u>Lotteries</u>
<u>Talk Today</u>
Money
Sports
Life
Tech
Weather

4. Move the mouse pointer over the blue underlined headings displayed along the left side of the USA Today page.

Notice the pointer changes shape to a white hand with the index finger pointing upward when it is positioned over underlined text. When the pointer takes this shape, it means you can click the left mouse button to jump to a related Web page (called a *hyperlink*).

5. Click the left mouse button over <u>World</u>.   Step 5 —

In a few seconds, the page with the top World news story is displayed.

6. Click the Back button 🔙 on the toolbar to return to the previous page.
7. Click the Forward button 🔜 on the toolbar to redisplay the World page (the page viewed prior to clicking Back).

Notice the Back and Forward buttons on the toolbar contain down-pointing triangles. Click the down-pointing triangle, and then click a Web site name in the drop-down list to jump to a page previously viewed.

8. Click the mouse pointer over the entry in the A<u>d</u>dress text box, key **www.microsoft.com,** and then press Enter.
9. Click one of the hyperlinks on the Microsoft home page to jump to a topic that interests you.
10. Continue exploring Web pages by keying URLs in the A<u>d</u>dress text box, clicking hyperlinks, the Back button, and the Forward button on the toolbar.
11. When you have finished exploring the Web, click the Close button ✖ at the right end of the title bar to exit Microsoft Internet Explorer. If necessary, disconnect from your ISP.

If you want to browse the Web by *topic,* rather than addresses, click the Search button on the toolbar. Click in the Find a Web page containing text box, key the topic you are interested in, and then click the Search button beside the box.

COMMUNICATING CLEARLY
Technology Terms: What do they mean?

a. application software
b. network
c. Web page
d. arithmetic/logic unit
e. Internet

f. binary
g. World Wide Web
h. software
i. personal computer
j. bit

k. ASCII
l. electronic commerce
m. register
n. hardware
o. supercomputer

1. A number system that uses combinations of zeros and ones (0s and 1s) to represent letters, numbers, and special characters.

2. A global system of linked computer networks that allows users to jump from one location to another location.

3. A worldwide network of computers linked together via communications software and media for the purpose of sharing information.

4. The smallest unit of data a computer can understand and act on.

5. Programs that enable a user to perform specific tasks.

6. A component of the ALU that temporarily holds instructions and data.

7. Internet technologies that enable the exchange of products and services between sellers and customers and between businesses.

8. An electronic document stored at a location on the Web.

9. A computer designed for use by a single individual and capable of performing its own input, processing, output, and storage.

10. Programs containing instructions that direct the operation of the computer system and the documentation that explains how to use the programs.

11. The largest, most powerful, and most expensive category of computers.

12. The part of the CPU that carries out the instructions and performs arithmetic and logical operations on the data.

13. A computer's physical components and devices.

14. A coding scheme used on most computers, including personal computers, to represent data.

15. A group of two or more computers, software, and other devices connected by means of one or more communications media.

Techno Literacy: How can new knowledge be used?

1. What is a new way to use the Internet?
   At your school or local library, page through several computer magazines and find an article on an interesting Internet application that was not presented in the chapter. Prepare a detailed written explanation about the application. In your explanation, include an explanation of the application, including examples of how members of your class might use the application for their own benefit.

2. How important is the new Teledesic technology?

   Several articles have been written about the technology being developed by Microsoft Corporation and McCaw Communications called "Teledesic." Visit your school library and research the development of this proposed technology. Imagine that you are a technology marketing person for Microsoft. How would you convince a customer to buy this product? Prepare a marketing plan that describes your strategy. Then present your sales pitch orally to your class, picturing them as the management staff of a company interested in Teledesic.

3. What kind of personal computer would you buy?

   Identify your needs; then research possible system configurations that match your needs. Select the best choice and prepare a detailed written report describing the computer. Include the name of the manufacturer, price, the number and kinds of processors, speed, storage capacity, and accessories. If possible, add photos and/or drawings. Using your written report, and possibly pictures or drawings of the computer system, make an oral presentation to your class describing the computer you selected.

4. What is a new way to connect to the Internet?

   Find an article or advertisement describing a recently introduced device that can be used to connect to other people around the world. Prepare a detailed written explanation of the device. Include specific information about the device's price, features, limitations, and technical specifications. If possible, include a picture or drawing of the device. How popular do you predict this device will become? Which current devices will the new device displace in the market?

5. How will the Internet be used in the future?

   Research the topic of the future of computer and Internet technology. Select an intriguing trend or application not discussed in the chapter and write a description of it, including the market needs that will encourage the development of this trend or application.

CONNECTING WITH CONCEPTS
Technology Processes: What's right with this picture?

What process is this? Identify the process illustrated in this drawing and write a paragraph explaining the process.

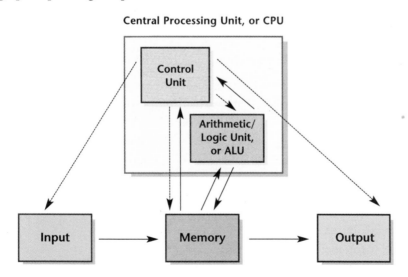

Central Processing Unit, or CPU

Control Unit

Arithmetic/ Logic Unit, or ALU

Input

Memory

Output

Key Principles: What's it all about?

1. The precursor to the Internet was the

   a) MilNet
   b) World Wide Web
   c) ARPANet
   d) Gopher Net

2. The uniqueness of a hypertext document lies in the fact that it

   a) combines text and graphics
   b) can be stored on a computer
   c) can be linked to other documents
   d) is created using a text editor

3. A CPU contains

   a) a card reader and a printing device
   b) an analytical engine and a control unit
   c) a control unit and an arithmetic/logic unit
   d) an arithmetic/logic unit and a card reader

4. The part of a computer that coordinates all its functions is called its

   a) ROM program
   b) system board
   c) arithmetic/logic unit
   d) control unit

5. A byte is equal to

   a) four bits, or one nibble
   b) six bits and one nibble
   c) two bits
   d) eight bits

6. Which of the following does *not* have a microprocessor?

   a) mainframe
   b) PC
   c) PDA
   d) terminal

7. The system clock inside a computer ensures that the

   a) user of the computer will always know the correct time
   b) computer will run faster than one without a system clock
   c) activities of the computer will be properly synchronized
   d) process will be able to address a 32-bit data bus

8. Storage devices are

   a) nonvolatile
   b) optical
   c) preformatted
   d) magnetic media

9. The parts of the information processing cycle are

    a) fetching, decoding, executing, storing
    b) fetching, comparing, interpreting, outputting
    c) input, interpret, processing, outputting
    d) inputting, processing, outputting, storing

10. Processing speed in microprocessors is measured in

    a) megabytes
    b) hertz
    c) kilobytes
    d) bits per second

MINING DATA

Conduct Internet searches to find information described in the activities below. Write a brief report that summarizes your research results. Be sure to document your sources, using the following format, which is recommended by the Modern Language Association (MLA):

- Author's name (if known)
- Title of document, in quotations
- Title of Internet page or online periodical, in italics (if not titled, put <u>Home Page</u> or give the name of the organization that created and maintains the page)
- Date of publication (for an article) or date site was last updated
- Date you accessed the site
- URL, in angle brackets

Example:
Sanders, Jill M. "The Space Agency Launches a Winner," *NASA News*, January 2001. March 2001<http://www.mit.edu:000/people/glenn.html>.

1. Select a current events topic that interests you and research the latest information on that topic in a variety of news sources, including *USA Today*.

2. What kinds of Internet-related information are available in newspapers and other news sources online? (Your summary should discuss the information available on a particular date.)

3. Research the topic of high-tech stock investments, as discussed in online news sources. What is the current trend as of the date of your research?

infolinks

citing sources:
www.bluewillowpages.com

MANAGING CHANGE

THINGS THAT THINK

1. The future holds that computers will be ubiquitous. For example, bridges will have computers that will alert city planners when part of a bridge is weakening or too stressed and in need of repair. What other objects can you think of that should have the same type of warning or notice capability built into the device?

2. Many futurists claim that we will be wearing computers in the future. What job problems could be addressed if we start wearing computers that are capable of collecting and analyzing data (tracking inventory, for example)?

PREDICTING NEXT STEPS

Look at the timeline below that outlines the major benchmarks in the development of wireless computing. Research this topic and fill in as many substeps as you can. What do you think the next steps will be? Complete the timeline through the year 2030.

1980s   Cellular phones are developed using analog technology, which varies the frequency of a phone's radio signals.

1990s   Second-generation cellular phones are developed using digital technology, which converts users' voices into streams of bits.

2000–   Third-generation broadband digital transmission is available, with transmission rates of 10 kilobits per second and higher.

SOLVING PROBLEMS

In groups or individually, brainstorm possible solutions to the issues presented.

1. Compared to previous decades, today's classrooms are made up of more diverse students and students with a wider range of performance capabilities. In fact, some theorists claim there is a 200 percent differential in the learning rate in our classrooms today. Imagine how computers will help instructors teach so many different types of students. Consider both traditional and distance learning modes.

2. Artificially intelligent robots are likely to play a large role in our future. What are some possible new applications of this technology in the areas of manufacturing, healthcare, and home maintenance?

EXAMINING ETHICAL ISSUES

Access the Computer Concepts Resource Center at EMC/Paradigm's Web site (www.emcp.com/college_division/ electronic_resource_center) and go to Computers: Exploring Concepts, then to Student Resources, then to the Ethical Issues page. Complete the activity for Chapter 1.

ANSWERS TO TECHNOLOGY TERMS AND KEY PRINCIPLES QUESTIONS

Technology Terms: 1 – f; 2 – g; 3 – e; 4 – j; 5 – a; 6 – m; 7 – l; 8 – c; 9 – i; 10 – h; 11 – o; 12 – d; 13 – n; 14 – k; 15 – b

Key Principles: 1 – c; 2 – c; 3 – c; 4 – d; 5 – d; 6 – d; 7 – c; 8 – d; 9 – d; 10 – b

CHAPTER 2

HARDWARE: ENABLING THE INFORMATION PROCESSING CYCLE

learning objectives

- Define hardware and give examples of hardware devices for input, processing, output, and storage

- Explain the role of the motherboard and the other components of a system unit

- Identify the major input devices for personal computers and rank them by use

- Categorize output devices and provide examples and uses of each type

- Identify the types of secondary storage and provide examples of devices for each type

- Conduct an Internet search using key words

THE PROCESSING CYCLE

PROCESSING

STORAGE

INPUT

OUTPUT

CYBER SCENARIO

Jenna Winbon is suddenly awakened by upbeat music coming from the speakers of the computer-controlled sound system in her home. The CD player, along with most of the appliances and electronic devices in her home, is managed by a computer system called a home information infrastructure.

Sitting on her bedside and thinking about the day's priority tasks at the office, she hears the coffeemaker brewing a pot of fresh coffee. In the bathroom the tub begins filling with water heated to a preprogrammed temperature. Settling into the warm bath, Jenna glances at the flat-panel TV screen on the wall as the announcer summarizes major headline and financial news reports recorded on the VCR from her favorite predawn newscasts. Hearing a report that one of her company's parts vendors is facing a worker strike, she picks up her cell phone and quickly sends an e-mail to the purchasing manager, noting the potential worker strike and suggesting that he order parts immediately.

Meanwhile, in the kitchen a robot serves Jenna's breakfast of cereal, milk, orange juice, and fresh fruit, and informs her of its nutritional and caloric content. As Jenna eats, the robot retrieves the vacuum cleaner and begins cleaning the living room carpet.

After finishing her breakfast, Jenna gathers her briefcase along with her Internet-enabled cell phone and heads for the garage. Her glancing at the wall clock in the utility room activates a scheduler device within the clock, and she is reminded on a digital display that she has an appointment with an advertising copywriter in 35 minutes.

Opening the door from the utility room to the garage automatically starts Jenna's car and opens the garage door simultaneously. As she backs out of the garage, she notices the car's interior temperature is approaching the 74 degrees she had selected on the Preferences menu of the controls system. Jenna drives down the freeway, enjoying her favorite music on the car's sound system without having to lift a finger.

"Now," she thinks, "if only my appointments and meetings at the office will go as smoothly."

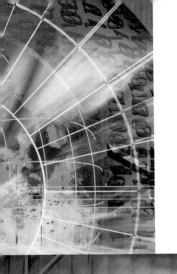

EMBEDDED COMPUTERS IN YOUR FUTURE

Computer systems such as the one in Jenna's home may soon become a reality within reach of average consumers. Major companies, including Matsushita Electric Industrial Company in Japan, are planning home computer networks that can manage not only the standard home appliances, but also electronic health checkers that allow users to send their health data to a clinic via an Internet-connected blood pressure cuff or thermometer. The company also foresees refrigerators linked to food catering services and doorbells linked to home security services. Systems such as these depend on the concept of embedded computers and sophisticated sensors, which are already common in household appliances and in a multitude of manufacturing equipment. As we move into the twenty-first century, we can expect to see increasingly complex computerized devices that make life easier at work as well as at home.

WHAT IS HARDWARE?

All computer systems, from handhelds to laptops to desktops to networks—and the Internet—require specific kinds of hardware. The word **hardware** refers to all of the physical devices, or equipment you can see, that make up a computerized system. The larger and more complex the system, for example, a mainframe computer, the larger the number of devices needed to support its functions.

PERSONAL COMPUTER HARDWARE

Along with the automobile and telephone, the personal computer is one of most important technological innovations of the past century. It is also the type of computer most widely used in business, government, home, and academic arenas.

You learned in Chapter 1 that among the categories of computers (supercomputers, mainframes, minicomputers, and personal computers), the **personal computer** is a relatively small and less expensive computer designed for an individual user. Personal computers range in price from a few hundred dollars to thousands of dollars. Specific model prices depend upon a number of factors including processor type, amount of memory, add-on boards, and peripheral devices. All of these factors are hardware-related.

TYPES OF HARDWARE DEVICES

Hardware devices can be grouped according to how and where they are used in the four parts of the information processing cycle:

- system unit devices (processing)
- input devices
- output devices
- storage devices

Within each group are several device choices that users select from to create, or configure, a complete personal computer system, as shown in Figure 2-1.

FIGURE 2-1: Personal Computer System

A desktop personal computer system, consisting of a CPU for processing, a keyboard and mouse for input, a monitor and speakers for output, and a hard drive (hidden) and floppy drive for storage

SYSTEM UNIT HARDWARE

The main part of a personal computer, called the **system unit,** is the hardware component that processes information (see Figures 2-2A and 2B). Within the system unit is the motherboard, which is the major circuit board in the computer.

MOTHERBOARDS

The **motherboard** is a thin sheet of fiberglass or other material with electrical pathways, called **traces**, etched onto it. These traces connect components that are soldered to the motherboard or attached to it by various connectors. The following components are typically found on the motherboard in contemporary personal computers (as shown in Figure 2-2A):

- a microprocessor
- sockets for connecting the RAM, or random access memory, chips that contain the temporary memory in which programs and data are stored while the computer is in use
- ROM, or ready-only memory, chips that contains the computer's permanent memory in which various instructions are stored
- ports for connecting devices such as a keyboard, a mouse, a modem, and a printer
- expansion slots for attaching expansion boards, or cards, that add various capabilities to the computer, such as the ability to access files over a network or to digitize sound or video

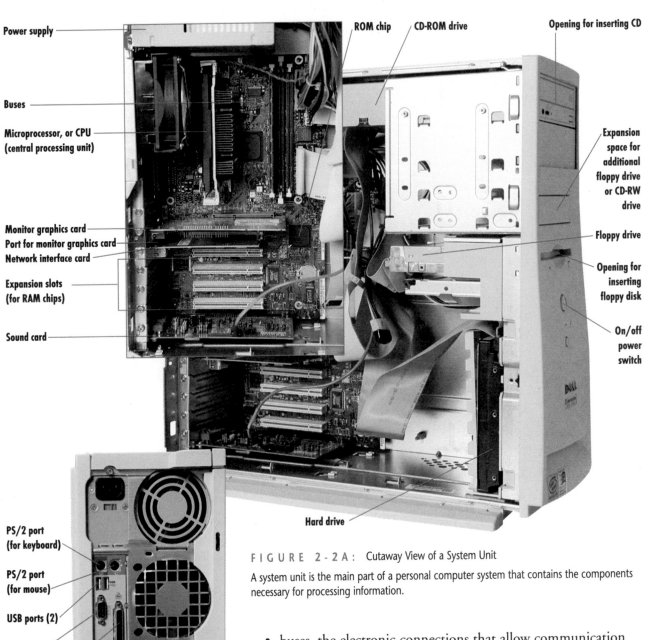

Power supply

Buses

Microprocessor, or CPU (central processing unit)

Monitor graphics card
Port for monitor graphics card
Network interface card

Expansion slots (for RAM chips)

Sound card

ROM chip   **CD-ROM drive**

Opening for inserting CD

Expansion space for additional floppy drive or CD-RW drive

Floppy drive

Opening for inserting floppy disk

On/off power switch

Hard drive

F I G U R E 2 - 2 A : Cutaway View of a System Unit

A system unit is the main part of a personal computer system that contains the components necessary for processing information.

PS/2 port (for keyboard)

PS/2 port (for mouse)

USB ports (2)

Serial port

Parallel port

Monitor card

Network interface card

Sound card

F I G U R E 2 - 2 B :
Rear View of a System Unit

Several devices plug into ports on the back of the system unit.

- buses, the electronic connections that allow communication between components in the computer
- a system clock (and battery) to synchronize the computer's activities
- a power supply to provide power to the computer

MICROPROCESSORS

The real intelligence of a personal computer resides in its **microprocessor,** also called a **processor** or **CPU (central processing unit) chip**. *(Note: The term* central processing unit *is sometimes used to refer to the case that contains the microprocessor and everything else within this case. Technically, however, the CPU is the microprocessor chip.)* In a personal computer, the microprocessor is a single chip, an integrated circuit containing millions of electrical transistors, packed onto a surface that may be smaller than a postage stamp (see Figure 2-3).

A variety of microprocessors with varying speeds and capabilities are available. Newer microprocessors are extremely fast and powerful and offer exceptional capabilities. For example, Intel Corporation's Pentium® 4 processor, introduced in 2000, contains 42 million transistors and has a clock speed of up to 1.5 gigahertz. Contrast that capability with Intel's 80286 processor, introduced in 1982, which had a clock speed of 6–12 megahertz and a total of 134,000 transistors.

The Celeron™ processor is another popular Intel chip that was revised in 2000 to create three new versions: a 600 MHz chip and a 650 MHz chip for full-sized laptop computers and a 500 MHz chip for the ultralight handhelds needing fast processing speed and low power consumption. The 500 MHz Celeron™ chip consumes less than 2 watts of electricity.

FIGURE 2-3:
Microprocessor

A microprocessor, connected to the motherboard, processes data entered by the user.

KEY TERMS

clock speed the pace of the microprocessor's internal clock, which determines how fast operations are processed within the CPU; clock speed is measured in megahertz (MHz)

RAM Chips

RAM (random access memory), also called **main memory**, consists of a group of electronic chips inside the system unit used to store programs while they are being executed and data while it is being processed (see Figure 2-2A). A computer can process only the data that is in main memory. Therefore, every program being executed (such as a word processor) and every file you access (such as a document) is copied by the computer from a storage device (such as a floppy disk or hard disk) into RAM.

The amount of main memory in a computer is important. Large programs require lots of main memory, and unless your computer contains enough main memory, you may be unable to use the program. With most computers, additional RAM chips can be installed inside the system unit.

Think of RAM as a basic workspace, similar to a drawing board. More RAM allows you to create a larger drawing table to work on. With more RAM, you can lay out more of your project at one time, and work on all of it at once. Also, you can work on multiple projects concurrently, moving back and forth among them. With too little RAM, you may be unable to work on even a single large project.

The amount of RAM varies among different kinds and sizes of computers. Obviously, supercomputers contain more RAM than handhelds. Table 2-1 shows the amount of RAM typically contained in various types of computers.

HOT WIRED

Is there a pocket for my cell phone?
For the fashion-conscious who want to stay wired on the go there is now the Java Jacket, a homemade wearable computer. Donald Sutherland, a staff engineer at Sun Microsystems, has designed a leather jacket that lets him monitor his e-mail, adjust the water temperature in his aquarium, and operate the lights at his home. The Java Jacket can also monitor the pollution in water, check the relative humidity, and measure surrounding wind speed.

This style of the future operates on batteries and contains a 166 MHz Pentium-powered motherboard, a GPS receiver and antenna, and a camera lens. It uses three wireless networking standards. The cuff contains a six-button keypad.

Sutherland plans to add a keyboard, a graphics display, and a head-mounted apparatus so that he can view maps, GPS coordinates, and other data. And Sutherland - a true Californian - wants to eventually incorporate the ability to monitor carbon dioxide levels and earthquake tremors.

Sutherland designed the Java Jacket so that he could enjoy the benefits of technology without being confined to a building. It's sure to be a trend-setter.

Source: Witt, Sam, and Durkin, Sean. "Net Software," *Wired,* July 2000.

TYPE OF COMPUTER	NUMBER OF PROCESSORS	AMOUNT OF MEMORY (RAM)
Handheld	Usually one	16 – 32 MB or more
Notebook (laptop)	Usually one	64 – 128 MB or more
Desktop	Usually one	128 – 512 MB or more
Minicomputer	Several	6 – 12 GB or more
Mainframe	Hundreds	Hundreds of GB or more
Supercomputer	Hundreds to thousands	Hundreds of TB to several PB (1 petabyte = 1,024 TB)

T A B L E   2 - 1 : Computer Memory Comparisons

CACHE MEMORY

A secondary type of processing storage used with RAM is cache memory. **Cache memory** is a holding area in which the data and instructions most recently called from RAM by the processor are temporarily stored. When a processor needs an instruction from RAM, it first looks for the instruction in cache memory and, because some instructions are called frequently, finds it there often enough to speed up processing. Some personal computers have cache memory chips hardwired onto the motherboard. Operating systems also are typically capable of setting aside a portion of RAM to be used as cache memory, and the size of that cache can be set by the user.

ROM CHIPS

ROM (read-only memory) chips contain instructions, information, or data placed on the chip by the manufacturer. Once data has been recorded on a ROM chip, it cannot be altered or removed and can only be read by the computer. A typical PC (refer to Figure 2-2A) contains ROM chips on which essential programs have been stored. One

such program is the **BIOS (basic input/output system)**, the program that boots (starts) the computer when it is turned on and controls communications with the keyboard, disk drives, and other components. Also activated with the startup of the computer is a **POST (power-on self test)** chip, which contains instructions that check the physical components of the system to make certain they are working properly.

PORTS

A **port** is a plug-in slot on a computer to which you can connect a device, such as a printer or, in the case of accessing the Internet, a telephone line (refer to Figure 2-2B). Personal computers have various types of ports, including:

- a **serial port**, also called a **communications (COM) port**, for connecting devices such as the keyboard, mouse, and modem; serial ports transmit data one bit at a time
- a **parallel port**, for connecting printers and scanners; parallel ports transmit data eight bits at a time
- a **video port**, which connects a monitor and may be built into the computer or provided by a **video card** placed in an expansion slot
- a **USB (Universal Serial Bus) port**, widely used for high-speed modems, scanners, and digital cameras; a single USB port can accommodate more than 100 peripheral devices connected together in sequence

Due to size constraints, most personal computers have a limited number of ports, which restricts the number of devices that can be connected. Some laptop computers can be inserted in a **docking station**, an accessory that provides additional ports plus (typically) a charger for the laptop's battery, extra disk drives, and other peripherals.

EXPANSION SLOTS

The system unit for most computers contains internal expansion slots. An **expansion slot** is an opening in a computer motherboard where an **expansion board**, also called **add-on board** or **add-in board**, can be inserted to add new capabilities, including RAM memory boards to increase the amount of main memory or a modem card to facilitate communication over a telephone line. Other examples include sound, video, network and graphics boards, and boards that allow you to capture and enter photos into your computer. Figure 2-4 shows an example of an expansion board.

Reaching Mongolia

"Outer Mongolia" is almost a synonym for inaccessible and remote. And, indeed, Mongolia is both. Fewer than three million people are spread across a vast expanse. Horses are the main mode of transportation on the limited network of roads. Almost half the population are nomadic herders who lead lives untouched by the twenty-first century.

A communist revolution in 1924 left Mongolia cut off from the outside world. Years of dependence on Russia resulted in a crumbling infrastructure, but also a literacy rate of 97 percent. Another revolution in 1990 ushered in democracy and a hope that the Internet can be used to overcome the country's isolation. The Mongolian government aims to make the Internet accessible to every citizen and to put 90 percent of the businesses and government services online, within a decade.

Currently, there are three Internet services in Mongolia. The cost is $50 a month, twice the average monthly income, which makes the Internet a luxury few can afford. The market is stepping in to fill the void. Internet cafes and public access Internet centers are cropping up for those who cannot afford a computer. And eventually, Mongolia's nomads will be able to roam virtually as well as physically.

Source: Sly, Liz. "Mongolia's Nomads Roam World on Internet," *Chicago Tribune,* July 16, 2000.

FIGURE 2-4:
Expansion Board

An expansion board is a circuit board that can be installed inside a system unit, usually on the motherboard. An example is a network expansion board, shown at left.

PC CARDS

Notebook and other portable computers are often too small to accommodate large motherboards, expansion boards, and other components. As a result, a type of expansion board called a **PC card** has been developed specifically for the smaller PCs. The PC card plugs into the side of a notebook or portable computer. Most are about the size of a credit card, only thicker, and can be unplugged and removed when no longer needed. Type I cards provide additional memory. Type II cards typically provide networking or sound capabilities, and Type III cards provide a removable hard drive. See Figure 2-5 for two examples of Type II cards.

FIGURE 2-5:
PC Cards

PC cards are small devices plugged into a small computer, such as a notebook computer, to add memory or to provide additional capabilities such as networking or sound.

BUSES

How does data move from one component to another inside a computer? The answer is that every computer contains buses that connect various components. A **bus** is a collection of tiny wires through which data, in the form of "0s" and "1s," is transmitted from one part of the computer to another.

One way to visualize a bus is to think of it as a highway that allows data to travel from one location to another. The more lanes in the highway, the greater the number of "vehicles" ("0s" and "1s") that can travel on the highway at one time. In computer terminology, this is referred to as **bus bandwidth**. The higher the bandwidth, the greater the amount of data that can be transmitted at the same time.

INPUT HARDWARE

An **input device** is any hardware component that enables a computer user to enter data and programs into a computer system. Keyboards, point-and-click devices, and scanners are among the more popular input devices, and a desktop or laptop computer system usually includes at least two input mechanisms.

thics

Votes for Sale?

Although inordinate amounts of money are spent trying to influence how people vote, it is illegal to buy or sell a vote outright in this country. But in the elections of fall 2000, you could do just that on the Web site Voteauction.com. According to its designers, the site was aimed at disillusioned voters who probably were going to sit out the election anyway. Voteauction.com further justified its actions by claiming that vote-purchasing started in the days of George Washington. Calling the entire political scene corrupt, the site argued that since millions of tax dollars and corporate and special interest contributions are spent to purchase votes, the taxpayers have the right to get their share.

Here's how the process worked: voters first register by giving their name and address. The highest bidder then chooses the candidate for whom the group will vote en masse via absentee ballot. Winnings are split equally among each state's voters. Votes from heavily populated states with more clout in the electoral college are worth more than those from less populated ones. In the 2000 presidential election, over 500 people in Illinois alone agreed to sell their presidential votes. The top bid was $8,500, giving each voter about $17.

Naturally, this auction has attracted the attention of both the Department of Justice and the Federal Elections Commission. Voteauction.com is undeterred. Citing the 1976 Supreme Court decision *Buckley vs. Valeo*, which said that to limit campaign spending was to violate free speech, it intends to continue operating under the motto "Bringing Democracy and Capitalism together."

Sources: Abramson, Ronna. "Wanna Buy My Vote? Fuhgeddaboutit," *The Standard,* August 21, 2000; Kornblum, Janet. "Chicago acts to end online sale of votes," *USA Today,* November 2, 2000; Connor, Chris. "Straight Talk from voteacuction.com," AuctionWatch.com, August 18, 2000.

KEYBOARDS

The **keyboard**, the most common input device, is an electronically controlled hardware component used to enter alphanumeric data (letters, numbers, and special characters). The keys on most keyboards are arranged similarly to those on a typewriter. Without a keyboard, using a computer would be difficult, if not impossible.

Although the number and placement of keys on the keyboard vary among manufacturers, most keyboards contain—in addition to keys for the letters of the alphabet—the following special groups of keys:

- function keys
- special-purpose keys
- cursor-control keys
- numeric keypad

Figure 2-6 shows a typical keyboard with the special key groups and their functions.

Function keys, labeled F1, F2, F3, and so on, allow a user to quickly access commands and functions.

Numeric keypad, which performs the same functions as a calculator, is used for entering numbers quickly.

Special-purpose keys, such as Control, Alternate, and Delete, are used in conjunction with another key to enter commands into the computer.

Cursor-control keys govern the movement of the cursor on the screen and include the Up Arrow, Down Arrow, Right Arrow, and Left Arrow keys on most keyboards.

FIGURE 2-6: A Typical Computer Keyboard

A keyboard, similar to a typewriter keyboard, is used to enter alphanumeric data (words and numbers) into a computer.

SPECIAL-FUNCTION KEYBOARDS

Special-function keyboards are designed for specific applications involving simplified, rapid data input. For example, cash registers in most fast-food restaurants are equipped with special-function keyboards. Rather than key the name and price of a specific sandwich, the employee needs only to press the key marked "Ham Sandwich" to record the sale (see Figure 2-7). Special-function keyboards enable fast-food employees, ticket agents, and retail clerks to enter transactions into their computer systems very quickly.

FIGURE 2-7:
Employee Using a Special-Purpose Keyboard

Special-purpose keyboards, like the one shown, are used by many businesses to increase user efficiency.

DRIVERS

In 1984, a 19-year-old University of Texas student named Michael Dell had a simple idea to sell custom-made computers directly to customers. Previously, computer manufacturers sold their machines to retailers, who marked up the price for consumers. Michael decided a better way was to assemble computers from inexpensive surplus parts, then produce high-quality machines to the exact requirements of his customers.

Michael's manufacturing and marketing concept of producing made-to-order computers and selling them directly to consumers is still working today. The only difference is that today his company, Dell Computer Corporation, is earning billions of dollars annually and employs more than 25,000 people.

Michael Dell showed entrepreneurial tendencies early on. At age 12, he earned $2,000 by forming a direct-mail marketing company to auction stamps. He followed this feat with a stint of selling newspaper subscriptions, earning $18,000, with which he bought a BMW. Trying to juggle both college and his made-to-order computer business, Michael caused parental worries to the point where he promised to quit his computer venture and devote himself full-time to his studies if his business didn't perform well. By the end of the year, his company was making $50,000–$80,000 a month. Dell incorporated his business and dropped out of college.

Two years later, Dell offered the first toll-free technical support and onsite service in the personal computer industry, services that later became standard practice. Dell Computer Corporation was also one of the first companies to sell computers over the Internet. In July 1996, the company offered online purchasing without any promotions or advertisement. Soon, the site was selling 30–60 computers a day. By the late 1990s, the company was selling an average of nearly $20 million worth of computers a day online and proving to skeptics that online commerce could bring in huge revenues.

Source: <http://www.biography.com>.

THE MOUSE AND OTHER POINT-AND-CLICK DEVICES

Operating systems such as Windows and Macintosh use a graphical interface containing buttons, drop-down menus, and icons to represent program features and commands. The user issues commands by pointing at an icon or menu item with a **mouse**, which after the keyboard is the second most common input device (see Figure 2-8). A mouse operates by moving the cursor (often called a **mouse pointer**) on the computer screen to correspond to movements made with the mouse (see Figure 2-9). If you visualize the computer mouse as a small oval with a long cable tail, you can understand how it got its name.

FIGURE 2-8:
Mouse and Mouse Pad

A mouse is an input device that, when moved about on a flat surface, causes a pointer on the screen to move in the same direction.

MOUSE POINTER
When the user moves the mouse (below) on the mouse pad, a pointer on the display screen moves in the same direction.

interface the connection between a user and software, between two hardware devices, or between two applications

icon a graphic symbol that represents a software program, a command, or a feature

MOUSE PAD
The user slides the mouse on the smooth surface of the mouse pad.

FIGURE 2-9: How a Pointer Works with the Windows Operating System

A mouse pointer allows a user to make selections from a menu and to activate programs represented by icons displayed on the screen.

FIGURE 2-10:
Optical Mouse
An optical mouse tracks movement with a light sensor.

A mouse plugs directly into the computer or into the keyboard. Mice used on the Macintosh generally have one button, while mice used on PCs generally have two (although three-button models also are available). The button on the left side is used to signal a choice. The button on the right side is used to display special options and menus. On the underside of a mouse is a rubber-coated round ball that glides over a rubberized pad with a smooth fabric surface, called a **mouse pad** (see Figure 2-8). An **optical mouse** (see Figure 2-10) contains no mouse ball and instead uses a light-based sensor to track movement. This mouse can be moved around on nearly any smooth surface, except glass, and thus no mouse pad is required. A **foot mouse** allows people with carpal tunnel syndrome or other hand or wrist injuries to use a computer.

TRACKBALLS

An input device similar to a mouse is the trackball. A **trackball** is a plastic sphere sitting on rollers, inset in a small external case, or in many portable computers, in the same unit as the keyboard (see Figure 2-11). The trackball is often described as an upside-down mouse, although, unlike the mouse, it remains stationary. The user moves the ball with her fingers or palm. One or more buttons for choosing options are incorporated into the design of the trackball.

The main advantage of using a trackball is that it requires less desk space than a mouse, and is therefore a good choice for people working in confined areas. The trackball also requires less arm movement, making it a useful device for those with limited arm mobility.

Portable computers are often packaged with trackballs. Some are made to mount on the side of a laptop or notebook computer so you can use the device while sitting in an airplane seat or another confined area. Other portable computers now come with built-in miniature trackballs. In either case, you can install a regular desktop mouse if you find the trackball inconvenient.

KEYTERMS

carpal tunnel syndrome the condition of weakness, pain, or numbness resulting from pressure on the median nerve in the wrist; the syndrome is associated with repetitive motion, such as typing or using the mouse

FIGURE 2-11:
Trackball

The ball in a trackball is contained on top of the device rather than on the bottom side, as in a mouse. Rolling the ball moves the pointer about on the screen.

FIGURE 2-12:
Notebook Computer with Touchpad

With a touch pad, the user traces a finger on the pad, letting the finger function as the mouse. The touch pad also includes a button for clicking commands.

TOUCH PADS AND TOUCH SCREENS

A **touch pad** feels less mechanical than a mouse or trackball because the user simply moves a finger on the pad. A touch pad has two parts: one part acts as a button, while the other functions like the smooth surface of a mouse pad on which the user traces in the direction he wants the cursor to move on the screen. People with carpal tunnel syndrome find touch pads and trackballs easier to use than mice. Many portable computers have built-in touch pads as the input device, as shown in Figure 2-12.

A **touch screen** allows the user to choose options by pressing a finger (or fingers) on the appropriate part of the screen. Touch screens are widely used in bank ATMs and in kiosks at retail outlets.

JOYSTICKS

The **joystick** (named after the control lever used to fly older fighter planes) is a small box that contains a vertical lever that, when pushed in a certain direction, moves the graphics cursor correspondingly on the screen (see Figure 2-13). It is often used for computer games. Some joysticks have a button in the tip near the user's thumb. Pressing this button performs such actions as firing a game weapon at an object on the screen.

FIGURE 2-13: Joystick

A joystick is an input device used for moving objects about on the computer screen. Many types of computer games require a joystick.

Recently, users of notebook computers have become accustomed to a new type of joystick, called a "pointing lever" or simply a "pointer." It is small (about the size of a pencil eraser), and, as shown in Figure 2-14, fits between the G and H keys of the keyboard. By placing the index finger on top of the lever, the user can slightly push or pull to adjust the pointer on the screen. This type of joystick eliminates a bulky external mouse or joystick and allows the hand to remain close to the keyboard.

FIGURE 2-14: Pointing Lever on Notebook Computer

The keyboard on some notebook computers contains a small lever used to move a pointer about on the screen. Pushing or pulling lightly on the lever adjusts the pointer on the screen.

Subzero Meteor Hunting

Antarctica is a meteorite hunter's paradise. Meteorites erode rapidly in most climates, but survive indefinitely in the cold, dry climate of the South Pole. Searching for meteorites in such inhospitable terrain is a daunting task, but not for Nomad, the four-wheeled robot with a nose for meteors.

Nomad was first tested in the deep freeze at a refrigerated warehouse, a place normally used for storing frozen meats or foods about to be flash frozen. Its cameras and its main body of electronics are heavily insulated and provided with heaters. Cables and connectors designed for subzero temperatures, lubricants rated for extreme temperatures, and rubber tires instead of metal ones enable Nomad to withstand the extreme conditions on the frozen continent.

Weighing 1,200 pounds and about the size of a Volkswagon Beetle, Nomad has a pair of video cameras and a laser rangefinder to steer itself. Nomad uses computer vision, light spectroscopy, and magnetic sensors to detect areas potentially loaded with meteorites.

Like a bloodhound searching a trail, Nomad drives back and forth across a targeted area. Upon spying a rock, the robot photographs it, classifies it, and then uses a built-in database to estimate the probability of the rock being a meteorite. When Nomad determines a rock to be a meteor, it radios its exact coordinates to human researchers so they can retrieve the rock to confirm the designation and study it further.

Nomad was developed by Carnegie Mellon University, in collaboration with NASA. If Nomad proves successful in Antarctica, it will be used for future exploration of other planets.

Sources: Spice, Byron. "A cold, dry run: Robot tests well before expedition to Antarctica," *PC News,* October 11, 1998; Roach, John. " 'Nomad' combs no-man's-land for meteors," *Environmental News Network,* Jan. 22, 2000.

PENS AND TABLETS

Some people complain that drawing with a mouse is rather like drawing with a bar of soap, although exquisite computer art has been generated using a mouse. Artists, engineers, and others needing precise control over an input device may choose instead to use a **digitizing pen** and a **drawing tablet** to simulate drawing on paper. Owners of personal digital assistants (PDAs) like the PalmPilot and the Handspring Visor also may use a special pen to choose menu options and to write information in the screen (see Figure 2-15).

FIGURE 2-15:
Visor Handheld Computer

GRAPHICS TABLETS

A **graphics tablet** is a flat tablet used together with a penlike stylus or a crosshair cursor (see Figure 2-16). Embedded in the tablet surface are hundreds of tiny wires. To capture an image, the user grasps a stylus or crosshair cursor and traces an image or drawing placed on the tablet surface. Mapmakers find the precision tracing capabilities of graphics tablets very helpful. After tracing in streets, parks, and highways, they can then use the keyboard to label the locations with names.

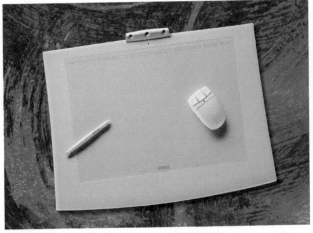

FIGURE 2-16:
Graphics Tablet

Graphics tablets, like the one shown, are widely used by engineers, drafters, and others who need to create precise, detailed drawings.

OPTICAL SCANNERS

An **optical scanner**, often called simply a **scanner**, is a light-sensing electronic device that can read and capture printed text and images, such as photographs and drawings, and convert them into a form a computer can understand. The scanned text or image is created and stored as a file rather than a paper document. Once scanned, the text or image can be displayed in the screen, edited, printed, stored on a disk, inserted into another document, or sent as an attachment to an e-mail message.

Two popular types of scanners are handheld scanners and page scanners (also called flatbed scanners). **Handheld scanners** are used for scanning small or curved areas. **Page scanners** look similar to tabletop copy machines. Pages are either laid face down on the scanner's glass surface or fed through the scanner by means of a side-feed device. Figure 2-17 contrasts the two types of scanners. Figure 2-18 illustrates how a scanner works.

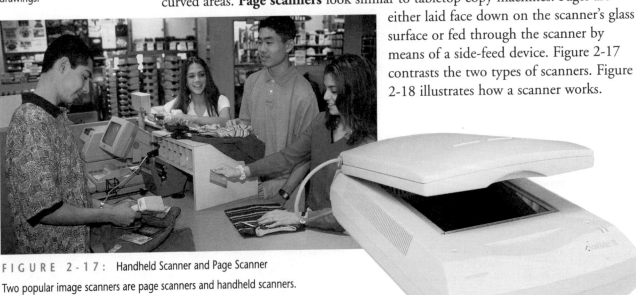

FIGURE 2-17: Handheld Scanner and Page Scanner

Two popular image scanners are page scanners and handheld scanners.

When text or a photo is scanned, it is stored as a matrix of rows and columns of dots, called a **bitmap**. Each dot consists of one or more bits of data. The greater the number of bits comprising a dot, the clearer the scanned image. The density of each dot helps determine the quality, called **resolution**, of the captured image. Modern scanners can capture text and images at resolutions ranging from 30 to 48 bits per dot. Resolution also depends on the number of dots, or **pixels**, per inch. The higher the number of dots (pixels), the sharper and clearer the captured image when displayed or printed. Resolution is measured in **dots per inch (dpi)** and expressed as the number of rows and columns. For example, a scanner with a dpi of 600 x 1,200 has a capacity of 600 columns and 1,200 rows of dots. Most modern scanners for home or office use a resolution of at least 1,200 dpi. Commercial scanners offer higher resolutions and are more expensive.

KEYTERMS

pixel the smallest picture element that a computer monitor or other device can display and from which graphic images are built

resolution a measurement of the sharpness of an image displayed on a computer monitor or other output device; resolution is measured in dots per inch (dpi), both vertically and horizontally, with higher resolution achieved by more dots per inch

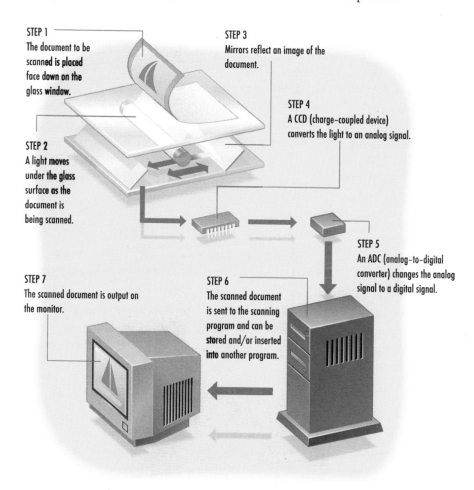

STEP 1
The document to be scanned is placed face down on the glass window.

STEP 2
A light moves under the glass surface as the document is being scanned.

STEP 3
Mirrors reflect an image of the document.

STEP 4
A CCD (charge-coupled device) converts the light to an analog signal.

STEP 5
An ADC (analog-to-digital converter) changes the analog signal to a digital signal.

STEP 7
The scanned document is output on the monitor.

STEP 6
The scanned document is sent to the scanning program and can be stored and/or inserted into another program.

F I G U R E   2 - 1 8 :   How a Scanner Works

A scanner captures text and/or graphical images and stores them as a bitmap, a matrix of rows and columns of tiny dots. Each dot represents one or more bits of data.

A particular scanner may be either a "dumb" scanner or an "intelligent" scanner. A **dumb scanner** can only capture and input a scanned image. Once entered into a computer, the image cannot be edited or altered. By contrast, an **intelligent scanner** uses **optical character recognition (OCR)** software that allows a captured image to be manipulated (edited or altered) with a word processor or other application program. Depending on the scanner model, the OCR software may be included in the package, or the software may need to be purchased separately.

BAR CODE READERS

Almost everything for sale today on the retail level is marked with a bar code, also known as a **Universal Product Code**, or **UPC**. The lines and spaces in a bar code contain symbols that a computer translates into a number. The computer then uses this number to find information about the product, such as its name and price, in a computerized record known as a **database**. **Bar code readers** can be found in every supermarket and in the larger chain stores (see Figure 2-19). Sometimes the reader takes the form of a pen. At other times it is placed below a glass cover at the end of a conveyor belt. Using bar codes greatly increases accuracy in recording sales and enables retail stores to update inventory files automatically. Overnight shipping services such as Federal Express and United Parcel Service (UPS) often use bar codes to identify packazges.

KEYTERMS

database a collection of information (data) about a subject that is organized in categories to make the information meaningful

FIGURE 2-19: Bar Code Reader

A bar code reader uses photo technology to "read" the lines in the bar code. The lines and spaces contain symbols that the computer translates into a number.

AUDIO INPUT

The process of entering (recording) speech, music, or sound effects is called **audio input**. Your personal computer must contain a sound card if you want to record or play high-quality sound. You will also need speakers and a sound-capturing device, such as a microphone, audio CD player, or tape player plugged into a port on the sound card. Finally, you will need special software, such as Windows Sound Recorder. Figure 2-20 shows a personal computer with a sound system.

FIGURE 2-20: Computer with Speakers

With the appropriate software and a microphone, sound is entered into a computer. Speakers allow captured or stored sound, such as music, to be played back.

Speech recognition, also called **voice recognition**, provides another type of audio input. Although a microphone is necessary for this type of input, the major element required is special software called a speech recognition program, for example, IBM's *Via Voice* or Dragon's *Naturally Speaking*. Speech recognition programs do not actually understand spoken words; they only understand a vocabulary of specific words ranging from a few words to several thousand words.

A particular speech recognition program may be either speaker-dependent or speaker-independent. A **speaker-dependent program** is one whereby the computer captures and stores your own voice as you speak words slowly and clearly into the microphone. Each spoken word is stored as a digital pattern of the word. After your words have been recorded, each word you speak is compared to those recorded earlier. The computer will recognize the word you speak only if it matches an already recorded word. A **speaker-independent program** contains a built-in vocabulary of prerecorded word patterns. The computer can recognize only spoken words that match a word contained in the built-in list of vocabulary words.

VIDEO INPUT

Video input occurs with a special type of video camera attached to the computer and plugged into a **video capture card** in an expansion slot, which converts the analog video signal into a digital signal (see Figure 2-21). It is also possible to connect an ordinary video camera directly to a

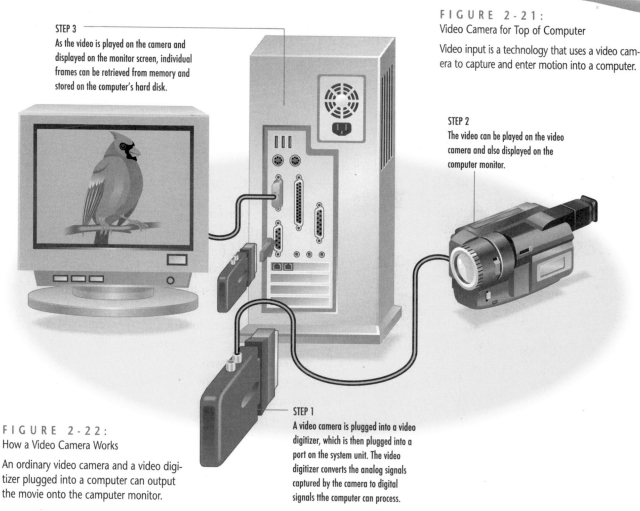

STEP 3

As the video is played on the camera and displayed on the monitor screen, individual frames can be retrieved from memory and stored on the computer's hard disk.

FIGURE 2-21:
Video Camera for Top of Computer

Video input is a technology that uses a video camera to capture and enter motion into a computer.

STEP 2

The video can be played on the video camera and also displayed on the computer monitor.

STEP 1

A video camera is plugged into a video digitizer, which is then plugged into a port on the system unit. The video digitizer converts the analog signals captured by the camera to digital signals tthe computer can process.

FIGURE 2-22:
How a Video Camera Works

An ordinary video camera and a video digitizer plugged into a computer can output the movie onto the camputer monitor.

analog continuous, not broken into bits; said of telephone signals, sound waves, temperatures, and all other signals that are not discrete

digital composed of separate bits (1's and 0's)

Macintosh or PC and to digitize incoming video by means of a special processing board attached to one of the computer's expansion slots (see Figure 2-22). Incoming video can be live or come from a previously recorded videocassette. With video-editing software, it is possible to view each frame of the video and to edit a video sequence.

APPLICATIONS FOR VIDEO INPUT

Businesses, government, and organizations are discovering numerous video-input applications. For example, book publishers can now include a small printed image on a book cover or within a magazine ad that will allow an order to be placed when a person holds the image up to a video camera on the computer. The camera captures the printed image, enters it into the computer, and transmits the order over the Internet to the publisher.

Some banks have begun using advanced video-input systems to identify customers. A camera captures an image of a would-be customer and quickly compares the image to those stored in a computer, thereby eliminating the necessity of checking a person's driver's license or other identification. Similar systems that store an image of a person's eye or fingerprints are used in high-security situations requiring quick employee identification, such as military installations and government facilities.

Manufacturers use video technology for quality control. For example, a product moving along an assembly line can be photographed and instantly compared with an already stored photograph of the "perfect" product. If a missing or broken part is detected, the computer rejects the product before it is packaged for shipment.

Experimental driver-less military vehicles use a **vision-input system** to avoid obstacles such as trees and ditches while driving over rough terrain. Similar vision-input technologies may soon be available for civilian vehicles. Vision-input offers great promise for the future.

FIGURE 2-23:
Digital Cameras

A digital camera looks much like a standard camera but captures and stores an image in digital format that can be processed by a computer.

DIGITAL CAMERAS

While conventional cameras capture images on film, **digital cameras** record and store images in a digitized form that can be entered into and stored by a computer. In appearance, digital cameras resemble traditional film-based cameras (see Figure 2-23). Most are portable, although some models are stationary and are connected directly to a computer. This connection allows recorded images to be altered, cropped, enlarged, or reduced.

A digital camera can capture a variety of images, including people, scenery, documents, and products. Newer models can even take short movies. Most digital cameras store captured pictures directly on a storage medium such as a floppy disk, from which the picture can be copied into the computer. You can then edit the picture using photo-editing software, print the picture, copy it into another document, post it on a Web site, or e-mail it to another computer. Some digital cameras allow you to view and edit pictures in the camera or connect the camera to a television for viewing or to a printer for printing. Figure 2-24 illustrates how a digital camera works.

As with a scanner, the quality of a digital camera's photos is measured by the number of bits stored in a dot, and the number of dots (pixels) per inch. Ads for the newer digital cameras talk about resolution in terms of megapixels (millions of pixels). A camera with a resolution of 2.1 megapixels produces high-quality pictures for the typical consumer. Professional photographers will probably gravitate toward a new digital camera introduced by Eastman Kodak in the fall of 2000. Kodak's camera uses a chip that can capture digital images with a resolution of 4096 x 4096 pixels (about 16 megapixels), which is about twice the resolution of 35-millimeter film and approximates the clarity achieved by the high-end 4 x 5 film cameras made by companies such as Hasselblad. What's even more exciting for computer users is that the new image-sensing technology used in the digital cameras may find its way into cellular telephones, because researchers are developing techniques to mass-produce the chips cheaply.

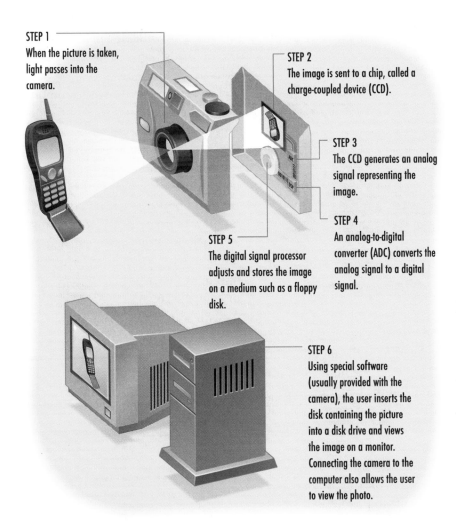

STEP 1
When the picture is taken, light passes into the camera.

STEP 2
The image is sent to a chip, called a charge-coupled device (CCD).

STEP 3
The CCD generates an analog signal representing the image.

STEP 4
An analog-to-digital converter (ADC) converts the analog signal to a digital signal.

STEP 5
The digital signal processor adjusts and stores the image on a medium such as a floppy disk.

STEP 6
Using special software (usually provided with the camera), the user inserts the disk containing the picture into a disk drive and views the image on a monitor. Connecting the camera to the computer also allows the user to view the photo.

FIGURE 2-24: How a Digital Camera Works

A digital camera captures images that are converted from analog to digital format and stored on a floppy disk or another storage medium. Once captured and stored, a picture can be printed or inserted into a document such as a sales brochure.

OUTPUT HARDWARE

Output is processed data, usually text, graphics, or sound, that can be used immediately, or stored in computer-usable form for later use. Two general categories of output are hard copy and soft copy. **Hard copy** is a permanent version of output, such as a letter printed on paper. **Soft copy** is a temporary version of output, typically the display of data on a computer screen. For example, the information displayed on a bank teller's computer terminal screen during the checking of your account balance is considered soft copy. Voice output such as the telephone company's computerized directory assistance is another form of soft copy, since soft copy includes any output that cannot be physically handled.

MONITORS

Monitors, a fundamental component of every single-user computer system, are the most common soft-copy output device. Available in various shapes, sizes, costs, and capabilities, a **monitor**, also called a **display screen** or **CRT (cathode ray tube)**, can display text, graphics, and images in brilliant color, often with exceptionally high resolution (see Figure 2-25).

The most common type of monitor for personal computers is the CRT monitor. However, flat-panel monitors are becoming increasingly popular. CRT monitors use the same cathode ray tube technology used in television sets, so they are fairly large and bulky. The screen of a CRT monitor is arranged as a grid of tiny pixels. Each pixel can be illuminated or not illuminated to produce an image on the screen, as shown in Figure 2-26. As with scanners and digital cameras, the number of pixels in the display determines the monitor's quality, or resolution. The greater the number of pixels, the higher the resolution and the better the image. Screen resolutions typically range from 640 x 480 to 1600 x 1200 or more. Although most monitors sold today offer the higher-range resolution, manufacturers are continually making technological improvements to provide even sharper images.

FIGURE 2-25:
Dell Monitor and NEC Monitor

A variety of monitors are used with computers. Shown here are examples of popular types.

FIGURE 2-26: Pixels on screen

Images are displayed in pixels on the monitor screen. The greater the number of pixels, the sharper the image.

Flat-panel displays use a variety of different technologies that allow them to be smaller, thinner, and lighter so they can be used with small computers, such as notebook computers, personal digital assistants (PDAs), and other devices. Their popularity is also increasing among desktop computer users as a result of improved resolution and because they take up less space. Figure 2-27 shows a notebook computer with a flat-panel display.

Another type of monitor that will likely grow in use is a set of **display goggles**. Highly effective for computer games, display goggles may become a standard feature of some of the new mobile computer devices such as belt-top computers or other systems worn on the body.

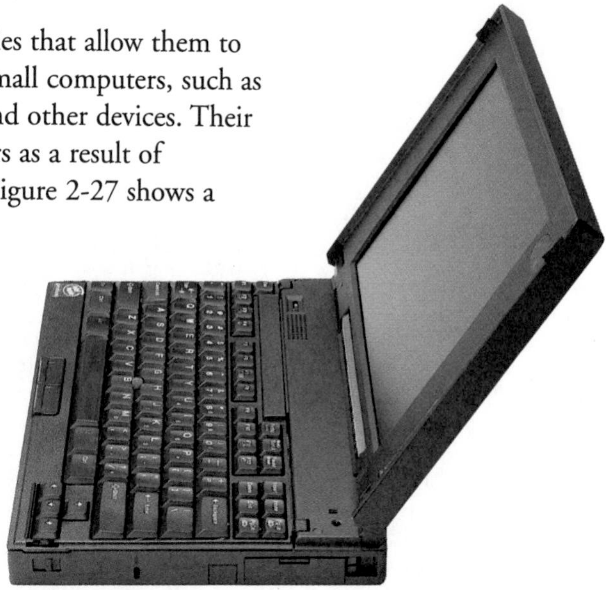

FIGURE 2-27: Notebook Computer with Flat-Panel Display

Notebook (laptop) computers such as the one shown above use flat-panel displays because they are thinner than CRT monitors.

PRINTERS

A **printer** is the most common type of hard-copy output device. Printers are separated into two main categories: impact and nonimpact. **Impact printers** print much like a typewriter, by striking an inked ribbon against the paper. **Nonimpact printers** use electricity, heat, laser technology, or photographic techniques to produce output. Three main types of printers for personal computers are dot-matrix printers, ink-jet printers, and laser printers. Table 2-2 lists printer types and examples of each kind.

PRINTER TYPE	EXAMPLE	USES	ADVANTAGES	DISADVANTAGES
Dot-matrix	Epson LQ570e	Print draft copies and multiple copies for large organizations with heavy printing workloads	Less costly than other types; useful for printing forms	Noisy; requires expensive ribbons; output quality inferior to other printer types; prints only in black
Ink-jet	HP Deskjet 990cse	Print documents for homes and small businesses	Capable of printing in color; high-quality output	Uses expensive ink cartridges; cannot print multiple copies
Laser	HP Laserjet Series	Print documents for homes and for businesses of all sizes	Prints in color or in black ; high-quality output; very quiet	Toner cartridges are expensive, especially the color toner

TABLE 2-2: Types of Printers

Dot-Matrix Printers

A **dot-matrix printer** is an impact printer that forms and prints characters in a manner similar to the way numbers appear on a football scoreboard. If you look closely at a scoreboard, you will see that each number consists of a pattern of

DRIVERS

The 2000 Nobel Prize in Physics was awarded to 76-year-old Jack Kilby for his work on the integrated circuit, which paved the way for the technological revolution that became known as the "Information Age." The development of the integrated circuit permitted gigantic gains in computer power.

Kilby's first integrated circuit, about the size of a thumbnail, was built in 1958. His novel idea was to develop the numerous electrical transistors in the chip's circuit from a single block of material, rather than assembling them with wires and other components. Kilby's work led to the integrated circuits of today, shrunk in size and loaded with millions of transistors. Without the integrated circuit, the personal computers of today would not have been possible.

Also credited with co-inventing the pocket calculator, Kilby worked for Texas Instruments until 1970 and then became a freelance inventor. He holds more than 60 patents and has been awarded honorary degrees from three universities. Kilby says he had no idea how much his microchip would expand the field of electronics. At home he still listens to music on a turntable and does not own a cell phone.

Kilby will get half of the $915,000 prize. The other half will be shared by two physicists who invented semiconductor heterostructures. The Nobel Prize is usually awarded for an abstract theoretical insight or an experimental technique. This is the first time the award was given for engineering rather than pure science. As a nod to the worldwide impact of the Internet, the Royal Swedish Academy of Sciences gave the prize to three men whose work enabled the growth of computer technology.

Sources: Johnson, George. "The Nobels: Dazzled by the Digital Light," *The New York Times,* October 15, 2000; Glanz, James. "3 Men Vital to Internet Share Physics Prize," *The New York Times,* October 11, 2000; Crissey, Mike. "Texan's Microchip Speeds Info Age," <http://www.news.excite.com/news/ap/001010/19/nobel-reax>.

lighted bulbs. By observing print produced on a dot-matrix printer, you can see that each letter or number consists of a series of tiny dots arranged to represent that letter or number, as shown in Figure 2-28.

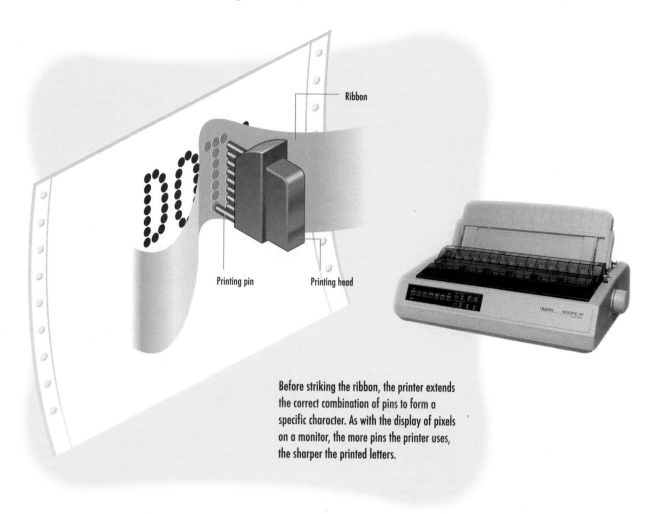

Ribbon

Printing pin

Printing head

Before striking the ribbon, the printer extends the correct combination of pins to form a specific character. As with the display of pixels on a monitor, the more pins the printer uses, the sharper the printed letters.

FIGURE 2-28: How a Dot-Matrix Printer Works

A dot-matrix printer prints characters in matrix format similar to the way numbers are displayed on a football scoreboard.

Dot-matrix printers are often used for printing multi-part forms, such as forms with the original copy plus carbon, or NCR, copies. For example, colleges and other schools typically use dot-matrix printers for printing class rolls and grade reports. For most other printing applications, however, nonimpact printers, including ink-jet and laser printers, are widely used. Technological improvements and declining prices have made these two types the printers of choice among personal computer users.

KEYTERMS

matrix a rectangular arrangement of elements into rows and columns

Ink-Jet Printers

An **ink-jet printer** is a nonimpact printer that forms images by spraying thousands of tiny droplets of electrically charged ink onto a page (see Figure 2-29). The printed images are in dot-matrix format, but of a higher quality than images printed by dot-matrix printers.

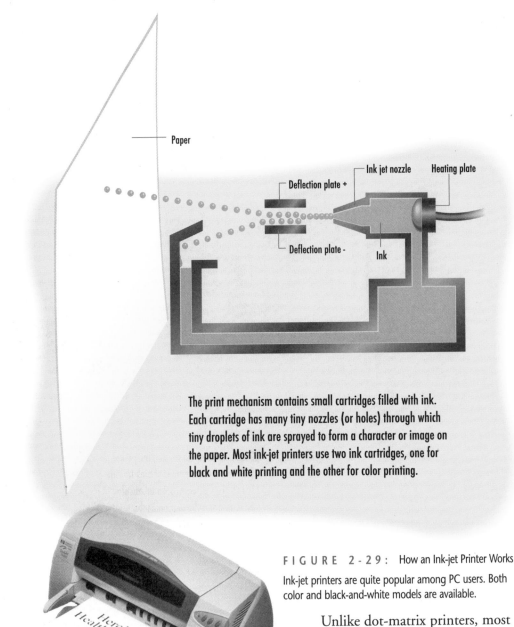

Paper

Deflection plate +

Ink jet nozzle   Heating plate

Deflection plate -

Ink

The print mechanism contains small cartridges filled with ink. Each cartridge has many tiny nozzles (or holes) through which tiny droplets of ink are sprayed to form a character or image on the paper. Most ink-jet printers use two ink cartridges, one for black and white printing and the other for color printing.

FIGURE 2-29: How an Ink-jet Printer Works
Ink-jet printers are quite popular among PC users. Both color and black-and-white models are available.

Unlike dot-matrix printers, most ink-jet printers are relatively quiet and can print images in a variety of colors. Their affordable price has made them the printer of choice for producing attractive color output. However, the cost of the replaceable ink cartridges can add up over time. Although their print quality is high, it is not as good as that produced by most laser printers.

Laser Printers

A **laser printer** is a nonimpact printer that produces output of exceptional quality using a technology similar to that of photocopy machines (see Figure 2-30). Their speed and their ability to produce clear, crisp text and images have made them the fastest growing segment of the printer market. Prices range from a few hundred dollars for a black-ink printer to a thousand dollars and up for a color printer.

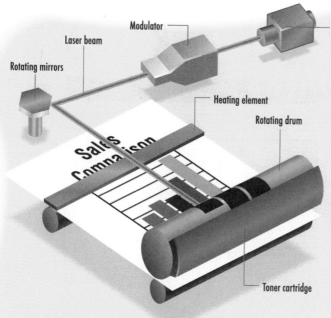

During priniting, characters are read by a mechanism inside the printer and relayed to the laser mechanism. Then, the laser mechanism sends light impulses through a series of reflective mirrors to the drum. The impulses, in the form of tiny dots, produce tiny magnetic fields on the drum in the shape of characters or images. As the drum rotates, the magnetic fields attract an ink-like powder, called toner. The toner on the drum is pressed onto the paper as the drum rotates.

FIGURE 2-30: How a Laser Printer Works
Laser printers produce output of exceptional quality and are among the most popular printers.

Laser printers form images in dot-matrix format and can produce text and images of exceptional quality. For example, with a 600 x 600 printer the output image is broken down into square-inch segments, each consisting of a 600 x 600 matrix of tiny printed dots. This means that each square inch of printed output consists of as many as 360,000 dots, resulting in exceptionally good resolution.

PLOTTERS

A **plotter** is a hard-copy output device used to output special kinds of hard copy, including architectural drawings, charts, maps, diagrams, and other images. Mapping applications might include housing subdivision plans, traffic patterns, topographical terrains, or demographics (for example, average age or family incomes). Plotters are also used to create engineering drawings for machinery parts and equipment. Figure 2-31 shows an example of a plotter.

FIGURE 2-31: Plotter
Engineers often use plotters like this one for producing high-quality, detailed prints of building, process, and machine designs.

DRIVERS

Steve Jobs is the prototype of America's computer industry entrepreneur. A college dropout fascinated with the counterculture and Eastern thought, Jobs transformed himself into a millionaire by the age of 30. Job's efforts changed the computer from a huge machine accessible only to big business and government into a small, user-friendly tool for the masses. In doing so, he revolutionized the computer industry.

Jobs started his career as a video game designer at Atari. He and a friend, Steve Wozniak, built their first computer in Job's basement. Then they each sold a few prized possessions to raise $1,300 to start their new company. Fondly recalling a summer working at an orchard in Oregon, Jobs named the company Apple Computer. Apple went public in 1980 and was soon worth $1.2 billion.

Apple originally had the personal computer market to itself, but when IBM started elbowing in, the company faltered. Jobs got involved in a power struggle and was eventually forced to resign. Jobs spent ten long years and almost his entire $100 million fortune in an effort to match the success of Apple. When his animation company Pixar went public after the release of the hit movie *Toy Story*, Jobs became a billionaire.

An even bigger coup was his invitation in 1996 to return to the floundering Apple as an informal advisor. Jobs has been the driving force behind the iMac computer and Apple's complete turnaround. In September 1999 at the Macworld convention, he was once again named CEO of Apple Computer. It was a long road back to what he calls "the best job in the world."

Source: "How Jobs Gets It Done," *talk*, October 2000; "Steve Paul jobs," <http://ei.cs.vt.edu/~history/jobs.html>.

SPEAKERS

Most personal computers have built-in **speakers** that produce warning sounds to alert the user to errors or other matters that require attention. A computer equipped with a powerful sound card like Creative Labs' Sound Blaster Pro can output high-quality sound from CD-ROMs, MIDI (Musical Instrument Digital Interface) keyboards, or the Internet through attached speakers (see Figure 2-32). Applications for which speakers are particularly important include computer games, multimedia distance learning programs, audio e-mail, and videoconferencing.

STORAGE DEVICES

Recall that main memory (RAM) provides temporary storage of data while it is being processed. Information contained in main memory is lost when the computer is turned off. Therefore, other hardware storage devices and media, called **secondary storage**, are needed for permanently storing important information such as computer programs, files, and data. Also called **auxiliary storage** or **external storage**, secondary storage devices and media provide the capability of reentering and reusing stored information.

A secondary storage system consists of two main parts, a storage device and a storage medium. A **storage device** is a hardware component that houses a **storage medium** on which data is recorded (stored), similar to the way a VCR is used for recording a television program on the tape inside a cassette. Some kind of secondary storage device is usually built into the system and is not visible unless you remove the case housing the CPU and related components. There are two main types of storage systems: magnetic and optical.

FIGURE 2-32:
Computer Speakers and Subwoofer

Computer speakers allow a user to hear sound effects from a computer game or an instructor's voice in a multimedia educational course. The satellite speakers handle mid- and upper-range tones, while the subwoofer handles the low tones.

MAGNETIC STORAGE DEVICES

Magnetic storage devices, the most commonly used secondary storage, are classified broadly as nonremovable (permanently installed) or removable (interchangeable). A **magnetic storage device** works by applying electrical charges to iron filings on revolving media, orienting each filing in one direction or another to represent a "0" or a "1." Data is stored and retrieved, or accessed, either sequentially or directly. **Sequential access** means that data can be retrieved only in the order in which it is physically stored, just as musical selections on a cassette tape are recorded and accessed one after the other. **Direct access** means that data can be retrieved in any order, regardless of the order in which it was stored. This type of access acts like a CD player. Although the songs are stored one after another, you can play any song by selecting its number.

TYPES OF MAGNETIC STORAGE MEDIA

Magnetic storage devices are popular because they provide an inexpensive means of recording large amounts of information. Furthermore, the media used by magnetic storage devices can be read, erased, or rewritten, and can therefore be used over and over. There are three main types of magnetic storage media:

- floppy disks
- hard disks
- cartridge tapes

Floppy and hard disks provide direct-access storage, while cartridge tapes provide sequential-access storage.

FLOPPY DISKS AND DISK DRIVES

A **floppy disk**, also called **diskette** or simply **disk**, is a thin, circular mylar wafer, sandwiched between two sheets of cleaning tissue inside a rigid plastic case (see Figure 2-33). When in use, the wafer spins and exposes its recording surfaces to the disk drive's read/write heads. Each disk surface contains millions of tiny metallic particles, representing bits. As the disk rotates, the read/write heads move back and forth across the disk surface. Specific particles are either magnetized or not magnetized, representing 0 and 1 bits. A magnetized particle represents a 1 bit and a non-magnetized particle represents a 0 bit. Recall from Chapter 1 that a combination of 0 and 1 bits represents a byte; that is, a letter, number, or special character. Figure 2-34 illustrates how a floppy disk drive works.

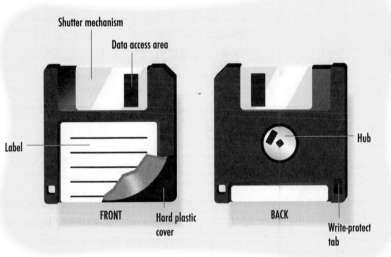

FIGURE 2-33: Floppy Disk and System Unit with Floppy Drive
Nearly all personal computers sold today come with a floppy disk drive.

Data is stored along the tracks and in the sectors of a floppy disk. A **track** is a numbered concentric circle. A **sector** is a numbered section or portion of a disk similar to a slice of pie. A group of sectors is called a **cluster**, which is the smallest unit of storage space that is assigned a memory address. As programs or data are stored along the tracks on the disk, the computer automatically maintains a file directory on the disk to keep track of the disk's contents. This directory shows the name of each file stored on the disk, its size, and the sector in which the file begins.

Floppy disks for early personal computers provided only 360KB of storage. As hardware capabilities increased, floppy disk capacity increased to 720KB, and today PCs typically use floppy disks with storage capacities of 1.44MB. Physically, the disks measure 3.5 inches in diameter, although other less commonly used sizes are also available. Table 2-3 lists the main types of floppy disks along with their storage capacities and related storage devices.

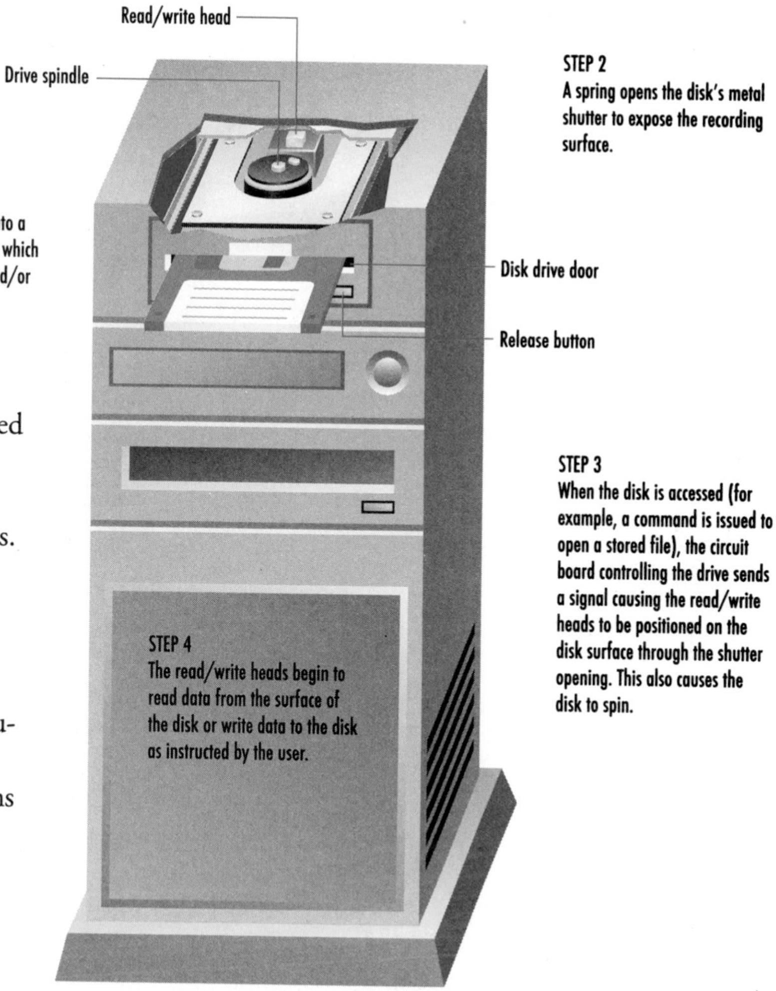

Higher-Capacity Floppy Disks

Until recently, a storage capacity of 1.44 megabytes was sufficient to handle most files of information. However, the increasing popularity of multimedia programs that include video files and desktop publishing applications requiring graphics files has created a need for ever-greater storage capacities. To accommodate these needs, manufacturers have developed higher-capacity storage devices such as the **SuperDisk** drive, the **Zip®** drive, and the **HiFD (High-Capacity FD)** disk drive. The SuperDisk uses both floppy and hard disk technology and requires specially formatted floppy disks. See Figure 2-35 for examples of the high-capacity floppy disks. Note that the high-capacity drives can also write to and read from standard 3.5-inch floppy disks.

STEP 1
The user inserts the disk into a device, called a disk drive, which records data to the disk and/or reads data from the disk.

STEP 2
A spring opens the disk's metal shutter to expose the recording surface.

STEP 3
When the disk is accessed (for example, a command is issued to open a stored file), the circuit board controlling the drive sends a signal causing the read/write heads to be positioned on the disk surface through the shutter opening. This also causes the disk to spin.

STEP 4
The read/write heads begin to read data from the surface of the disk or write data to the disk as instructed by the user.

Read/write head
Drive spindle
Disk drive door
Release button

FIGURE 2-34: How a Floppy Disk Drive Works

Once the floppy disk is inserted into the drive, data is recorded onto the disk or retrieved from it by means of read/write heads inside the drive.

DISK TYPE	STORAGE CAPACITY	EQUIVALENT NUMBER OF SINGLE-SPACED PAGES OF TEXT	STORAGE DEVICE
High Density (HD)	1.44 MB	480	Floppy disk drive
SuperDisk	120 MB	40,000	SuperDisk drive
Zip® disk	100-250 MB	33,333-83,333	Zip® drive
HiFD	200 MB	66,666	HiFD drive

TABLE 2-3: Types of Floppy Disks

CHAPTER 2

FIGURE 2-35: Zip Disk and External Zip Drive
Higher-capacity floppy disks such as the Zip disk, the SuperDisk, and the HiFD disk provide large secondary storage capacities.

Uses of Floppy Disks

Floppy disks are widely used for backing up, or saving, copies of files and programs; sharing files with other computer users; and installing, or loading, commercial software (although most programs are now shipped on CD-ROMs). Nearly every desktop computer or laptop/notebook comes installed with a floppy disk drive, which is accessed by inserting a floppy disk into a slot on the outside of the computer case.

Formatting a Disk

Before data can be stored on a disk, the disk must be prepared for use, a procedure called **formatting**, which can be done by the manufacturer or the user. The disk drive and the operating system software being used determine how the disk is formatted. During the formatting process, the disk surface is arranged into tracks, sectors, and clusters (see Figure 2-36), ready for the storage of data.

address the number or bit pattern that identifies a file and a specific location on a storage medium

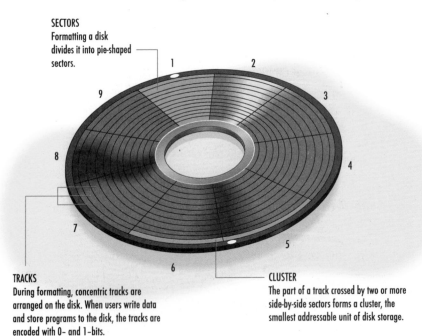

SECTORS
Formatting a disk divides it into pie-shaped sectors.

FIGURE 2-36: Cross Section of a Formatted Floppy Disk

The process of formatting a floppy disk results in the disk being arranged into tracks and sectors. Data is stored in sectors along the tracks.

TRACKS
During formatting, concentric tracks are arranged on the disk. When users write data and store programs to the disk, the tracks are encoded with 0- and 1-bits.

CLUSTER
The part of a track crossed by two or more side-by-side sectors forms a cluster, the smallest addressable unit of disk storage.

Proper Handling of Disks

It is important that floppy disks be cared for properly to prevent damaging the contents. Figure 2-37 illustrates guidelines for handling and storing floppy disks.

HARD DISKS AND DISK DRIVES

A **hard disk** system consists of one or more rigid metal platters (disks) mounted on a metal shaft and sealed in a container that contains an access mechanism (Figure 2-38). The container is sealed to prevent contamination from dust, moisture, and other airborne particles and to allow the system to operate more efficiently. Hard disks range in size from 1 to 5.25 inches in diameter. Storage capacity ranges from 4 GB to more than 30GB. People frequently use the terms *hard disk* and *hard drive* to mean the same thing, even though in technical terms the drive is the storage device and the disk is the magnetic storage medium. A hard disk unit may be either nonremovable (fixed) or removable (interchangeable). Most personal computers arrive from the factory with a fixed hard drive installed within the system unit housing. Some also include an interchangeable hard drive that functions like a floppy disk drive. Iomega Corporation's **Jaz® cartridge**, for example, is a removable hard disk that offers 1 GB of storage. Figure 2-38 shows how a hard drive retrieves information.

DO:

1. Do insert the disk into the drive carefully.
2. Do store the disk in a safe place when not in use

DO NOT:

1. Do not open the disk's shutter or touch the recording surface on the disk.
2. Do not place heavy objects on the disk.
3. Do not eat, drink, or smoke near a disk.
4. Do not expose the disk to heat, sunlight, or cold.
5. Do not place the disk near magnetic fields, such as TVs, radios, monitors, or calculators.

FIGURE 2-37: Guidelines for Handling Floppy Disks

The hard plastic cases of floppy disks do not totally protect the circular wafers inside. Stored data can be damaged by improper handling of disks.

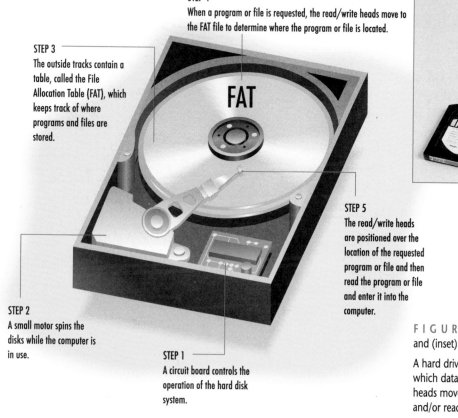

STEP 4
When a program or file is requested, the read/write heads move to the FAT file to determine where the program or file is located.

STEP 3
The outside tracks contain a table, called the File Allocation Table (FAT), which keeps track of where programs and files are stored.

FAT

STEP 5
The read/write heads are positioned over the location of the requested program or file and then read the program or file and enter it into the computer.

STEP 2
A small motor spins the disks while the computer is in use.

STEP 1
A circuit board controls the operation of the hard disk system.

FIGURE 2-38: How a Hard Drive Works and (inset) a Jaz Cartridge and Drive

A hard drive contains one or more hard disks on which data is stored. When activated, read/write heads move in and out between the disks to record and/or read data.

Comparing Hard Disks and Floppy Disks

Hard disks offer far greater storage capacities and operate much faster than floppy disks. Thus, hard disks greatly improve a PC's efficiency. Storage capacities of hard disks are stated in terms of gigabytes, or billions of bytes of data, whereas floppy disk capacities are stated in megabytes, or millions of bytes of data. Computers sold today often contain hard disks with 30 or more gigabytes of storage capacity.

A hard disk rotates faster and continues spinning while the computer is in operation, whereas a floppy disk spins only when data is being stored or accessed. Continuous spinning of a hard disk provides faster access because it enables the disk surface(s) to move past the read/write heads faster (refer to Figure 2-38). This speeds up the computer's operation as important system commands and functions, such as a command to save a file, are executed more quickly.

Hard disks contain many more tracks and sectors than do floppy disks. Prior to being sold, hard disks are formatted by the manufacturer unless instructed otherwise by the purchaser. A preformatted hard disk for personal computers can be reformatted by the user. However, inexperienced users should never attempt to reformat a hard disk, since a PC's operating system is installed on the computer's hard disk and reformatting a disk destroys all of the previous contents.

Tape Cartridges and Tape Drives

One of the first secondary storage media for computers was magnetic tape on which programs and data were stored. Today, **tape cartridges,** consisting of a small plastic housing containing a magnetically coated ribbon of thin plastic, are used mainly for backing up the contents of a hard drive and for archiving large amounts of data that are no longer actively used but need to be saved for historical purposes. Similar to a pocket-size tape recorder, a **tape drive** is used to write data to, and read data from, the tape (see Figure 2-39). Administrators of local area networks (LANs) might use magnetic tape cartridges to back up a company's data on a daily basis. Tape cartridges provide a relatively inexpensive, sequential-access type of storage.

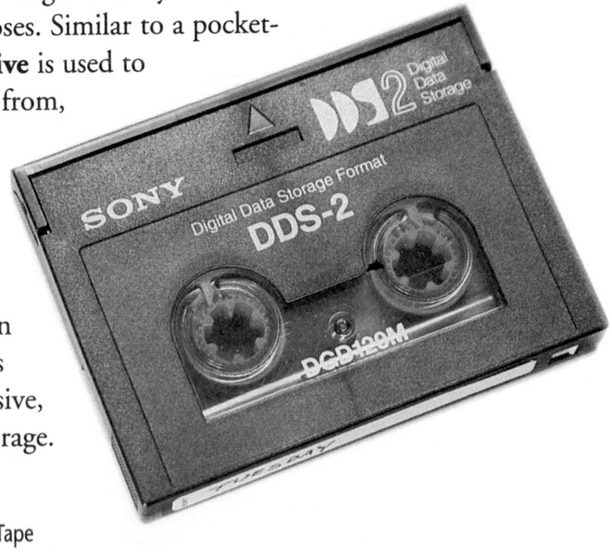

FIGURE 2-39: Cartridge Tape

Cartridge tape is used with personal computers mainly for backing up the contents of a hard drive. The tape is housed in a small plastic container that also contains a tape reel and a take-up reel.

OPTICAL DISKS AND DISK DRIVES

Optical disk systems are a popular storage device among PC users. An **optical disk** is a secondary storage medium on which data is recorded and read by two lasers: a high-density laser that records data by burning tiny indentations, or pits, onto the disk surface, and a low-intensity laser that reads stored data from the

disk into the computer (see Figure 2-40). An optical disk can store several gigabytes of data. Common types, which are explained in the following sections,
include:

- CD-ROM (compact disk, read-only memory)
- CD-R (compact disk, recordable)
- CD-RW (compact disk, rewritable)
- DVD (digital video disk)

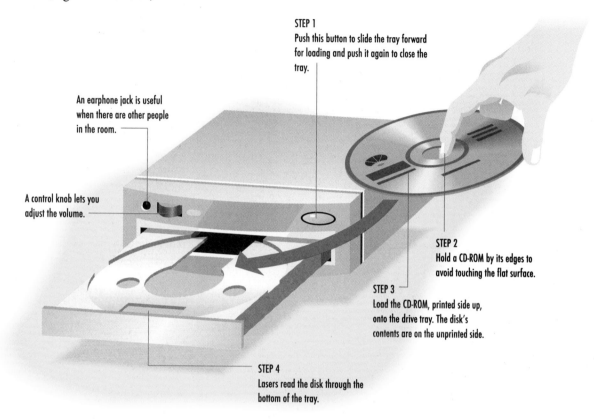

STEP 1
Push this button to slide the tray forward for loading and push it again to close the tray.

An earphone jack is useful when there are other people in the room.

A control knob lets you adjust the volume.

STEP 2
Hold a CD-ROM by its edges to avoid touching the flat surface.

STEP 3
Load the CD-ROM, printed side up, onto the drive tray. The disk's contents are on the unprinted side.

STEP 4
Lasers read the disk through the bottom of the tray.

FIGURE 2-40: Using an Optical Disk Drive

Optical disk systems are used when there is a need for very large storage capacity. Various types of optical disks are available in addition to the standard CD-ROM.

Advantages of Optical Disk Storage

Optical disk technologies are not compatible with one another and each requires
a different type of disk drive and disk. Within each category there are varying
storage formats, although CD-ROMs are relatively standard (Table 2-4 compares
the storage capacities of optical disks). All three systems offer the following advantages over floppy disks, hard disks, and tape cartridges:

- greater storage capacity
- less expense, bit for bit
- greater durability

CD-ROM Disks

Most optical disk systems are of the CD-ROM (pronounced *see-dee-rom*) type.
Like an audio CD you might listen to in your car, a **CD-ROM (compact disk,
read-only memory)** comes with data already coded on it. The data is permanent
and can be read many times, but the data cannot be changed. To access the stored

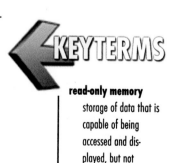

KEYTERMS

read-only memory
storage of data that is capable of being accessed and displayed, but not changed and resaved

OPTICAL DISK	STORAGE CAPACITY	FEATURES
CD-ROM	650–700 MB	Can be written to only once: used for distributing digital data such as computer software and for storing large data and graphics files
CD-R	650 MB	Used mainly in small businesses for creating one-of-a-kind CDs
CD-RW	650 MB	Allows rewriting; used mainly for backing up important files
DVD-ROM	4.7 GB	Can be written to only once; typically used to create master copies of movies
DVD-RAM	4.7 GB	Allows rewriting
DVD-Video	4.7–9.4 GB	Used in the entertainment industry for recording movies that are sold or rented

TABLE 2-4: Types and Capacities of Optical Storage

data, you need a CD-ROM drive. Since CD-ROM disks conform to a standard size and format, any CD-ROM disk can be used with any CD-ROM drive. Computer CD-ROM drives are also capable of playing audio CDs. CD-ROMs are well suited for storing large computer applications that include graphics, sound, and video. Consider, for example, that the entire 32-volume set of the *Encyclopedia Britannica 2001* can be stored on two CD-ROM disks.

CD-ROM drives are classified by spin speed, which is measured relative to the speed of the original CD standard created in the 1980s. Speeds of today's drives are typically 24X (twenty-four times the speed of the original CD standard), 32X (thirty-two times the original speed), and 40X (forty times the original speed).

CD-R Disks

The **CD-R (compact disk, recordable)** was developed to allow average PC users, including businesses, to create their own CDs using a peripheral device called a CD writer. This device writes once to the CD-R disk, and the resulting audio CD or CD-ROM will run in any CD-ROM drive. CD-R disks are rapidly being displaced by the more versatile CD-RW. Figure 2-41 shows CD-R disks ready for recording.

KEYTERMS

recordable capable of having files of information stored on, or written to

rewritable capable of having files of information stored on and overwritten, or restored

FIGURE 2-41: CD-R Disks

CD-R disks offer an inexpensive way for individuals and businesses to create their own CDs.

CD-RW Disks

A newer type of optical disk storage technology is **CD-RW (compact disk, rewritable)** that uses an erasable disk on which a user can write multiple times. Thus, a CD-RW disk acts the same as a floppy disk or hard disk that allows you to write and rewrite data to the disk many times. To use a CD-RW system you must have a CD-RW drive and special CD-RW software. CD-RW disks are often used in the movie industry for making original copies of movies. Once perfected, the movie is copied to other optical disks that cannot be changed.

DVD-ROM Disks

Many of today's complex applications demand huge amounts of storage capacity, often requiring several standard CD-ROMs to store the applications. To overcome this limitation, DVD-ROM technology was developed. **DVD-ROM (digital video disk-ROM)** is an extremely high capacity disk capable of holding several gigabytes of data (see Figure 2-42). In fact, an 18 GB disk can hold the entire contents of a telephone book listing every resident in the United States.

DVD-ROM technology was initially developed to store the contents of full-size movies. However, the disk can also store text, graphics, images, and sound. This technology requires the use of a DVD-ROM drive or player. Due to its backward compatibility, you can access data stored on a standard CD-ROM with a DVD-ROM drive.

KEYTERMS

backward compatibility being able to work with earlier versions of a program or earlier models of computers

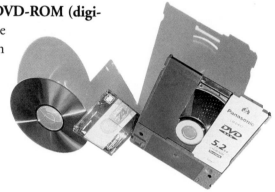

FIGURE 2-42: DVD Disk
A DVD-ROM disk looks like its relative, the CD-ROM.

LARGE COMPUTER HARDWARE

Large computer systems, such as mainframe and minicomputer systems, typically incorporate many of the same hardware devices found in personal computers, although in multiples. The central processing unit (CPU) of a mainframe or minicomputer, for example, often includes several processors and coprocessors. A supercomputer may contain hundreds of processors that work together to process huge amounts of data, such as census data or bank transactions. Multiple processors allow a computer to execute programs and to process data faster because they work in teams—each processor working on a particular program segment and its accompanying data.

A **coprocessor** is a special type of dedicated processor designed to perform certain kinds of processing, such as processing large amounts of numerical data. High-end personal computers may also contain a coprocessor, called a **math coprocessor**, dedicated to processing numerical data.

WWW infolinks

top 500 supercomputers:
www.top500.org

STORAGE DEVICES

Large computer systems typically use magnetic disk and magnetic tape secondary storage devices and media. Magnetic disk storage consists of a disk drive that houses multiple hard disks contained in a rigid plastic container called a **disk pack**. A disk pack is mounted inside a disk drive. A metal shaft extends vertically through the center of the vertically aligned disks. When activated, electromagnetic read/write heads record information and/or read stored data by moving inward and outward between the disks, as shown in Figure 2-43.

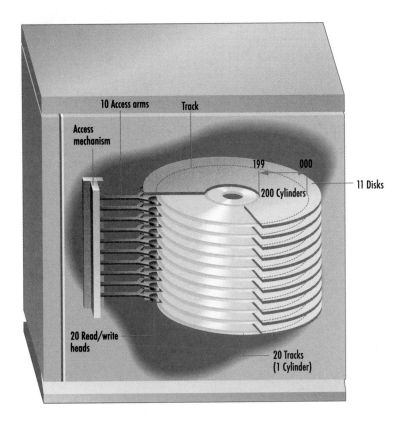

Disk storage provides a user with direct, or random, access to stored data. Disk storage is preferred when the user needs to access, and perhaps update, the stored information quickly. For example, disk storage allows bank and utility company employees to quickly access and update customer accounts.

Another type of secondary storage for large computer systems is **magnetic tape storage** using removable reels of magnetic tape, somewhat similar to a reel-to-reel stereo system (see Figure 2-44). The tape contains tracks that extend the full length of the tape. Each track contains metallic particles representing potential 0 and 1 bits. As is true of magnetic disks, combinations of bits are magnetized, or not magnetized, to represent bytes of data (see Figure 2-45).

FIGURE 2-43:
Disk Pack

A disk pack houses multiple vertically aligned disks in a rigid plastic container and placed inside a disk drive. When activated, read/write heads read and/or record on the disks by moving inward and outward between them.

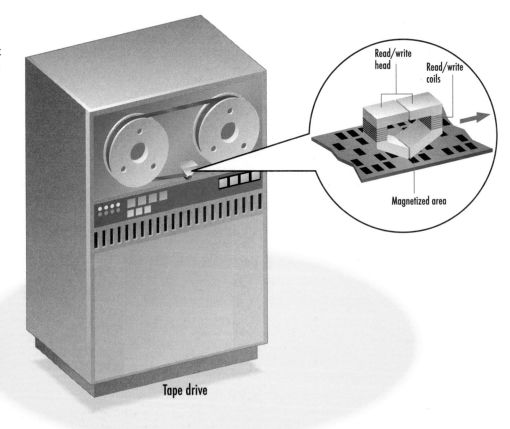

FIGURE 2-44: Tape Drive

A tape drive records and reads data from a reel of magnetic tape. Many large businesses and organizations use this sequential-access storage medium for backing up important programs and data.

Because magnetic tape is a sequential storage technology, information is accessed and/or updated in sequential order. For example, if the user wants to access the 20th record on the tape, the previous 19 records must first move past the read/write heads before the 20th record can be accessed. Magnetic tape storage is typically used in situations where large amounts of information, such as all employee payroll records, are to be updated. In this case, all records are to be updated and the order in which individual records are processed is not important.

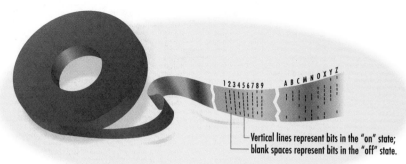

Vertical lines represent bits in the "on" state; blank spaces represent bits in the "off" state.

FIGURE 2-45:
Data Stored on Magnetic Tape

Data is stored as magnetic particles along tracks that extend the full length of the tape.

Magnetic tape storage may be used for other kinds of applications. Information stored on magnetic disk is often backed up onto tape and stored in a safe place in case it is needed. For example, a serious fire could damage or destroy disk drives, tape drives, and other equipment. Having a backup copy of the data can eliminate the need to reconstruct important information.

WORM DISKS

A type of optical laser disk, the **WORM (write once, read many) disk** is a very high capacity storage device that is often used by companies to store huge amounts of data, particularly images. These disks are mostly used in mainframe applications.

Numerous other hardware devices may be used with large computer systems including servers, terminals, and printers. The specific hardware devices used will vary from one business or organization to another and are determined by the specific needs of the enterprise. Chapter 4 discusses network hardware, including servers and related devices.

Computers in Your Future?

The Online Job Search

Instead of pounding the pavement, job hunters now search for jobs online. Posting a resume and scanning for employment is the first step. But which Web sites produce results?

The large sites such as Monster.com, HotJobs.com, and Headhunter.net have huge databases and extra tools such as salary calculators, but their size—some millions of job listings—may prove cumbersome to comb through. Also, the big sites require resume data in a standard format, usually chronological order, which may not be ideal for those who want to emphasize unique skills or experience. Another drawback to big sites is that half of their postings come from headhunters, who don't reveal the name of a potential employer.

If you already have a dream company in mind, start by looking at their Web page. Some big corporations, such as Lucent Technologies and Sun Microsystems, have developed their own recruiting sites for prospective employees.

Niche boards, such as telecomcareers.net, offer more focused listings and may give users more control over how their resumes look. Some limit headhunters' listings. Niche listings also tend to have more mid- and upper-management jobs. Look for niche boards that are offshoots of trade publications, professional organizations, or networking groups.

Another way to job hunt is to focus on a site that organizes jobs by location. For example, craigslist.com lists technology jobs by locality. It currently has nine U.S. sites and two in Australia.

Source: Salkever, Alex. "A Better Way," *Business Week,* October 9, 2000.

ON THE HORIZON

Scientists, computer engineers, and entrepreneurs of all stripes are working almost feverishly to develop new and improved hardware devices that will make information access faster and easier. After all, much is at stake—the great satisfaction that comes with creating something new and better, plus the millions and billions of dollars in revenue to be shared by the successful individuals and companies. Several trends are worth watching.

WIRELESS, WIRELESS, AND MORE WIRELESS

WWW infolinks

Wireless LAN Association: www.wlana.com

Wireless Resource Center: www.informationweek. com/center/wireless

Consumers and businesses are discovering the enormous advantages of being able to access the Internet anytime, anywhere using handheld computers and Internet-enabled cell phones. Industry watchers estimate that some one billion people will be using cell phones by 2003. The applications for the new wireless devices grow more exciting almost daily.

Imagine being able to watch movies on your cell phone or being able to make your airline reservations and almost instantly receive your e-mail ticket. Salespeople could check inventories, transmit an order, and bill the customer—all on the run. Wireless devices in the form of medical sensors with access to the Internet could alert your doctor to potentially life-threatening conditions, such as a heart attack, before you felt the first twinge of angina.

INCREASED MAGNETIC DATA STORAGE CAPACITIES

Chip manufacturers are facing the problem of size limitations—how small can chips become without self-destructing because of the energy generated? Scientists expect to be able to increase magnetic storage capacities up to 100 times their present limit before entirely new technologies will be needed.

IMPROVED MONITORS

Expect computer monitors to become ever thinner and more flexible. Using new materials will enable manufacturers to create monitors that can be rolled up like a piece of paper. At the same time, monitor resolution will continue to increase, and within a decade we may be able to see multiple Web documents simultaneously on the screen, eliminating the current problem of having to scroll while reading documents at Web sites.

MORE SMART CARDS

WWW infolinks

Smart Card Resource Center: www.smart-card.com

Smart Card Industry Association: www.scia.org

The use of **smart cards**—something like a credit card embedded with a computer chip—will probably increase, particularly in the United States where their use is far less than in Europe. Dataquest, a research firm, projects that worldwide sales will grow from $2.4 billion in 2000 to $8.1 billion by 2004. The growth in wireless Internet access and the need for improved security during online transactions and data sharing are factors driving the growing popularity of smart cards. Their security advantage is that, unlike a standard credit card, an account number is not saved and stored at a commercial Web site during a transaction. Instead, the user slips the smart card into the computer slot and enters a password that allows the transaction to proceed.

Consumers likely will use smart cards to both order and pay for products over the Web and to manage their banking. Smart cards also could contain complete personal data, such as health, insurance, driving, and social security records. Large companies could use smart cards as a security device against hackers.

BIOMETRIC AUTHENTICATION DEVICES AS SECURITY MEASURES

The need for enhanced security and privacy protection while on the Internet is also creating a larger market for hardware devices that establish a person's identity based on unique physical attributes. Fingerprint recognition hardware along with voice and face recognition devices are expected to be more widely used in the future to confirm a customer's identity during an Internet order and purchase or to control user access to protected information. Interestingly, though, experts predict that eye-recognition devices will fall out of the picture because people tend to feel more protective about their eyes than, for example, their fingerprints, and will be reluctant to allow the recording of their irises as an identification mechanism.

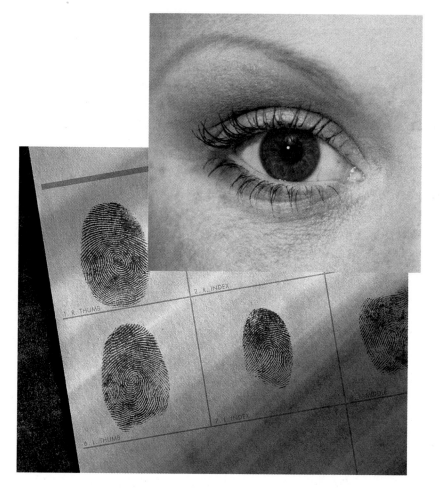

Leading by a Nose

Of all the senses, the sense of smell is the most complex and has the quickest path to our hearts and brains. Consider that there are four genes for vision, as compared with 1,000 genes for olfaction. Also, while all of the other senses follow an indirect route, smell goes straight to the part of the brain responsible for feelings and memories. Despite its emotional punch, this sense has been largely overlooked by computer technology.

Enter a company named DigiScents, which has developed a computer peripheral called the iSmell to allow users to access scents, aromas, and odors. The iSmell contains a palette of 128 chemical odors that can be combined to generate any number of smells. Its software is programmed with the mathematical models of specific odors, enabling users to download specific smells or even create new ones.

The power of smell leads to infinite applications for such a product: cooking magazines could offer tantalizing hints of recipes; travel agents might tempt customers with salty ocean air. Proctor & Gamble, sniffing out opportunity, has negotiated with DigiScents to share its research.

Other companies are quickly jumping on the smell bandwagon. AromaJet.com is collaborating with video game companies to add smell as a sensory element to their products, and TriSenx has developed scent-producing hardware that will allow users to print scent sheets on cards.

Source: "Now on the Small Screen: The Scent of a Kitchen," *The New York Times,* Sept. 13, 2000.

1936
John Dvorak designs an easy-to-use keyboard

1940

1944
IBM markets a type-writer with proportional spacing

1950
Douglas Engelbart pro-motes the idea of using monitors instead of paper to view computer output

1950

1956
MIT researchers experi-ment with keyboard input for computers; IBM's hard disk is first on market

1960

1963
Douglas Engelbart is awarded a patent on a pointing device for com-puters

1969
The barcode scanner is invented; Intel offers a 1KB RAM chip

1970

1971
The LCD monitor appears on the market; IBM debuts the floppy disk, an 8-inch disk called a "memory disk"

1972
CD technology is developed

1980

1983
Microsoft introduces its Mouse for the IBM PC; Sony and Philips pro-duce a CD-ROM, based on the audio CD

1990

1993
Intel releases the Pentium microprocessor

1998
The DVD-RAM drive is available

2000

2000
Sony Corporation intro-duces a PDA with a slot for its Memory Stick memory card; Intel launches the Pentium 4 chip with clock speed of 1.5GHz or more

- **What is Hardware?** All systems including computers, networks, the Internet, and the World Wide Web require hardware. The word **hardware** refers to all of the physical devices that make up a computer system. The larger the system, the more devices needed to support the system.

- **Personal Computers.** A **personal computer**, also called **microcomputer** or simply **PC**, is a relatively small and inexpensive computer designed for an individual user. Personal computer types include **desktop**, **notebook**, and **handheld** computers.

- **Personal Computer Hardware.** A personal computer system includes hard-ware devices for each part of the information processing cycle: processing (system unit), input, output, and storage.

- **System Unit Hardware.** The **system unit** is the component that processes information. It consists of the **motherboard**, also called **system board**, which houses a **microprocessor**, **memory boards and chips**, **storage interfaces**, **ports**, **expansion slots**, and **expansion boards** that allow peripheral devices such as the **monitor**, **keyboard**, **mouse**, and **disk drives** to function properly. A **microprocessor**, or CPU chip, processes data. **RAM (random access memory)** chips inside the system unit are used to store programs while they are being executed and data while it is being processed. **ROM (read-only memory)** refers to chips on which instructions, information, or data has been prerecorded. Once data has been recorded on a ROM chip, it cannot be altered or removed and can only be read by the computer. A **port** is a plug-in slot on a computer to which you can connect a device, such as a printer. An **expansion slot** is an opening in a computer where a circuit board, called an **expansion board**, can be inserted to add new capabilities to the computer. A **PC card** is a small expansion board that plugs into the side of a notebook or portable computer. A **bus** is a collection of tiny wires through which data is transmitted from one part of the computer to another.

- **Input Hardware.** An **input device** enables a user to enter data and pro-grams into a computer system. Common input devices include **keyboards**, **point-and-click devices**, and **scanners**. Examples of point-and-click devices include a **mouse**, **joystick**, **trackball**, and **graphics tablet**. Another popular input device is a **scanner**.

- **Input via Video and Digital Cameras.** A variety of photographic, audio, and video devices can be used to enter multimedia data. **Video input** involves capturing and entering action motion into a computer and storing the motion (movement) on a storage medium. This technology uses a spe-cial type of video camera plugged into a **video capture card** installed in an expansion slot inside the computer. A **digital camera** can capture images of people, scenery, documents, and product records in a form that can be entered and stored by a computer. The process of entering (recording) speech, music, or sound effects is called **audio input**. **Speech recognition**, also called **voice recognition**, refers to a computer system's capability to rec-ognize and capture spoken words using a speech recognition program.

- **Output Hardware**

  Output. is processed data, usually text, graphics, or sound, that can be used immediately, or stored in computer-usable form for later use. Two general categories of output are hard copy (permanent) and soft copy (temporary). A **monitor**, also called a **display screen** or **CRT**, is a soft-copy output device. A **printer** is the most common type of hard-copy output device. Three main types of printers for personal computers are **dot-matrix printers**, **ink-jet printers**, and **laser printers**. Other output devices include **speakers** and **plotters**.

- **Secondary Storage Hardware.** **Secondary storage**, also called **auxiliary storage** or **external storage**, is the permanent storage of computer programs, files, and data using secondary storage devices and media. Once stored using these devices and media, the stored information can be reentered into the computer and used again and again. Common secondary storage devices include **floppy disks**, **superdisks**, **hard disks**, **optical disks**, and **cartridge tapes**.

- **Large Computer Hardware.** Large computer systems typically include a variety of devices including a **central processing unit (CPU)**, **processors**, **coprocessors**, and secondary storage devices including **disk drives** and **tape drives**. Numerous other hardware devices may be used with large computer systems including **servers**, **terminals**, and **printers**.

KEYTERMS

audio input, 18
bar code reader, 18
BIOS (basic input/output system), 8
bitmap, 17
bus, 10
bus bandwidth, 10
cache memory, 8
CD-R (compact disk, recordable), 35
CD-ROM (compact disk, read-only memory), 35
CD-RW (compact disk, rewritable), 37
cluster, 30
coprocessor, 37
database, 18
digital camera, 20
digitizing pen, 16
direct access, 29
disk pack, 37
display goggles, 23
docking station, 9
dot-matrix printer, 23
dots per inch (dpi), 17
drawing tablet, 16
dumb scanner, 17
DVD-ROM (digital video disk-ROM), 37
expansion board, 9
expansion slot, 9
flat-panel display, 23
floppy disk, 30
foot mouse, 14
formatting, 32
graphics tablet, 16
handheld scanner, 16
hard copy, 22
hard disk, 33
High-Capacity FD (HiFD) disk drive, 31
impact printer, 23
ink-jet printer, 25
input device, 10
intelligent scanner, 17
Jaz® cartridge, 33
joystick, 15
keyboard, 11

laser printer, 26
magnetic storage device, 29
magnetic tape storage, 39
math coprocessor, 37
microprocessor, 6
monitor, 22
motherboard, 5
mouse, 13
mouse pad, 14
mouse pointer, 13
nonimpact printer, 23
optical character recognition (OCR), 17
optical disk, 34
optical mouse, 14
optical scanner, 16
page scanner, 16
parallel port, 9
PC Card, 10
pixel, 17
plotter, 27
port, 9
power-on self test (POST), 8
printer, 23
resolution, 17
secondary storage, 29
sector, 30
sequential access, 29
serial port, 9
smart card, 40
soft copy, 22
speaker-dependent program, 19
speaker-independent program, 19
speakers, 29
special-function keyboard, 11
speech recognition (voice recognition), 19
storage device, 29
storage medium, 29
SuperDisk drive, 31
system unit, 5
tape cartridge, 34
tape drive, 34

touch pad, 14
touch screen, 15
trace, 5
track, 30
trackball, 14
Universal Product Code (UPC), 18
Universal Serial Bus (USB) port, 9
video capture card, 19
video input, 19
video port, 9
vision-input system, 20
WORM (write once, read many) disk, 39
Zip® drive, 31

INTERNET

TUTORIAL 2

CONDUCTING A SIMPLE SEARCH

In the previous Internet topic, Web sites were explored by keying the Web address (URL) for a specific company. Another method used to find information is by entering a keyword or a phrase and then browsing through a series of Web pages that were found. Several search engines are available to assist users with locating Web sites by *topic*. A search engine is a company that uses specialized software to continually scan the Web to index and catalog the information that is published. These companies have created Web sites where the user begins a search by keying the word or phrase they would like to find information on. The search engine then lists the Web pages that contain the word or phrase as links, which are called *hits*. Some search engines maintain category indices where the user clicks through a series of categories and subcategories until they reach the desired list of Web pages.

In this topic, you will find information on the Web by entering keywords and then conduct another search by browsing through a list of categories.

Steps

1. Start Internet Explorer. If necessary, connect to your ISP and enter your username and password.

2. Click the Search button on the Internet Explorer toolbar.

A Search pane opens at the left side of the Internet Explorer window with categories displayed that can be searched and a text box to enter the keyword or phrase to find. The default category selected is Find a Web page. The default search engine that will be used on the computer you are using may vary.

3. Key **space station** in the Find a Web page containing text box and then click the Search button.

In a few seconds, a list of Web pages will be displayed as hyperlinks in the Search pane. These pages are Web sites that the search engine has indexed to the text you specified.

4. Click the down-pointing triangle at the bottom of the vertical scroll bar to scroll down the Search pane and view the search results.

5. Click the <u>next>></u> at the bottom of the Search pane to display the next 10 sites.

6. Click one of the links in the Search pane to view the related Web page.

As you position the mouse pointer over a hyperlinked Web page, the name of the link changes color and the URL displays in the Status bar.

7. Scroll the search pane and then click another link to view another related Web page.

Another way to search for information is to use a search engine's category index. In the next steps, you will close the Search pane, key the URL for a search engine, and then browse the category index.

8. Click the Search button on the Internet Explorer toolbar to close the Search pane.

If you prefer to use the full screen for viewing Web pages, close the search pane and then go directly to the search engine's URL.

9. Key **www.yahoo.com** in the A<u>d</u>dress text box and then press Enter.

Yahoo is a popular search engine that maintains category indices and can also be used to search for a topic by keywords.

10. Scroll down the Yahoo Web page and then click <u>Science</u>.

<u>**Education**</u>
<u>College and University</u>, <u>K-12</u>...

<u>**Regional**</u>
<u>Countries</u>, <u>Regions</u>, <u>US States</u>...

<u>**Entertainment**</u>
<u>Cool Links</u>, <u>Movies</u>, <u>Humor</u>, <u>Music</u>...

<u>**Science**</u>
<u>Animals</u>, <u>Astronomy</u>, <u>Engineering</u>...

11. Scroll down the Yahoo Science category page and then click <u>Space</u>.

- <u>**Research**</u> *(162)*
- <u>**Science and Technology Policy**</u> *(66)*
- <u>**Space**</u> *(1261)* NEW!
- <u>**Sports@**</u>
- <u>**Web Directories**</u> *(42)*

12. Scroll down the Yahoo Space category page and then click <u>Space Stations</u>.

13. Click the <u>Skylab</u> link on the Space Stations category page.

14. Click one of the links on the Skylab page and then view the Web page.

15. Click the Back button on the Internet Explorer toolbar, click another link from the Skylab page, and then view the Web page.

16. Close Internet Explorer. If necessary, disconnect from your ISP.

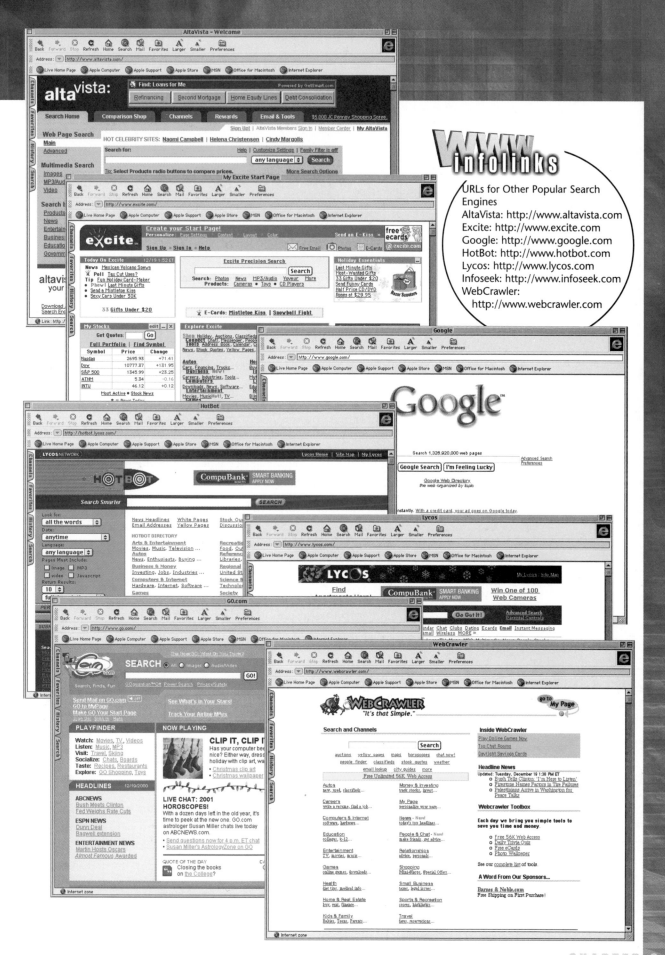

CHAPTER 2

COMMUNICATING CLEARLY
Technology Terms: What do they mean?

a. mouse
g. laser printer
b. port
h. hardware
c. cartridge tape
i. diskette
d. expansion board
j. monitor
e. formatting
k. main memory (RAM)
f. motherboard
l. image scanner

1. A term that refers to computer devices or components, including the system unit, input devices, output devices, and storage devices.

2. The main electronic circuit board inside the system unit.

3. A group of electronic chips inside the system unit used to store programs while they are being executed and data while it is being processed.

4. An interface on a computer to which you can connect a device.

5. A printed circuit board you can insert into a computer to give the computer added capabilities.

6. A handheld point-and-click input device whose movement across a flat surface causes a corresponding movement of its on-screen pointer.

7. A device that enables a user to capture and enter images including text, photographs, drawings, forms, or any combination of these items into a computer.

8. An output device that displays a copy of the output on the computer screen.

9. A hardware device that produces high-quality hard-copy output using a technology similar to that of photocopy machines.

10. The procedure of preparing a floppy disk for use.

11. Another name for a floppy disk.

12. A storage medium, contained in a small plastic housing, capable of holding large amounts of data and used mainly for backing up the contents of a hard drive.

Techno Literacy: How can new knowledge be used?

1. What is inside the computer case?
   Ask your instructor to allow you to open up a computer in the computer lab and look at the components inside. Using paper and pen, draw the components that you recognize and label each one. At a minimum, include the microprocessor chip, memory chips (RAM and ROM), expansion slots, expansion boards, and ports. Ask your instructor to explain other components you do not recognize. Label each one and write a brief summary of the component's function.

2. How many ways can a user input data?
   Page through a computer magazine such as *PC World* or visit a computer store and select a personal computer that interests you. Research and describe all of the different input devices that could be used with that particular computer system.

3. Which features should be considered when you purchase a printer?
   Hewlett-Packard is a major manufacturer of printers for personal computers. Visit the company's Web site at www.hp.com, where you can learn about the various kinds of printers HP produces. Select one printer and write a brief report describing the following features of the printer:

   a. type of printer (ink-jet, laser, and so on)
   b. model number
   c. printing speed
   d. color printing capability
   e. amount (if any) of storage capacity inside the printer
   f. graphics printing capability

4. Is a computer in the hand worth two on the desk?
   Handheld computers are available in a variety of styles. Research the major brands and models, paying particular attention to their screen displays and other features. Create a table that compares the various handhelds. Then identify the one that would best meet your needs, and explain why. How would you use it?

5. Who's in charge?
   Picture the future when sophisticated home information infrastructures such as the one described at the beginning of the chapter will be available. Which appliances, systems, and devices would you want connected and managed electronically in your home? Is there anything you would not want included? Do the benefits of these computerized management systems outweigh any potential drawbacks? How?

CONNECTING WITH CONCEPTS
Technology Processes: What's right with this picture?

What process is this? Identify the process illustrated in the drawing below and write a paragraph explaining it.

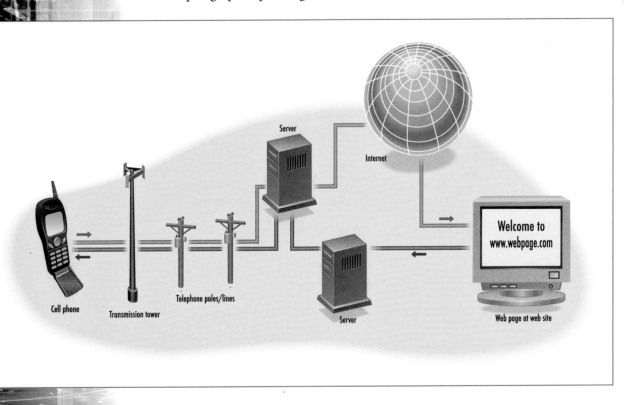

Key Principles: What's it all about?

1. A(n) _____ is a relatively small and inexpensive computer designed for an individual user.

2. A computer system consists of various physical devices or components, called _____.

3. A(n) _____ is a component inside the system unit that processes information.

4. A(n) _____ is any device that enables a computer user to enter data and programs into a computer system.

5. A(n) _____ is an electronically controlled device used to enter alphanumeric data (letters, numbers, and special characters) into the computer.

6. Processed data, usually text, graphics, or sound, that can be used immediately, or stored in computer-usable form for later use, is called

   _____.

7. _____ is a term that refers to media for the permanent storage of computer programs, files, and data.

8. A thin, circular mylar wafer sandwiched between two sheets of cleaning tissue inside a rigid plastic case is a(n) _____.

9. A(n) _____ system consists of one or more rigid metal platters (disks) mounted on a metal shaft and sealed in a container that contains an access mechanism.

10. A(n) _____ is a secondary storage medium on which data is typically recorded by means of a high-density laser.

MINING DATA

Conduct Internet searches to find information described in the activities below. Write a brief report that summarizes your research results. Be sure to document your sources, using MLA format. (See Chapter 1, page A-39, to review MLA style guidelines.)

1. Renting data storage, a service called "data warehousing," is becoming a hot trend among large companies that generate huge amounts of data. Using the techniques you learned in the Internet Tutorial at the end of the chapter, locate information that explains data warehousing and discusses the benefits, costs, and potential growth rate for this service.

2. Using the Yahoo search engine, select an interesting topic listed under the category of science and find information that analyzes the latest developments in that area.

THINGS THAT THINK

TEAMWORK

1. Scientists have invented the first prototype of a computerized scalpel that can tell a surgeon when to stop cutting during surgery to remove cancerous tumors so that only the diseased tissue is removed. This technology would allow doctors to save healthy tissue, thus potentially improving the patient's odds for survival. What other areas could benefit from this development? Think not only of medical applications, but of possible uses in various industries.

2. Smart cards, plastic cards the size of credit cards with tiny chips embedded in them, are growing in popularity among several major U.S. corporations because of their ability to protect personal information, such as account numbers, during Internet business transactions. With a Web-enabled cell phone, a user could access a company Web site, order a product, and then pay for it by inserting a smart card into a slot in the phone. Can you think of other ways in which this intelligent plastic could be used? Brainstorm applications in business and beyond.

PREDICTING NEXT STEPS

Look at the timeline below that outlines the major milestones in the development of PDAs (personal digital assistants), such as the PalmPilot and the Visor. Research this topic and think of what the next steps will be. Complete the timeline through the year 2010 or later, if the research warrants it.

1980s	The first small portable computers appear on the computer scene.
1993	The first PDA, Apple's Message Pad, is introduced to the mass marketplace.
1996	U.S. Robotics introduces the first PalmPilot model.
1998	Manufacturer 3Com offers several PalmPilot models that capture 41.4% total marketshare.
1999	Palm Computing launches their wireless Palm VII, providing access to the Internet with a single device.
2000	Sony Corporation introduces a PDA that includes a slot for its Memory Stick® memory card, which allows users to add extra memory and to transfer files to the device.

SOLVING PROBLEMS

In groups or individually, brainstorm possible solutions to the issues presented.

1. Computers currently offer both visual and audio communication. Under development are devices and technologies that will allow users to smell various types of products while looking at them in the computer screen. What are some new applications of this technology for the food industry? Can you think of other industries that could use this capability?

2. Picture yourself working in the Information Technology department of a mid-sized company. Your responsibilities include evaluating employees' computer system needs and recommending equipment purchases. Recently, the company president hired a new employee and you must evaluate her computer system needs. The new employee is Sondoles Marquez, the national sales manager, who will travel approximately three weeks of each month but needs to stay in daily contact with the home office and be able to access its network server for sales data such as daily product sales and warehouse inventory totals. During her one week a month in the office, Marquez uses her computer to prepare graphics-intensive reports and slide-show presentations for training the sales force. She also researches competitors' products and other information on the Internet.

    Considering that you have a budget of $5,500 for equipping Sondoles Marquez with the computer system (or systems) she needs, research possible configurations and prepare a report outlining your recommendations, including costs. Assume that for the office she needs a complete system, including a system unit, monitor, printer, speakers, keyboard, and mouse. *(Hint: Check computer magazines, retail stores, and Internet sites such as www.gateway.com for ideas.)*

EXAMINING ETHICAL ISSUES

Access the Computer Concepts Resource Center at EMC/Paradigm's Web site (www.emcp.com/college_division/ electronic_resource_center) and go to Computers: Exploring Concepts, then to Student Resources, then to the Ethical Issues page. Complete the activity for Chapter 2.

ANSWERS TO TECHNOLOGY TERMS AND KEY PRINCIPLES QUESTIONS

Technology Terms: 1 – h; 2 – f; 3 – k; 4 – b; 5 – d; 6 – a; 7 – l; 8 – j; 9 – g; 10 – e; 11 – i; 12 – c

Key Principles: 1 – personal computer; 2 – hardware; 3 – microprocessor; 4 – input device; 5 – keyboard; 6 – output; 7 – secondary storage; 8 – floppy disk; 9 – hard disk; 10 – optical disk

CHAPTER 3

SOFTWARE: OPERATING SYSTEMS AND PRODUCTIVITY APPLICATIONS

learning objectives

- Discuss the roles of the major types of software in a computer system

- Explain the concept of an operating system and identify its main functions

- Identify the features common to graphical user interfaces (GUIs) and explain their significance relative to software

- Compare the uses of the main types of productivity software

- Analyze the factors leading to the development of software suites

- Conduct an advanced search on the Internet

THE SOFTWARE CONNECTION

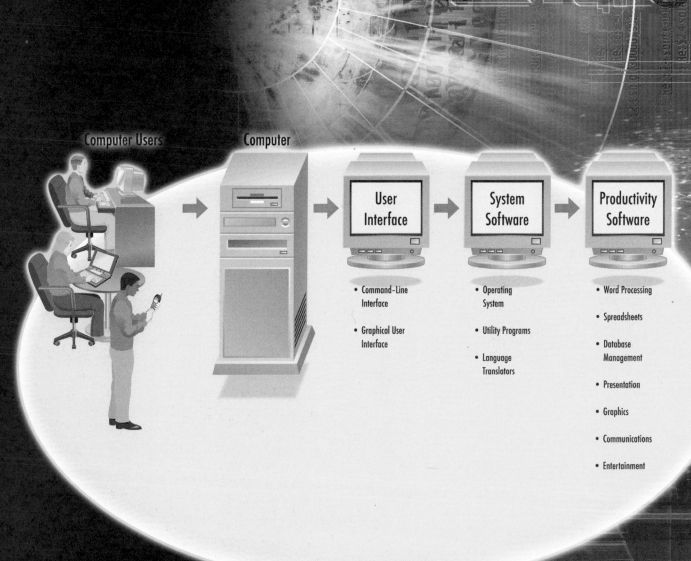

Computer Users

Computer

User Interface
- Command-Line Interface
- Graphical User Interface

System Software
- Operating System
- Utility Programs
- Language Translators

Productivity Software
- Word Processing
- Spreadsheets
- Database Management
- Presentation
- Graphics
- Communications
- Entertainment

CYBER SCENARIO

Shortly after sunrise, Vincente Chamarro boards the high-speed train that will take him to his biweekly meeting with other staff members at InterMed, a designer and manufacturer of pacemakers and other medical devices that can be monitored over the Internet. Vincente, a product manager in the Cardiac Devices division, has telecommuted from his mountain home for more than three years, meeting face to face with the marketing team every two weeks to maintain personal contact and to resolve any issues that cannot be handled well with remote communication.

Arriving in the city at 7:30 A.M., Vincente steps off the train and heads for the company headquarters building two blocks away. Walking down the street, he pulls a cell phone from his pocket and speaks a Web address, www.ananova.com, toward the mouthpiece. Almost instantly, the virtual face of Ananova appears on the high-resolution screen of the cell phone. Vincente says, "News," and Ananova begins her newscast with the latest headlines from around the world.

As he walks into his office on the ninth floor of the InterMed building, Vincente remembers that he needs to check his bank balance. Commanding his computer with the words, "Turn on and go to the Web site for Fidelity National Bank," he continues his request with, "This is Vincente Chamarro. What's the balance in my checking account?" The bank's automated teller system recognizes his voice and promptly reports that he has $1,956 in his account. "Good," he thinks, "no need to transfer any funds from savings."

Today, the marketing team will meet about plans for exhibiting at the international trade show for cardiac surgeons to be held in Zurich, Switzerland, in three months. Reflecting on his communication needs for the trade show, Vincente decides to buy a new handheld that will allow him to track all of the materials his company ships via express courier to Zurich, plus provide current cultural events and street locations for Zurich and other European cities. Vincente accesses a Web site where he can purchase the most powerful handheld on the market. A Web cam enabled with advanced pattern recognition software captures his image and quickly compares it with a database of identification images. "Hello, Vincente," says a human-sounding voice. "Would you like to place an order?" He tells the automated ordering system what he wants. The order is repeated back to him for confirmation, and the purchase is deducted from his bank account. He can expect to receive his new "toy" in two days.

The meeting with his marketing manager and team members proceeds without a hitch. They approve his plan to use the company's Ananova-like synthetic character, Jillian, to pitch their new devices over computer monitors at the international trade show. Vincente has outlined a script for Jillian. Now he just needs to write it. Vincente stays late to finish a rough draft, dictating to his computer until 8 P.M. Finishing the script, he directs the computer to send copies to team members and leaves to catch the 8:50 train home.

A Dog with a Byte

If you want a loving, obedient, and loyal pet but don't want one that sheds, chews on the sofa, or has accidents on the carpet, then consider adopting an AIBO from Sony. AIBO (the name is a combination of *Artificial Intelligence* and *Robot* that coincidentally means *companion* in Japanese) looks like a black, metallic dog. AIBO stands over 10 inches high and weighs 1.5 pounds. But this wildly popular breed doesn't come cheap—a non-furry friend will cost you approximately $1,600.

Sony announced the first generation of AIBOs in June of 1999. All 5,000 sold within four days. By the time the next litter of 10,000 were "born," more than 135,000 orders had been received.

Sony's second generation of AIBOs have been bred for enhanced capabilities. Each AIBO has a built-in stereo microphone, voice-recognition technology, and a speaker allowing it to respond to its owner with an electronic tonal language that mimics the sounds it hears. Twenty motorized joints enable AIBO to sit, walk, lie down, flap its ears, and even wag its tail. A small camera in the nose gives it sight. Sensors on its head, chin, and back enable AIBO to respond to touch. And one glance at AIBO's LED eyes will melt any owner's heart.

AIBO learns from experience. Its first steps are as wobbly as a puppy's, and it slowly learns whatever name it is given. AIBO likes to perform, play, and, of course, be fed—that is, have its battery recharged. As with any pet, AIBO's behavior is formed by its interaction with humans. Acting on instinct and free will, it will respond to attention by repeating positive behavior. Scolding and discipline will teach it to refrain from undesirable habits. AIBO can express happiness, sadness, anger, fear, surprise, and dislike. And so far, no human has reported an allergy to AIBO.

Source: "Introducing Sony's Second Generation autonomous robot companion!" The Sharper Image Gift Catalog, 2000.

SOFTWARE FOR A SOFT JOB?

Vincente Chamarro's job is made easier through advances in speech recognition, natural language processing, and artificial intelligence technologies. Those same developments are poised to bring a whole new level of "customer care" and individualization to computer users worldwide. Driving the change is an intricate interaction among computer hardware manufacturers, scientists, and software developers.

WHAT IS COMPUTER SOFTWARE?

In the broadest sense, **software** is a set of programs that tell a computer what to do and how to manage the computer's resources, including all hardware devices. A **program** is a set of instructions for a series of actions that take place in a certain order. Programs tell computers how to process data into information.

A popular expression in computer circles is that "software drives hardware." This statement is quite true because without software, the hardware of a computer system is merely a physical structure of metal, silicon, wires, and other materials. When it is turned on, the computer by itself can do little more than search for some essential program files, which direct the computer to load additional software. It is the software that launches information processing and puts the hardware to work. There are two main categories of software:

- **system software:** programs that manage basic operations such as starting and shutting down the computer and saving and printing files
- **application software:** programs that perform specific tasks such as word processing, spreadsheet analysis, and database management

SYSTEM SOFTWARE

System software includes those programs that control the operations of a computer system, meaning the system unit and all components and devices that comprise the computer system. System software performs a number of essential functions, including starting the computer, formatting disks, copying files, and enabling an application, such as a word processor program, to work smoothly with your computer. Thus, system software serves as the gateway between the user, the user's application software, and the user's computer hardware (see Figure 3-1). Three main types of system software are operating systems, utility programs, and language translators.

OPERATING SYSTEMS

An operating system (OS) is the most important piece of software on a personal computer system. Typically, the OS is installed on the computer's hard disk and is loaded into RAM (random access memory) when the computer is started. An **operating system** performs several interdependent functions related to the input, processing, output, and storage of information:

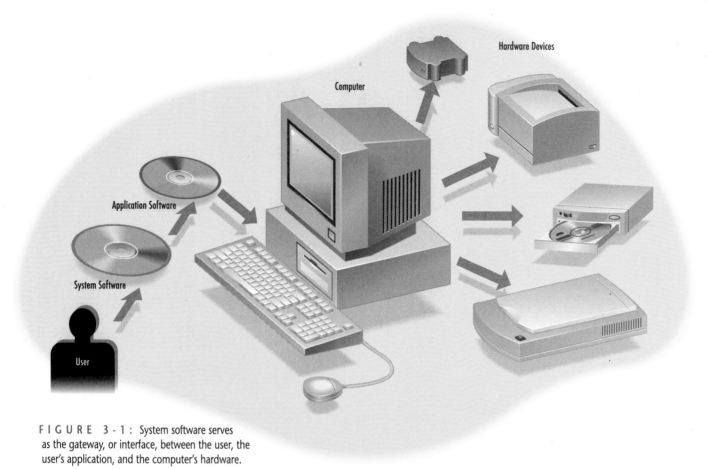

FIGURE 3-1: System software serves as the gateway, or interface, between the user, the user's application, and the computer's hardware.

- manages main memory, or RAM
- configures and controls peripheral devices
- manages essential file operations, including formatting disks and copying, renaming, and deleting files
- monitors system performance
- provides a user interface

Table 3-1 lists the operating systems commonly used on personal computers today.

Manage Memory

When the computer is first started (called **booting**), only a portion of the operating system is automatically loaded from the hard disk into the computer's main memory (RAM). The loaded portion contains the most essential instructions for operating the computer, such as instructions for displaying output on the monitor. Other, less frequently used, instructions remain on the hard disk until they are called up. Instructions for formatting a floppy disk, for example, remain on the hard disk until the user issues a command to format a disk. Managing memory in this way ensures that the maximum amount of RAM is available at all times for processing data.

As information is being processed, the operating system assigns the applications programs and data to specific areas of RAM. The operating system reserves and manages sections of memory, called **buffers**, that hold information and data waiting to be transferred to or from an input or output device. When the information

KEYTERMS

cold boot process of starting a computer by turning on the unit's power switch

warm boot process of restarting a computer while power is on; clears the memory and reloads the operating system

buffer a temporary storage place to which part of data to be displayed, printed, or transmitted is written

Operating System	Developer	Computer Designed For	Type of Interface
Macintosh OS 8	Apple Computer	Macintosh	Graphical User Interface
Macintosh OS 9	Apple Computer	Macintosh	Graphical User Interface
Windows 95	Microsoft Corp.	IBM PC & compatibles	Graphical User Interface
Windows 98	Microsoft Corp.	IBM PC & compatibles	Graphical User Interface
Windows NT	Microsoft Corp.	IBM PC & compatibles	Graphical User Interface
Windows CE	Microsoft Corp.	Handheld computers & other mobile devices	Graphical User Interface
Windows 2000 Professional Edition	Microsoft Corp.	IBM PC & compatibles	Graphical User Interface
Windows 2000 Me	Microsoft Corp.	IBM PC & compatibles	Graphical User Interface
OS/2	IBM	IBM PC & compatibles	Graphical User Interface
UNIX X-Windows	AT&T, MIT, GE	IBM PC & compatibles	Graphical User Interface
Linux (modified for PC)	Linus Torvalds	IBM PC & compatibles	Graphical User Interface
Java	Sun Microsystems	IBM PC & compatibles; Macintosh	Graphical User Interface

TABLE 3-1: Commonly Used Operating Systems for Personal Computers

or data residing in the buffers is no longer needed, it is erased (cleared) by the operating system.

An important part of managing RAM is allowing an individual user to work on two or more applications at the same time. This capability is called **multitasking.** If you are using a multitasking operating system, such as Microsoft Windows, it is not necessary to quit one application before working on another application. For example, if you have loaded both a Microsoft Word document and a Microsoft Excel spreadsheet into RAM, you can switch back and forth between the two of them as often as you wish. Figure 3-2 illustrates how Windows uses a computer's RAM.

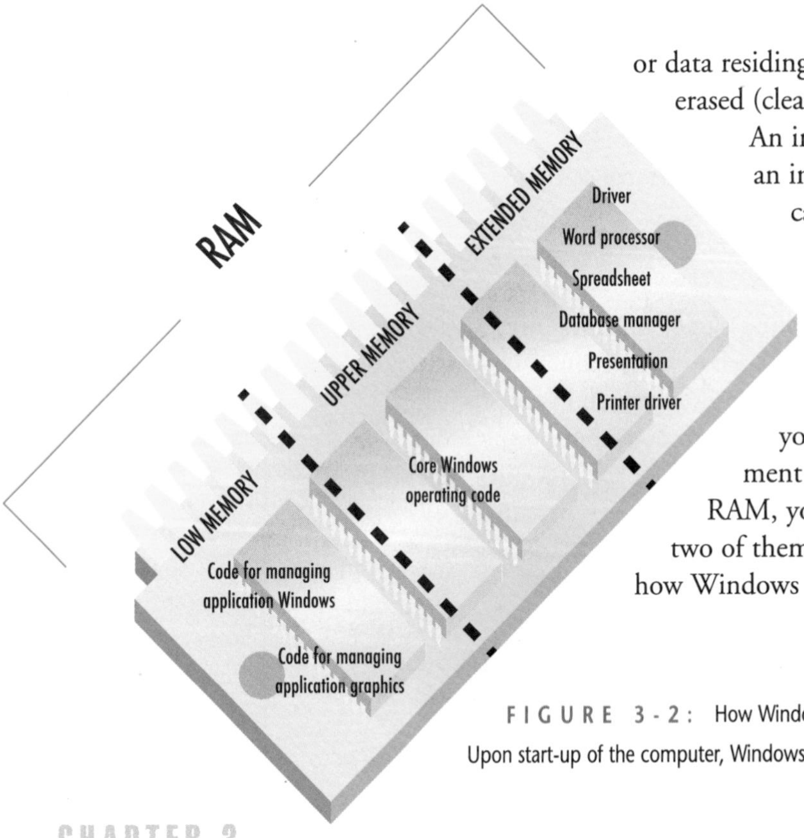

RAM

EXTENDED MEMORY
Driver
Word processor
Spreadsheet
Database manager
Presentation
Printer driver

UPPER MEMORY
Core Windows operating code

LOW MEMORY
Code for managing application Windows
Code for managing application graphics

FIGURE 3-2: How Windows Works with Memory
Upon start-up of the computer, Windows loads portions of code into all three areas of RAM.

Configure and Control Devices

Typically included with a computer's operating system are small programs called **drivers,** which enable the computer to communicate with keyboards, monitors, and other input and output devices. A keyboard driver recognizes input; a monitor driver directs the display of text and images. If a user decides to add other devices later, he will need to install a driver for that particular device. A driver program usually accompanies the device and is contained on a disk, along with easy-to-follow instructions that guide the user through the installation process.

Manage Essential File Operations

An operating system contains a program called a **file manager**, which performs basic file management functions. For example, a file manager keeps track of used and unused disk storage space. This program also allows a user to format a disk, to view stored files, and to copy, rename, delete, or sort them. Figure 3-3 shows the Microsoft Windows Explorer window, where files can be copied, deleted, moved, and otherwise manipulated.

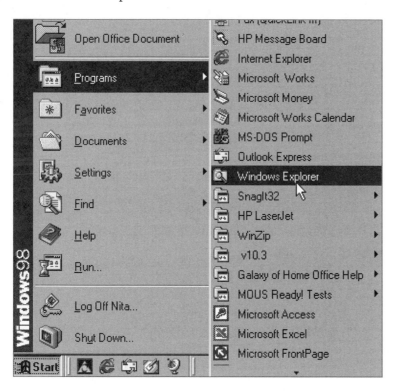

FIGURE 3-3: With Windows Explorer, a user can copy, delete, and move files.

Another program called a **print spooler** increases a computer's efficiency by holding a document in a buffer instead of sending it directly to the printer. A computer typically sends a document to a printer much faster than a printer can print the document. With **print spooling,** the document is held in the buffer until the printer is ready to print it, thereby enabling the printer to print at its own speed. When a document is placed in a buffer, the CPU is free to begin executing the next instruction or carry out the user's next command.

Monitor System Performance

An operating system typically includes a system **performance monitor** that monitors the computer system's speed and efficiency. A user can determine the performance of the CPU, memory, and storage disks. In Microsoft Windows, for example, this is done by clicking the command sequence of Start, Programs, Accessories, System Tools, System Monitor. Then, if programs seem to execute slowly or if downloads (such as e-mail messages and Web pages) are taking longer than expected, the user might decide to install additional RAM chips or upgrade the processor.

Provide a User Interface

Once loaded, the operating system takes over the computer, creating a display of visuals and text on the monitor that allow the user to issue commands and direct the operation of the software and hardware. This display and the tools it represents comprise the user interface.

SOFTWARE USER INTERFACES

Operating systems, along with every other type of software, contain a set of instructions called a **user interface** that allows the user to communicate with the software and the software to communicate with the user. Both the manner in which the user enters data and commands and the way information and processing options are presented on the screen are controlled by the program's interface. Application programs are written for use with particular operating systems. Therefore, the user interface of the operating system and the user interface of the application software must be compatible, that is, able to work together. Two types of user interfaces have been developed for personal computers:

- command-line interfaces
- graphical user interfaces (GUIs)

COMMAND-LINE INTERFACES

prompt a symbol, character, or phrase that appears on-screen to inform the user that the computer is ready to accept input

The early personal computer operating systems, including CP/M (Control Program for Microcomputers) and DOS (Disk Operating System), used what is known as a **command-line interface**. This interface presented the user with a symbol called a **prompt** (for example, C:\>), which indicated that the computer was ready to receive a command. The user would respond by typing in a line of codes telling the computer what to do. For example, the command

COPY A:\INCOME.STM C:

would tell the computer to copy the file named INCOME.STM, located on drive A, to drive C. Command-line interfaces were ideal for early personal computers with their limited graphical display capabilities, but they could also be complicated and difficult to learn. Often, the commands involved long sequences of codes, and a mistyped letter would lead to an error message, forcing the user to type the command again. Figure 3-4 illustrates the use of the DIR (directory) command in DOS.

```
MS-DOS Prompt                                    _ □ ✕

T  8 x 14 ▾   [:]  🗔 🗎 🔲   🗁 🖨  A

HEALTH     EXE       405,952   06-03-96  11:55a  HEALTH.EXE
HEALTH     ICO           766   08-15-95   9:34a  HEALTH.ICO
HEALTH     Z       2,266,038   06-03-96   2:34p  HEALTH.Z
HEALTH96   <DIR>               03-13-96   7:47p  HEALTH96
INTRO      BMP       153,516   08-18-95   2:58p  INTRO.BMP
IVI        BMP       308,280   08-04-95   2:26p  IVI.BMP
IVIPBW32   DLL       459,776   02-05-96  12:50p  IVIPBW32.DLL
IVIPUBW    DLL       280,123   05-16-96   2:43p  IVIPUBW.DLL
QTW        <DIR>               03-22-96  11:58a  QTW
README     DOC        29,696   03-01-96   2:59p  README.DOC
REVLOG     TXT           393   06-03-96  11:46a  REVLOG.TXT
SETUP      BMP       158,382   08-17-94   4:48p  SETUP.BMP
SETUP      EXE        44,064   05-15-96  10:15a  SETUP.EXE
SETUP      INI            65   04-22-96   4:33p  SETUP.INI
SETUP      INS        69,227   06-03-96   2:30p  SETUP.INS
SETUP      PKG           406   06-03-96   2:34p  SETUP.PKG
UNINST     EXE       269,312   09-02-95   3:57p  UNINST.EXE
_INST32I   EX_       312,294   05-15-96   5:03p  _INST32I.EX_
_ISDEL     EXE         8,192   09-08-95   1:22a  _ISDEL.EXE
_SETUP     DLL         5,984   04-29-96   8:25a  _SETUP.DLL
_SETUP     LIB       603,899   06-03-96   2:36p  _SETUP.LIB
          21 file(s)      5,383,575 bytes
           2 dir(s)                 0 bytes free

E:\>DIR_
```

Start   MS-DOS Prompt   2:39 PM

F I G U R E   3 - 4 :   The DOS command DIR shows a directory, or list of files, stored on a medium such as a hard disk or floppy disk.

GRAPHICAL USER INTERFACES (GUIs)

In 1983, Apple Computer introduced its Lisa computer, which had an entirely new kind of OS and screen display known as a **graphical user interface**, or **GUI** (pronounced *gooey*). Based on the OS of the Alto computer developed at the Xerox Corporation's Palo Alto Research Center, this new type of interface was graphics-based rather than command-based and much more intuitive and user-friendly than the old command-line operating systems were. Because of its high price and the few software applications available for it, the Apple Lisa was a commercial failure. Apple's next computer, the Macintosh, introduced in 1984, also incorporated a GUI; however, this computer was a marketplace success (see Figure 3-5). The Macintosh OS revolutionized personal computing.

information on the
Macintosh OS:
www.macos.apple.com

F I G U R E   3 - 5 : An Early Macintosh Computer

Introduced in 1984, Apple's Macintosh quickly became popular in the marketplace.

Today, the GUI is the most popular type of interface for personal computers. A graphical user interface is easier to use than a command-line interface because it enables the user to interact with on-screen simulations of familiar objects. Remembering long strings of commands is no longer necessary, since the screen itself becomes a virtual desktop on which the user's work (programs and documents) is spread out (see Figure 3-6). **Icons,** or thumbnail pictures, appear on the desktop and represent such familiar items as a trash can or recycle bin (for deleting or throwing away files) and file folders (for storing groups of files). In addition to representing common commands, special icons are used to symbolize programs and files. A calculating program, for example, can be represented by a tiny calculator in the screen, or a time management program can be represented

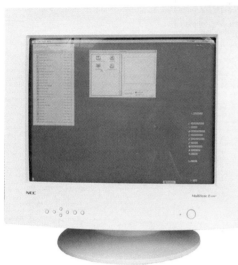

by a clock. GUIs are to operating systems what special keyboards are to cash registers in fast-food restaurants. Both use "pictures" or text symbols to stand for complex commands, thus simplifying and streamlining actions for the user.

Graphical user interfaces were made possible with the development of mouse technology and the introduction of more powerful computers and high-resolution graphics screens. Today, most new PCs arrive from the factory with a GUI operating system already installed and most application software is designed to work smoothly with a GUI. Once you know the features of a graphical user interface such as Windows, you already know how to print and save files, plus execute other fundamental operations of any Windows-based application because both the operating system and the application use the same icons and commands for basic operations.

FIGURE 3-6:
Graphical User Interface of the Mac

A Graphical User Interface allows a user to interact with familiar objects on the screen.

FEATURES OF A GRAPHICAL USER INTERFACE

A typical graphical user interface offers many features that make a user's tasks easier, including:

- menus of options for key features
- icons that represent common commands
- on-screen desktop
- display windows
- dialog boxes
- online help

Menus of Options for Key Features

A **menu** provides a set of options from which a user selects by clicking a highlighted option with a mouse or by typing one or more keystrokes. Making a selection launches an action, such as saving a document.

Many software programs display a menu bar, also called main menu, at the top or side of the screen when the program is activated. A **menu bar** is a horizontal or vertical bar that lists the highest-level command options by name (usually one or two words). Each high-level option may be accompanied by another menu, called a **pull-down menu** (or **submenu**), containing various lower-level options (see Figure 3-7). These submenus, in turn, may include yet another submenu level offering more precise choices.

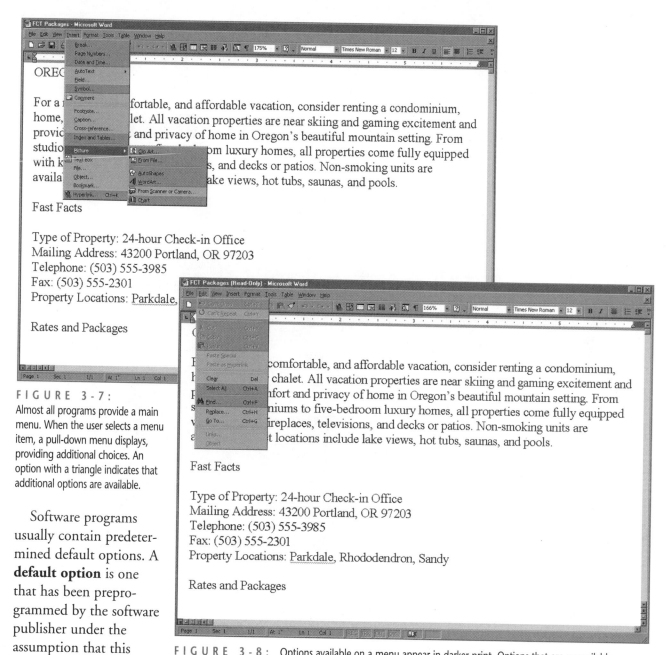

FIGURE 3-7:
Almost all programs provide a main menu. When the user selects a menu item, a pull-down menu displays, providing additional choices. An option with a triangle indicates that additional options are available.

FIGURE 3-8: Options available on a menu appear in darker print. Options that are unavailable appear in grayed-out print.

Software programs usually contain predetermined default options. A **default option** is one that has been preprogrammed by the software publisher under the assumption that this option is the choice most users favor. The newer versions of Microsoft Word, for example, include a default font of 10-point New Times Roman. However, a user can choose a different font by clicking the Format option on the menu bar.

Depending on the action being taken, some pull-down menu options may be unavailable to the user at certain times. Options that are available typically appear in darker type. Unavailable options usually appear grayed out, or dimmed, to let the user know the option cannot be chosen. Figure 3-8 shows a pull-down menu containing choices that are available and those that are not.

On pull-down menus, a small right-pointing triangle at the right of an option indicates that additional options are available. Pointing at the triangle displays the associated menu. A check mark at the left of an option indicates the option has been selected and is therefore active. Figure 3-9 shows a pull-down menu associated with the View option in Microsoft Word.

D R I V E R S

William (Bill) H. Gates III is a cofounder and, at present, chairman of the board of directors of Microsoft Corporation, the world's leading provider of software for personal computers. Born on October 28, 1955, Gates grew up in Seattle, Washington, where he attended public elementary school before moving on to the private Lakeside School in North Seattle. He began programming computers at the early age of 13.

In 1973, Gates entered Harvard University. While at Harvard, Gates developed a version of the BASIC programming language for the first microcomputer, called the MITS Altair. He dropped out of Harvard in his junior year to devote his full time to building Microsoft Corporation, a company he had started in 1975 with his boyhood friend Paul Allen. Guided by a belief that the personal computer would be a valuable tool on every office desktop and in every home, Gates and Allen began developing software for personal computers.

Twenty-five years later, Microsoft and Bill Gates (along with Allen and other early players) are worth billions. Under Gates's leadership, Microsoft has forged a mission to advance and improve software technology to make it easier, more cost-effective, and more enjoyable for people to use computers. The company is committed to a long-term view, which is reflected in its annual investments of millions of dollars for research and development. Gates and his wife, Melinda, have endowed a foundation with more than $21 billion to support philanthropic causes dedicated to worldwide health and education, such as providing vaccines for children in developing countries and scholarship programs for low-income high-achievers.

Microsoft has been quick to take advantage of opportunities created by the Internet. Gates has a substantial investment, along with cellular telephone pioneer Craig McCaw, in the Teledesic project, an ambitious plan to launch low-orbit satellites around the earth to provide a worldwide two-way broadband telecommunications service.

Source: <http://www.microsoft.com/billgates/bio.asp>.

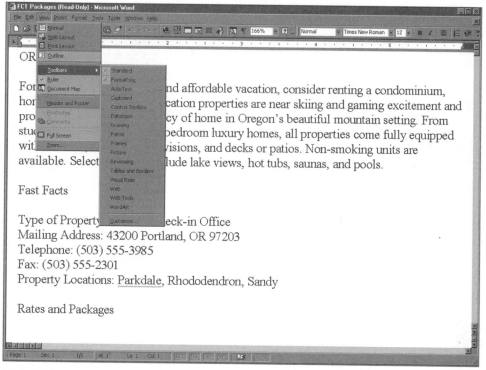

FIGURE 3-9: A check mark at the left of an option in a pull-down menu indicates that the option has been selected and is therefore active.

In Figure 3-9, notice the check mark at the left of the <u>R</u>uler option. This means the ruler option is selected and that the ruler is displayed at the top of the page or document. At the right of the <u>T</u>oolbars option, the triangle indicates an associated pull-down menu containing various toolbar options. The selected options, as indicated by the check marks, are Standard and Formatting.

ICONS THAT REPRESENT COMMON COMMANDS

A GUI uses icons to represent common actions such as opening, saving, or printing a file. These icons may be displayed in a row, called a **toolbar**, near the top of the screen. When the mouse pointer is positioned on an icon, a one- or two-word label (often called a Screen Tip) displays immediately below it to identify the icon. Clicking the icon launches the associated action. For example, Microsoft Word allows a user to print a document by clicking on a small printer icon in the toolbar (Figure 3-10). For many users, simply clicking on an icon is easier than having to remember and enter a series of keystrokes.

Like menus, some icons may be immediately unavailable and appear in ghosted or dimmed form. These icons usually represent actions that depend on a related, previous action. For example, Microsoft Word will not allow a user to select the scissors icon (for "cutting" or removing text) until the word or paragraph to be deleted has been selected (highlighted with the mouse).

Printer icon

FIGURE 3-10: A graphical user interface (GUI) uses pictures and symbols, called icons, to represent commands. Clicking the printer icon, shown above, prints a file.

FIGURE 3-11: Most PCs are preloaded with a GUI that uses the concept of an onscreen desktop, a work area displaying graphical elements such as icons, windows, and buttons. Graphical elements allow for faster, easier access to programs and commands.

FIGURE 3-12: Windows Desktop with the Start Button Selected

ON-SCREEN DESKTOP

Almost all personal computers are installed with software that uses the concept of an on-screen desktop. A **desktop** is a screen on which graphical elements such as icons, buttons, windows, links, and dialog boxes are displayed, much as manila folders, pens, scissors, and paper might be arranged on your desk at the office. Using a desktop containing these elements is easier for many users because it allows them to interact quickly and accurately with the computer. During the installation of a software application, the program may automatically add an icon representing the program to the desktop. Figure 3-11 shows the left half of a desktop displaying a variety of icons and buttons.

A **button** is a graphical element that, when selected, causes a particular action to occur. For example, clicking with a mouse on the Windows Start button in the lower left corner of the screen displays a menu of options related to starting and operating the computer (Figure 3-12). When a button is selected, the button appears pressed in, as though it has been pressed by a user's finger.

DISPLAY WINDOWS

The main feature of a graphical user interface is the display window. A **display window** is a rectangular area of the screen used to display a program or various kinds of data, such as text and numbers. At the top of each window is a horizontal bar, called the **title bar**, in which the window's name is displayed, as shown in Figure 3-13.

Most graphical user interfaces allow you to divide your display screen into multiple windows. Within each window you can work with a different application or display different data.

Windows are particularly useful in multitasking environments, which allow you to work with multiple programs and applications concurrently. By dividing the screen into windows, you can see and work with the output produced by each program. To work within a particular program—to enter data, for example—you simply click on the program's window to bring it to the forefront. Figure 3-14 shows multiple windows, each representing a different program.

Because documents are often too large for the entire document to be displayed in a window, **scroll bars** at a window's side or bottom enable a user to see and work with portions of the document that may be hidden. Small arrows at the tips of a scroll bar can be used to move the document horizontally or vertically. A small box between the two arrows can also be used to scroll through a document page by page.

DIALOG BOXES

Graphical user interfaces use several types of **dialog boxes** to provide information to a user and to request information from a user (see Figure 3-15). The dialog box is a window that displays temporarily and disappears once the user has entered the requested information.

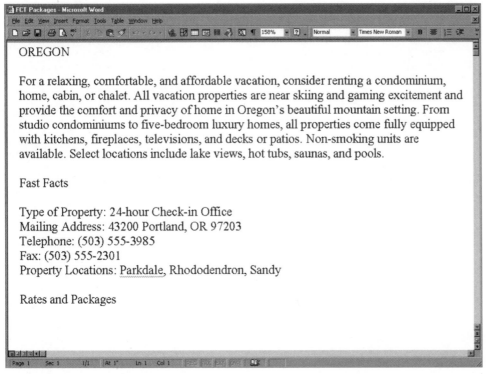

FIGURE 3-13: A display window, the main feature of a GUI, is a rectangular area on the screen used to display a program, data, or communications. A title bar at the top of the window shows its name.

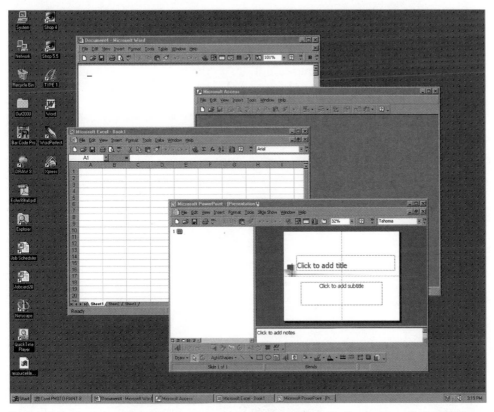

FIGURE 3-14: Most GUIs allow a user to work with multiple applications concurrently. Each application appears in its own window. A user can switch back and forth among applications by clicking on a window's title bar.

Interactions between the user and the software are carried out through various elements that allow choices. The following are some of the more common elements: tabs, option buttons, check boxes, and text boxes.

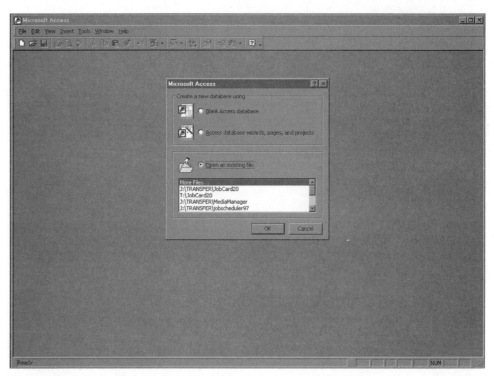

FIGURE 3-15: Dialog boxes provide information to a user and also request responses so commands can be executed.

- **Tabs.** Many dialog boxes offer several subsets of options, each of which is labeled as if it were a manila folder within a file drawer. The name of a subset of options is displayed in a **tab** at the top of the "folder." Clicking the tab brings that particular group of options to the front of the dialog box (the "file drawer"). Figure 3-16 shows a dialog box with tabs.

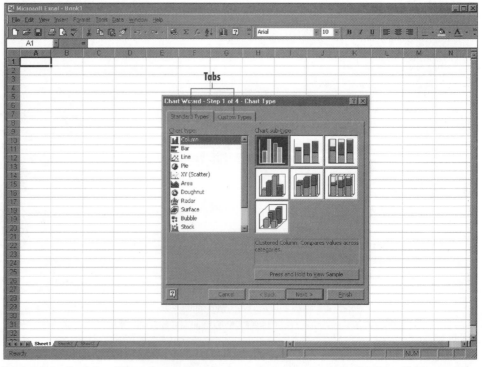

FIGURE 3-16: Tabs at the top of a dialog box indicate separate subsets of options. Clicking on a tab brings that group of options to the front of the dialog box.

- **Option Buttons.** Another standard element of a dialog box is an outlined box containing a set of buttons called **option buttons** (also called **radio buttons**). Named for their resemblance to the station-tuning buttons on transistor radios, these buttons offer a set of choices. Like those on a standard radio, only one button at a time can be activated. For example, clicking the printer icon in Microsoft Word displays a dialog box containing a set of buttons labeled All, Current page, Selection, and Pages (see Figure 3-17). You can select only one option at a time.

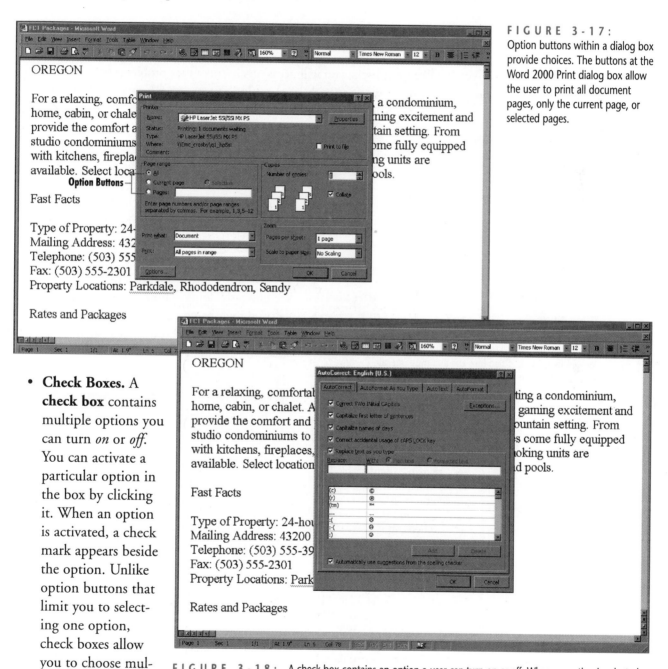

F I G U R E   3 - 1 7 :
Option buttons within a dialog box provide choices. The buttons at the Word 2000 Print dialog box allow the user to print all document pages, only the current page, or selected pages.

- **Check Boxes.** A **check box** contains multiple options you can turn *on* or *off*. You can activate a particular option in the box by clicking it. When an option is activated, a check mark appears beside the option. Unlike option buttons that limit you to selecting one option, check boxes allow you to choose multiple options at one time. Figure 3-18 shows a check box with multiple options that have been activated (checked).

F I G U R E   3 - 1 8 :   A check box contains an option a user can turn on or off. When an option is selected, a check mark appears beside it, indicating it is turned on.

- **Text Boxes.** As the name suggests, one enters information into a **text box** to allow the computer to continue or complete a task. For example, if you are using Microsoft Word and want to save a document, you first click on the File menu and then click Save or Save As to display the Save or Save As dialog box. Once the dialog box appears, you need to specify a drive where the document will be saved and type a file name for your document (see Figure 3-19).

Most dialog boxes also contain OK and Cancel buttons that allow the user to submit the information she has entered into a text box or a check box.

ONLINE HELP

If you are like most users, you will occasionally encounter problems or think of questions while you are working with an operating system or with a particular application. You can get help by clicking the Help button or by pressing a designated key.

Text box

FIGURE 3-19: A text box is used for entering information that will allow the computer to complete a specific task. At the Save As dialog box, the user must indicate the drive to be saved to plus the file name.

When you click on the Help button, a dialog box appears asking you to specify the kind of help needed. The program then searches its online documentation and displays a menu of topics from which you can choose. Selecting a topic causes a set of helpful instructions to display in the screen, as shown in Figure 3-20.

Some programs display Help messages based on where you are in the program and what you are presently doing. This kind of Help system is referred to as being **context sensitive**, as the system seems to "sense" your needs based on the tasks you are doing.

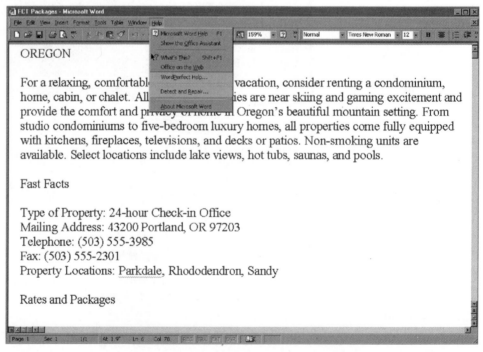

FIGURE 3-20: Clicking on the Help option on the menu bar displays a list of topics from which a selection can be made.

COMMONLY USED OPERATING SYSTEMS

Microsoft Windows is currently the dominant operating system for personal computers. According to some estimates, Windows is used on about 90 percent of all PCs. The remaining 10 percent are Apple Macintosh personal computers that use Apple's Mac OS operating system.

PLATFORMS

Not all operating systems will run on every computer. For example, an OS designed and written for the Apple Macintosh computer usually will not run on an IBM-compatible computer. The computers are said to have different platforms. A **platform** is, as the word suggests, a foundation or standard around which software is developed. The two determinants of a platform are the operating system and the processor type. Early versions of Windows, for example, were called 16-bit operating systems, meaning they supported microprocessors that could process 16 bits of data at a time. Later Windows versions, including Windows 95 and 98, supported 32- and 64-bit processors.

A platform determines which types of applications will run on a particular computer or clone of that computer. Operating systems and other software that run on a certain personal computer platform are referred to as *native* to that platform. Thus there is software native to the UNIX platform, to the PC platform, to the Macintosh platform, and to the Palm OS platform. In the personal computer category, the dominant platform is Windows for the PC. Over a period of about fifteen years, Microsoft Windows has evolved from a GUI/DOS combination (Windows 3.0 through 3.11) to a true graphical user interface with versions for all types of personal computers (Windows 2000).

WINDOWS 3.X

Microsoft embraced the term *windows* to describe the graphical user interface that it developed for use on PCs. Version 3.0, introduced in 1985, was the first version, followed shortly by versions 3.1 and 3.11, which contained significant improvements (see Figure 3-21). In the truest sense, the three versions were not actually operating systems. They were **operating environments**, meaning they were graphical interfaces on top of an underlying DOS kernel. Apple Computer unsuccessfully sued Microsoft, claiming that the latter company had copied the "look and feel" of the Mac OS. The failure of Apple's suit opened the door for the development of successive versions of Windows and of other graphical user interfaces such as UNIX X-Windows from the Massachusetts Institute of Technology (MIT) and IBM's OS/2, a GUI for PCs that made its debut in 1988. Though considered an excellent program, IBM's OS/2 has had little success in the marketplace. Today, various versions of Windows dominate the business PC market.

Keep 'Em Moving

New technology has allowed Los Angeleans to move their buses faster through town. Although one million people use the bus in Los Angeles every day, county transportation officials would like to lure even more drivers out of their cars. Survey results indicate that speed is the top priority of bus passengers. Research also shows that bus speeds have been declining in recent years, down to a mind-numbing 10 miles per hour. Buses were spending half their time idling at red lights or at bus stops.

Electronic antenna loops were installed in the pavement along two popular express bus routes. A transmitter in each bus sends a signal to the traffic light at the next intersection and to a central computer system that monitors bus position and speed. The software technology allows a green light to stay on longer if a bus is approaching. To avoid creating traffic snarls on the cross streets, green lights are extended for no longer than 10 seconds. At critical intersections, green lights can only be extended on alternating cycles.

The new system has cut up to 25 percent off the travel time. Although other changes have also been initiated, such as using buses that are designed for faster passenger access and cutting the number of stops on bus routes, almost half of the improvement can be attributed to the signal-timing computer technology.

Source: "Rolling on: System Lets Traffic Lights Wave Buses Through," *New York Times,* September 14, 2000.

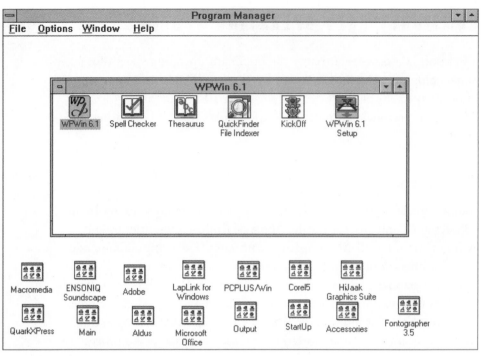

FIGURE 3-21: Loading Windows 3.1 caused the Program Manager screen to display. At this screen, users could click a program icon to launch it.

WINDOWS 95

Windows 95, a major release of the Microsoft Windows operating system in August 1995, was a significant improvement over its precursor, Windows 3.1. It offered a new user interface and Internet access. It supported newly written 32-bit applications, allowing them to run faster on this operating system. Many of the older DOS limitations, including the recognition of only 640 K of memory and the maximum file name length of eight characters, were removed. However, Windows 95 included some DOS programs and could run DOS-based applications. With its improved graphical user interface (see Figure 3-22), increased speed, and its ease of use, Windows 95 enjoyed immediate acceptance by users. Minimum system requirements for running Windows 95 were as follows:

- 486/25 MHz-based processor
- 8 MB of RAM
- 40 MB of available hard disk space
- VGA or higher-resolution display
- Microsoft Mouse or compatible pointing device

WINDOWS 98

An upgrade of the earlier Windows 95 version, **Windows 98** contained several new and improved features. It was easier to use in that applications could be started with a single mouse click instead of a double-click. Basic operations such as startup, the launching of applications, and shutdown were faster than in Windows 95. Windows 98 offered improved access to the Internet and Web through its Web browser, called *Internet Explorer*. It allowed a user to set up an **Active Desktop** in which icons could be used as links to the World Wide Web (see Figure 3-23). A Web Publishing Wizard enabled users to publish pages on intranets or the Internet. Equally important, Windows 98 provided support for multimedia devices, including DVD-ROM drives

KEYTERMS

wizard an application or part of an application that guides the user, step-by-step, through the completion of a task or that anticipates what a user might want to do and performs all or part of a task automatically

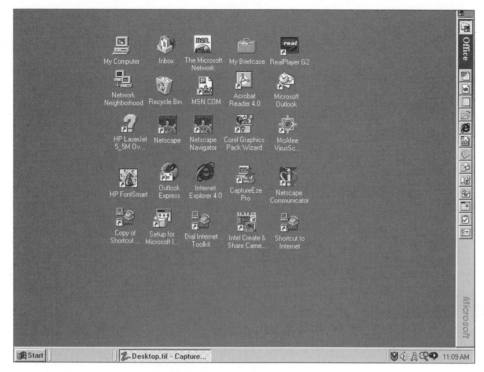

FIGURE 3-22: Windows 95 Desktop

and USB devices. It ran faster and capitalized on several new and improved features available with newer and more powerful computers.

The minimum system requirements for Windows 98 Second Edition are:

- 486DX/66 MHz or higher processor
- 24 MB of RAM
- 205 MB of available hard disk space (more for additional options)
- CD-ROM or DVD-ROM drive
- VGA or higher-resolution monitor
- Microsoft Mouse or compatible pointing device

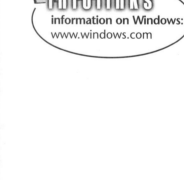

information on Windows:
www.windows.com

FIGURE 3-23: Windows 98 Desktop

WINDOWS NT

Windows NT is a powerful GUI operating system designed for executing large applications in networked environments. First released in 1993, the OS was available in two versions, a server version for the network's server computer and a workstation version for computers connected to the network (see Figure 3-24). Windows NT used the graphical user interface of Windows 95, but not its DOS features. It offered more powerful multitasking and memory management capabilities than Windows 95, and it could run programs written for both DOS and Windows. However, it was designed to take advantage of 32-bit processors and could be used with various processors. Windows NT accommodated multiple-networked computers processing applications concurrently.

System requirements for running NT on Intel-based systems were as follows:

- 486/25 MHz or higher Pentium-compatible processor
- 12 MB of RAM; 16 MB recommended
- 110 MB of available hard disk space
- CD-ROM drive or access to a CD-ROM over a computer network
- VGA or higher-resolution monitor
- Microsoft Mouse or compatible pointing device

India's Silicon Valley

India, with a population of more than 1 billion people, suffers from some large-scale problems. Its cities are burdened with overcrowded masses, many lacking access to water, electricity, and sanitation. Some 48 percent of Indians are illiterate, and only 30 percent make it to high school. But a glimmer of hope lies in the city of Bangalore.

Bangalore, on southern India's Deccan Plateau, is home to 5 million people. Fifty years ago, newly independent India chose Bangalore as the site for one of its weapons and aeronautics laboratories. The city grew into a hub of technology. Struggling to work on outdated equipment, Indian programmers became experts at writing precise, simple codes. In the 1990s India lowered its barriers to foreign investors, and when they came looking, they found a pool of talent waiting in Bangalore. And it was very affordable talent at that—the cost of labor in India is one-tenth of that in the United States.

Bangalore is now home to 300 high-tech companies that employ 40,000 people, some of whom have become millionaires, and even billionaires. All this has had a dramatic influence on the social hierarchies defined by India's caste system. In a country where the average annual income is less than $320, some Bangalore techies have made more money in the past ten years than their families earned in 500 generations. The industry is also changing the future for women. Forty percent of all new job applicants are women, and the industry is one of the rare few in this country that offers them equal pay for equal work.

Source: Wetzler, Brad. "Boomgalore," *Wired*, March 2000.

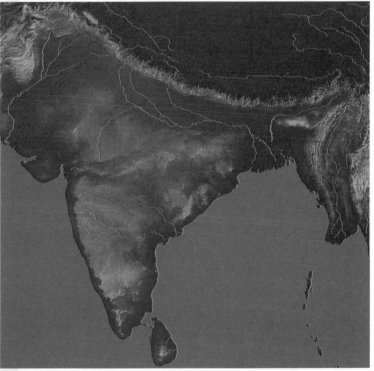

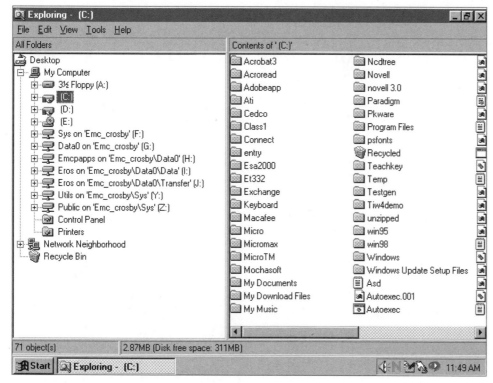

FIGURE 3-24: Windows NT Desktop

WINDOWS 2000 PROFESSIONAL

Windows 2000 Professional, introduced in late 1999, is designed for use with business desktop and notebook computers and thus is the main replacement for Windows 98 in office environments. Incorporating the networking power of Windows NT, Windows 2000 Professional (Figure 3-25) can be used for computers linked together in a network environment. This more advanced operating system is particularly well suited for newer, faster, and more powerful PCs. Thus,

FIGURE 3-25: Windows 2000 Professional Desktop

DRIVERS

Rarely does a computer programmer achieve the status of a hero, but many computer users have reason to grant heroic status to **Bill Atkinson**, the legendary programmer who created the first painting program for personal computers, **MacPaint**. Atkinson's concept for the program, which helped to popularize the first personal computer graphical user interface, was simple and clever: the user was presented with a white screen (a sketchpad) and a set of painting tools, including a paintbrush and a paint bucket. Selecting the paintbrush with the mouse cursor changed the cursor into a brush tip. When the brush tip was moved across the white screen with the mouse button depressed, it turned the pixels beneath it from white to black. By this means, shapes were formed on the screen. Selecting the paint bucket enabled the user to fill an area with a predefined pattern. Later, Atkinson and others developed color versions of painting programs based on the same concept.

Not content to rest with this significant accomplishment, Atkinson initiated a second software revolution by creating **Hypercard**, a program that enabled users to build customized programs, called **stacks**, without learning a complex programming language. To develop a program in Hypercard, a user first created a stack of cards, like the cards in an old-fashioned library card catalog, employing painting and text tools to design these cards. The user could then add buttons, icons, and text fields to the cards. The user could apply simple scripts in the **HyperTalk scripting language** to these objects. These scripts caused the buttons, icons, and text fields to perform such tasks as moving to another card, making mathematical calculations, importing text, animating graphics, and bringing up dialog boxes. Using Hypercard, nonprogrammers were able to create their own programs. Hundreds of thousands of Hypercard programs were created, including tutorials, gradebooks, statistical analysis applications, and slide shows.

Hypercard is not widely used today, but it was the program that first introduced many personal computer users to the concept of **hypertext**—pages containing text and graphics that are linked to one another in an associative rather than linear fashion. The same concept is today the basis of the World Wide Web. Hypercard was also ahead of its time because it gave ordinary computer users—people who were not programmers—the ability to assemble their own programs using **object-oriented programming**, in which user-definable objects, containing both instructions and data, were combined in erector set fashion to produce full-scale applications. In the future, it is likely that successors to Hypercard—programs that enable users to create individualized applications—will be widely used on corporate intranets, on the Internet, and on the network user interfaces that will replace older operating systems. For these reasons, many people consider Atkinson a visionary, one of those rare programmers whose work takes a quantum leap into the future.

Source: Introduction to Computers and Technology, Paradigm Publishing.

Windows 2000 Professional requires more disk space for storage and runs better on computers equipped with the latest microprocessors.

Minimum system requirements for Windows 2000 Professional are:

- 133 MHz or higher Pentium-compatible processor
- 64 MB of RAM
- 2 GB hard disk with a minimum of 650 MB of available space
- CD-ROM, CD-R, CD-RW, or DVD-ROM drive
- VGA or higher-resolution monitor
- Microsoft Mouse or compatible pointing device

WINDOWS 2000 SERVER

Microsoft's **Windows 2000 Server** is specifically designed to be used on a network server computer. It supports multitasking operations in which multiple computers on a network can process applications at the same time. It allows for the connection of various peripheral devices including hard drives and printers. The Server edition is designed to take advantage of the newest and fastest Intel-compatible microprocessors and to keep track of usage by each computer on the network. Installed on a properly equipped server computer, Windows 2000 Server provides for Internet access and for the development of Web pages. Some former Windows NT users have upgraded their operating systems with Windows 2000 server.

Windows 2000 Advanced Server and Datacenter Server are editions created for the largest network environments. Advanced Server supports up to 9 processors and up to 8 gigabytes of data, while Datacenter Server can support up to 32 processors and 64 gigabytes of data.

WINDOWS ME

Windows Millenium Edition (Me), introduced in 1999, is designed for users of less powerful PCs, such as those that may be found in homes and small offices. Although less expensive than the more powerful, feature-rich versions of Windows 2000, Windows Me supports the use of CD-ROM and DVD-ROM drives and is thus an ideal platform for games and other multimedia applications incorporating videos, photos, and music. It also offers home networking capabilities and provides Internet access with Microsoft's Web browser, Internet Explorer.

WINDOWS CE

The **Windows CE** operating system is targeted toward personal digital assistants (PDAs), wireless communications devices such as pagers and cellular phones, and next-generation smart consumer devices such as multimedia players and Web-enabled phones (see Figure 3-26). It is a 32-bit, multitasking, graphical user interface OS with special power management capabilities and built-in Internet and e-mail capability. It allows the interchange of information with desktop and networked Windows-based PCs. Windows CE is also particularly well suited for in-car computers and all devices that use embedded computer chips. *(Note: Unlike the name Windows Me, where Me stands for a term—Millenium—the CE in Windows CE has no particular significance, according to Microsoft.)*

FIGURE 3-26:
Windows CE on a Web Phone

FIGURE 3-27:
Palm OS on a Handspring Visor

PALM OS

Palm Inc., manufacturer of one of the earliest calendar and time management devices on the market, has developed its own operating system for its handheld personal digital assistants. Called **Palm OS,** this system provides a simpler graphical user interface than the one included with Windows CE, but versions available in 2000 are also less powerful. The Palm OS is used in the Palm Pilot, in various versions of other Palm PDAs, and in the Handspring Visor (see Figure 3-27). Windows CE is also used in certain Palm computers and in handhelds made by Hewlett-Packard, Compaq, and Casio.

MACINTOSH OPERATING SYSTEM (MAC OS)

The **Macintosh OS,** first released in 1984 and since updated many times, was the first commercial GUI. It included a virtual desktop, pull-down menus, dialog boxes, and icons to represent common commands and programs. With its impressive graphics and ease of use, it quickly became the model for other GUIs. Soon after its introduction, manufacturers and users of IBM-PCs and compatibles wanted a comparable GUI for their computers. Within a short time, Microsoft introduced its first Windows product for IBM-PCs and compatibles.

The Mac OS runs only on Apple's Macintosh computers. It contains many impressive and useful features, including both the Netscape and Internet Explorer

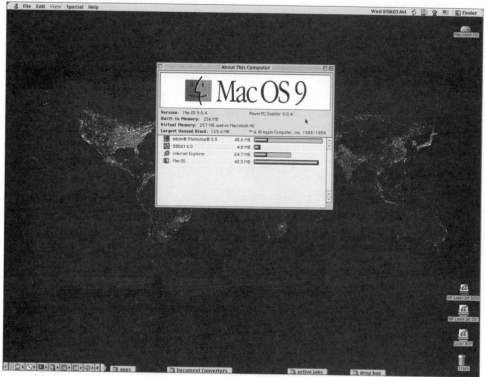

FIGURE 3-28: Mac OS 9 Interface

KEYTERMS

beta a prerelease version of a piece of software distributed so that users can test it to evaluate features and to identify any existing bugs

Web browsers. Its extraordinary graphics capabilities help make Apple's Macintosh computers the computers of choice among graphic designers, desktop production specialists, printing companies, and publishers.

Mac OS 9, the version widely available in 2000, contains several new and improved features (see Figure 3-28). It offers improved speech recognition, supports files up to two terabytes (two trillion bytes), provides for multiple users, allows for the encryption of files, and allows passwords to be entered by voice. An even newer version, Mac OS X, was released as a beta in the fall of 2000. Particularly noteworthy about this version are its new interface called Aqua and the news that it is based on the UNIX operating system, considered a highly stable and powerful system. More than 200 developers, including Microsoft, Adobe, IBM, Sun Microsystems, and Hewlett-Packard, have agreed to create software for the new system.

OS/2

IBM's **OS/2,** a graphical user interface operating system, can be thought of as the company's response to the market popularity of Microsoft Windows and Apple Computer's Mac OS. The latest version of OS/2 is called OS/2 Warp. In addition to running application programs native to it, OS/2 can also run programs written for DOS and Windows systems. The OS/2 operating system is designed mainly for business PC users running business applications. A version has been developed for use on network servers.

UNIX

Developed in the early 1970s by programmers at Bell Laboratories, the **UNIX** operating system was originally designed for large computer systems including minicomputers, mainframes, and supercomputers (see Figure 3-29). It uses a

FIGURE 3-29: UNIX is often the operating system of choice for minicomputers and mainframes.

complex command-line interface and offers some superb capabilities, including **time-sharing,** or simultaneous access by many users to a single powerful computer. From its inception, UNIX has been a **multiuser OS,** an OS that allows many people to use one CPU from remote stations. It is also a **cross-platform OS,** one that runs on computers of all kinds from supercomputers, mainframes, and minis to workstations and desktop machines. Because of its dominance in universities and laboratories, UNIX was the first language of the Internet. Today, many Internet Service Providers continue to use UNIX to maintain their networks. Several versions of UNIX are available for most kinds of computers, including PCs and larger computers.

LINUX

Based on AT&T's UNIX, the **Linux** operating system is a recent OS developed by a Finnish programmer named Linus Torvalds. Unlike most other operating systems, the original version of Linux is a nonproprietary operating system, meaning no single entity owns it. The programming code used in the initial development of Linux is available free to the public at several Web sites. Therefore, any programmer can alter the software, and knowledgeable users can make changes to meet their own requirements. The availability of programming code and the ability of developers to re-release their own versions of Linux make this operating system an **open-source** software program.

Linux software has quickly gained widespread acceptance and usage. One reason is that it can accommodate both Windows and Macintosh programs and is thus cross-platform compatible (see Figure 3-30). Another reason for its popularity is that it is free. Some companies, such as Red Hat and Corel, market their own versions of the software. Some computer professionals believe Linux is a strong competitor with other, more established operating systems. A testimony to the growing popularity of Linux is the plan announced in fall 2000 for Intel, IBM, Hewlett-Packard, and other computer companies to collaborate on creating a laboratory for developing and testing advances in Linux.

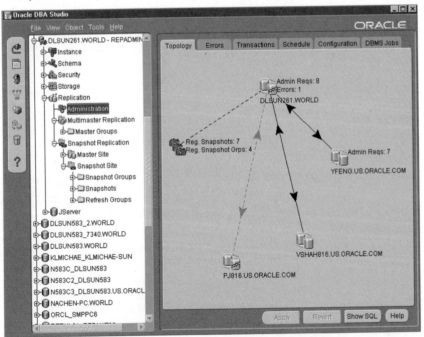

FIGURE 3-30: An Oracle application running on the Linux platform.

JAVA™

Developed by Sun Microsystems, **Java™** was originally a program of small applications, or **applets**, that could be run on all types of computers, including IBM PCs, Apple Macintoshes, handheld devices, network computers, and supercomputers. The program was created primarily to facilitate communication on the Internet among the array of users' platforms. Central to the software is a translator and **run-time version** called the **Java virtual machine**, which converts general Java instructions into commands that a specific device or computer can understand. Today, Java™ is built into most Web browsers. On embedded chip devices such as smart cards or Web-enabled cellular phones, Java works with the device's operating system or may be integrated directly into it. While Java may not meet the strict definition of an operating system, many computer industry experts consider it an important technology that fits within the OS category.

UTILITIES AND TRANSLATORS

System software may contain other special software, or allow for the use of specialized programs. Two important kinds of software are utility programs and language translators, which are explained in the following sections.

UTILITY PROGRAMS

Typically, an operating system includes several utility programs that are installed automatically at the factory. Users can also purchase and install additional utilities of their choice. A **utility program** performs a specific task, such as checking for viruses, uninstalling programs, and deleting data no longer needed (see Figure 3-31). A utility called *Scandisk*, for example, examines a disk and its contents to identify potential problems, such as bad sectors on the disk. Another popular

run-time version a program embedded with essential operating system features that allow the program to run unaccompanied by the complete operating system

Java technology:
www.sun.com

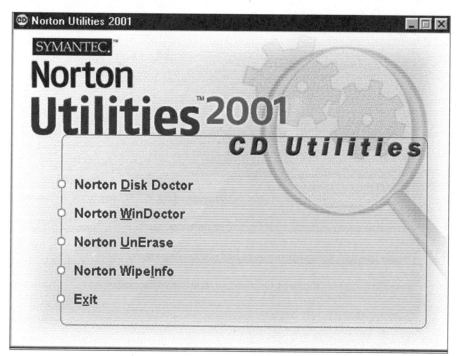

FIGURE 3-31: Norton Utilities is a utility program that can perform several tasks, including defragmenting a disk and checking for viruses.

Utility Program	What the Utility Does
Antivirus program	Protects the computer system from a virus attack
Backup utility	Makes a backup copy of files on a separate disk
Data compression utility	Reduces the size of files so they take up less disk space
Device driver	Allows hardware devices, such as disk drives and printers, to work with the computer system
Diagnostic utility	Examines the computer system and corrects problems that are identified
Disk optimizer	Identifies disk problems, such as separated files, and rearranges files so they run faster.
Disk tool kit	Recovers lost files and repairs any that may be damaged
Extender utility	Adds new programs and fonts to the computer system
File viewer	Displays quickly the contents of a file
Screen capture program	Captures as a file the contents shown on the monitor
Uninstaller utility	Removes programs and files, along with all the contents

TABLE 3-2:
Kinds of Utility Programs

utility program is Norton Utilities, which can be used to diagnose and repair some hard disk problems, to optimize hard drive performance, to restore deleted files, to erase deleted files permanently, to perform file management, and to rescue and restore files from a hard drive that has crashed. Along with the basic operating system, utility programs are usually stored on a hard disk and activated when needed by the user. Table 3-2 lists some popular kinds of utility programs.

Antivirus Software

One of the most important utility programs is a virus checker such as Norton Anti-Virus or McAfee VirusScan (see Figure 3-32). A virus is a programming code that is buried within a computer program or data and transferred to a computer system without the user's knowledge. Contamination of a computer system by a virus can have consequences varying in severity from the mildly annoying to the disastrous. Antivirus utilities perform many functions that keep a computer's software healthy. They scan new disks or downloaded material for known viruses, diagnose storage media for viral infection, monitor system operations for suspicious activities such as the rewriting of system resource files, and alert the user when such activities are occurring. Most businesses use antivirus utilities as a daily startup routine. Home computer users find them valuable as well. *(Note: The spread of viruses across the Internet, principally through attachments to e-mail messages, represents the major source of virus transmission. See Chapter 4 for a discussion of this topic.)*

Additional Types of Utilities

Productivity software (discussed in a following section) may also include utility programs that make a user's tasks easier. For example, a database application program may include its own built-in sort routine. A **sort routine** is an operation that rearranges alphabetical or numerical data in ascending or descending order.

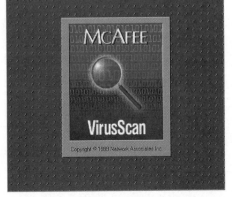

FIGURE 3-32: McAfee VirusScan is a popular virus-checking utility.

Another type of utility program that is widely used is a **file compression program** such as WinZip or Stuffit. Compression software reduces redundancies in files, such as the binary descriptions of rows of identically colored pixels in graphics files. Compression software can often reduce file size enormously and thus reduce the time that it takes to transfer a file over a network. The ability to compress and decompress files is especially helpful when sending or receiving large files over the Internet.

LANGUAGE TRANSLATORS

A computer cannot understand programming code written in a human language, such as English or Spanish. Instead, it can understand only binary code written in zeros ("0s") and ones ("1s"), which is called **machine language.** Operating systems and other system software programs may be written using machine language, which enables them to execute very quickly. However, machine language is difficult to learn and programmers find that writing machine-language programs is time-consuming. Because of this, application programs are usually written using more English-like programming languages, called **high-level languages**. Examples of high-level languages are COBOL, Java™, and Visual BASIC. However, these programs must be translated into machine-language format before the CPU can execute them. Thus, special programs called **language translators** are needed to translate (convert) high-level language programs into machine-language programs so they can be run by the computer. Microsoft Windows includes a version of BASIC for this purpose. Figure 3-33 shows a simple program created in DOS BASIC.

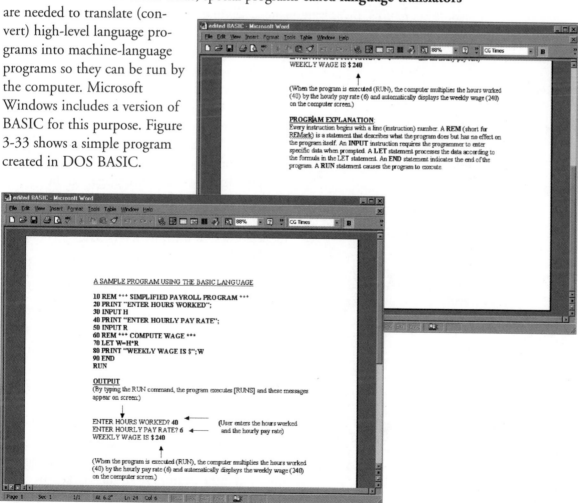

FIGURE 3-33: Sample Programming Code in DOS BASIC

Two types of language-translating software are interpreters and compilers. A **compiler** translates an entire program into machine language before the program will run. Each language has its own unique compiler. An **interpreter** reads, translates, and executes one instruction at a time.

Interpreters and compilers have advantages and disadvantages for programming. Since an interpreter acts on just one line of instruction at a time, it identifies errors as they are encountered, including the line containing the error, thereby making it somewhat more user-friendly. A compiler reads the entire program prior to execution and then displays a list of program errors that may be present. After the errors are corrected, a compiled program will usually execute more quickly than an "interpreted" program.

PRODUCTIVITY (APPLICATION) SOFTWARE

In the previous sections you leaned about one major category of software, called system software, which manages a computer system and serves as an interface between a user, the user's installed programs, and the user's computer system. Another major category of programs is productivity software, also called application software. The term **productivity software** refers to programs that allow users to perform specific tasks, such as creating letters and other documents, preparing income tax returns, managing finances, sending and receiving messages over the Internet, and designing new products. In short, productivity software enables a user to be more productive. Today, the market abounds with thousands of productivity software packages. Chances are that if you buy a personal computer for home use, it will come with some productivity programs already installed and ready for you to use. In the workplace, businesses regularly purchase and update productivity software.

Productivity software packages can be obtained from many sources, including the manufacturer, computer stores, bookstores, and mail-order houses, to mention a few. Programs can also be obtained over the Internet. Programs purchased through a retail source are typically contained on one or more CD-ROMs and are packaged with documentation and a registration card you can fill out and mail to register the product. Programs purchased and downloaded from a company's Web site to your computer typically include online documentation and an electronic registration form you can complete and e-mail to the company. Many application programs are commercially successful and are periodically upgraded, while others may appear briefly and then vanish from the market. In most situations, users quickly learn the true value of these programs.

CATEGORIES OF PRODUCTIVITY SOFTWARE

Productivity programs can be categorized in numerous ways. Table 3-3 illustrates a common way in which they are grouped, along with examples of specific programs for each group.

Category	Software Example	Common Uses
Word processing	Microsoft Word; Corel; WordPerfect	Write and format memos, letters, reports, tables
Spreadsheet	Microsoft Excel; Lotus 1-2-3; Corel Quattro Pro	Prepare financial spreadsheets and other accounting types of information
Database management	Microsoft Access; Corel Paradox	Organize, manage, and store textual and statistical information
Presentation	Microsoft PowerPoint	Create computerized slideshows to accompany speeches and other presentations
Graphics	QuarkXPress; PageMaker	Produce drawings; arrange text and graphics as pages
Communications	Eudora; Microsoft Outlook	Send e-mail messages over the Internet
Miscellaneous, including personal information management, entertainment, personal finance, and education	Lotus Organizer; Microsoft Outlook; Quicken; Doom; Microsoft Encarta; Automap; TripMaker	Track business and social appointments; play computer games; balance checkbook; learn new skills

TABLE 3-3: Productivity Software Categories

Productivity programs are available for almost any task. Some major types of software used by businesses include word processors, spreadsheets, databases, presentation software, software suites, personal information managers, money management programs, and tax software.

WORD PROCESSORS

Used to create letters, books, newsletters, business cards, and more, **word processors** are the most widely used of all software applications because they are central to communication. Communicating is a skill and a tool essential to nearly every business endeavor. At one time, computers appealed only to scientists and programmers. When computers advanced enough to allow the editing of documents without retyping, their utility for everyone became evident. Had it not been for word processing, computers would not play the central role that they do in our society today.

Of all computer applications, word processing is probably the easiest to learn and use, and almost all computers can run word processing software. Figure 3-34

infolinks
reviews of software:
www.pcworld.com/
reviews

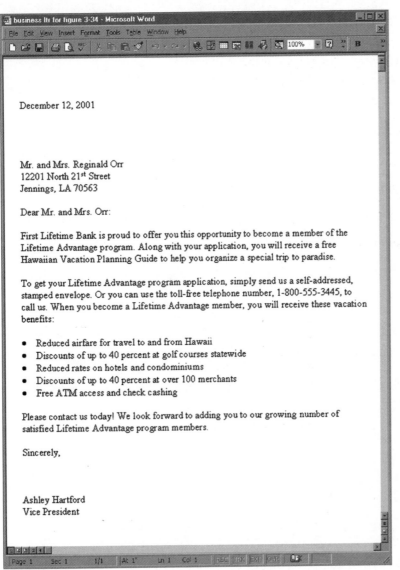

shows a sample business letter created using Microsoft Word, one of the most widely used word processors. Word processing programs are often available for more than one platform. Microsoft Word and Corel WordPerfect are available for DOS, Windows, and Macintosh computers. Another popular word processor is Lotus Development's Word Pro.

Regardless of the type of document a user creates with a **word processing** program, the essential parts of the procedure remain the same:

- Create (enter) text.
- Edit the text.
- Format the document.
- Save and print the file.

Creating Text

Creating refers to the development of a document, such as a letter or memo, by entering text and numbers, inserting graphical images, and performing other actions using one or more input devices, such as a keyboard or mouse. Documents can be created using a blank page or by using a previously created and stored form, called a **template**.

FIGURE 3-34:

Sample Business Letter

With a word processing program such as Word 2000, a user can create, edit, and print a variety of documents, including memos, letters, and reports.

Another feature called a **wizard** creates template-type documents that incorporate a user's specific information such as company name and address.

Editing Text

The process of altering the content of an existing document is called **editing**. You are editing a document anytime you insert, delete, cut, or copy and paste items into a document. Editing features allow you to make changes until you are satisfied with the content of the document.

Perhaps the most valued editing feature of a word processor is a **spelling checker**, which matches each word in your document to each word in its word list or dictionary. A spelling checker is not context sensitive and will not flag words spelled correctly but used incorrectly—for example, *their* when *there* would have been correct.

A **grammar checker** checks a document for common errors in grammar, usage, and mechanics. Grammar checkers are no substitute for careful editing by a knowledgeable human being, but they can be useful for identifying such problems as run-on sentences, sentence fragments, double negatives, and misused apostrophes.

Formatting Text

Word processing programs allow users to manipulate text in many different ways. One important feature of a word processor is that it allows a user to **format** text, or define its appearance. The following formatting features are found in many word processors:

- **Text formatting:** Text formatting features include changing fonts; applying styles such as bold, italic, and underline; changing the font size, color, and **leading** (the space between lines); and altering the **kerning** (the amount of space that appears between letters). Figure 3-35 shows a page of text with special formatting features applied.
- **Paragraph formatting:** Paragraph formatting changes how a body of text flows on the page. Features related to the appearance of a paragraph include

KEYTERMS

header in word processing, a line or more of repeated text such as a page number and a document's title that appears at the top of the document's pages

footer in word processing, a line or more of repeated text such as a page number and a document's title that appears at the bottom of the document's pages

leading in word processing and page layout programs, the space between lines of type

kerning in word processing and page layout programs, the space between the letters of a word

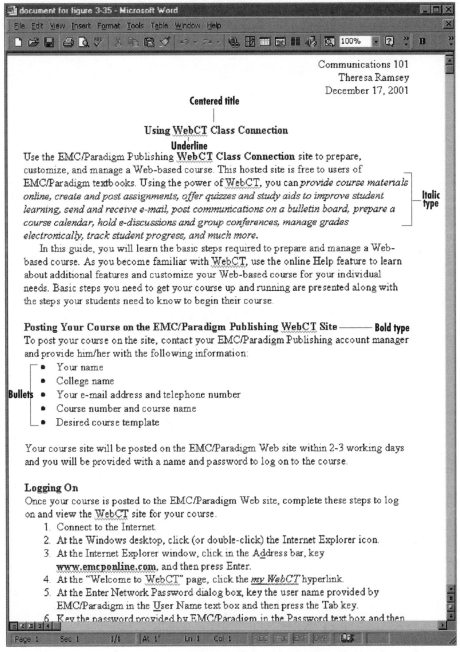

F I G U R E 3 - 3 5 : Word processing programs include several formatting features that can be applied to an individual word, a line, a paragraph, a page, or an entire document.

placing the text in columns or tables; aligning the text at the left, right, center, or as justified within the margins; and double- or single-spacing the text lines. In Figure 3-35, for example, the first paragraph is left-aligned, the course title and name/date are right-aligned, and the title is centered.

- **Document formatting:** Document formatting allows the user to specify the form of the document as a whole, defining, for example, where page numbers, **headers**, and **footers** will appear; the size of paper; and the widths of margins.

A special feature that allows a user to format text in a single step is the **style sheet**. This formatting feature allows a user to create some text, apply text and paragraph formatting to it, and then automatically apply that same complex of attributes (font, font size, leading, kerning, columns, and so on) to other sections of text. Figure 3-36 displays a page of a report with a footer containing the page number.

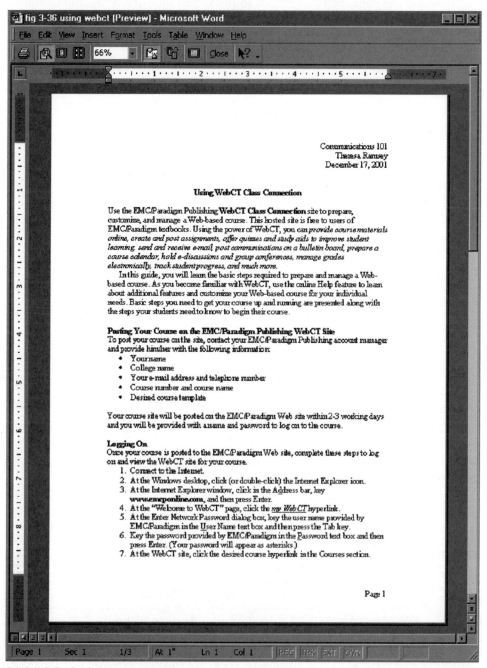

FIGURE 3-36:
Formatting features such as footers automatically add page numbers and other information of the user's choice.

Storing a copy of the displayed document to a secondary storage medium such as a floppy disk or hard disk is called **saving**. Once saved, a document (or portion of a document) can be retrieved and reused. Saving a document requires specifying the drive and assigning the document a file name. The three-character extension following the file name is generally added by the application.

Printing means producing a hard copy of a document on paper or other physical medium, such as transparency film. Although most documents are eventually printed, a document may be sent electronically over a network to another computer, where the receiver may choose to print the document.

SPREADSHEETS

An **electronic spreadsheet** is a program that provides a means of organizing, calculating, and presenting financial, statistical, and other numeric information similar to the way accountants used ruled worksheets in the past. Figure 3-37 shows a sample spreadsheet of student grade calculations using Microsoft's Excel spreadsheet program. Other widely used spreadsheets include Lotus 1-2-3 and Corel's Quattro Pro.

F I G U R E   3 - 3 7 : Student grades can be automatically calculated and stored in an Excel spreadsheet.

Businesses find spreadsheets particularly useful for evaluating several scenarios in making financial decisions. The spreadsheet uses "what if" calculations to evaluate possibilities. For example, a business might ask, "*What* happens to our profit *if* our sales increase by 50 percent?" or "*What if* our labor costs increase by 10 percent?" These types of questions can be answered quickly and accurately by entering **values** (data, such as numbers) and mathematical **formulas** into a spreadsheet. Calculations can be made almost immediately. The values can then be changed and the results recalculated almost instantly. Since the computer does all of the tedious calculations, the user can experiment with different combinations of data.

Other common business uses of the spreadsheet include calculating the present value of future assets (such as income), analyzing market trends and making projections, and manipulating statistics.

For the individual, spreadsheets can fulfill the following purposes:

- preparing and analyzing your personal, or business budget
- reconciling your checkbook
- analyzing your financial situation
- keeping track of and analyzing your investments
- preparing your personal financial statement
- estimating your taxes

Common Spreadsheet Features

technical support:
www.helponthe.net
www.answersthatwork.
com

Although spreadsheet programs differ somewhat, most offer the following characteristics and features:

- **Grid:** Spreadsheets display numbers and text in a matrix formed of columns and rows. Each intersection, or **cell**, has a unique address consisting of the column designation and the row designation—for example, A1, B1, or C3 (refer to Figure 3-37).
- **Number formatting:** Numbers may be formatted in a variety of ways, appropriate for everything from dates to dollars.
- **Formulas:** Formulas for processes from addition and multiplication to standard deviation can be entered into cells and can incorporate amounts from other cells. Formulas use other cells' addresses, not their contents. For example, a formula could direct the program to multiply cell F1 by cell A4. The use of cell addresses means that a spreadsheet can automatically update the result if the value in a cell changes.
- **Macros:** Most spreadsheets allow the user to create a **macro**, a set of commands that automate complex or repetitive actions such as checking sales figures to see if they meet quotas and then compiling all that do not into a separate chart.
- **Charting:** Spreadsheet programs allow the user to display selected data in chart form, such as in a line chart, bar chart, pie chart, or in other types of charts. A **chart** is a visual representation of data that often makes the data easier to read and understand. Figure 3-38 shows selected spreadsheet data displayed in bar chart form.

DATABASE MANAGEMENT SOFTWARE

Prior to computers, records such as employee employment information, voter lists, and customer names and addresses were typically placed in file folders and stored in a metal cabinet, along with perhaps thousands of other folders. Even if the records were stored in an organized manner, locating a particular folder could prove time-consuming and frustrating. Many of these manual systems have been replaced by electronic database systems that use a computer and appropriate software to manage stored data more efficiently. Although the first electronic database systems were developed for large computer systems, today's database software is also available for personal computers. Microsoft's Access, Lotus Development's Approach, and Corel's Paradox are among the more popular and best-selling database programs for personal computers.

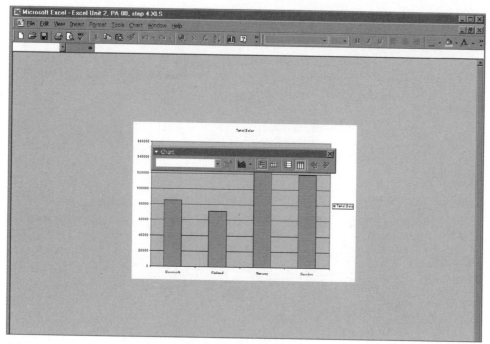

FIGURE 3-38: Microsoft Excel 2000 includes several charting options. A bar chart is useful for showing individual figures at a specific time or variations among components.

A **database** is a collection of data organized in one or more tables that consist of **fields** (individual pieces of information) and **records** (a collection of fields for a particular unit). Figure 3-39 shows an example of a table created in a database program. Typically, a commercial database program allows a user to create a **form** for entering data into a database. Figure 3-40 shows a form for entering information that will become a record in the table shown in Figure 3-39. Users can add, remove, and change the stored data. In a computerized database system, data is stored in electronic form on a magnetic storage medium, such as a hard disk or floppy disk.

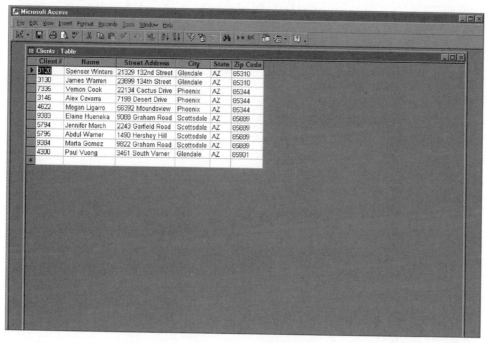

FIGURE 3-39: Within a database program, data is organized into one or more tables, each with its own name. A table consists of columns and rows. A complete row of information is called a record.

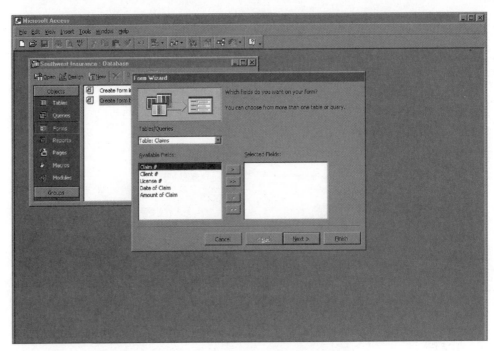

FIGURE 3-40: Forms provide an efficient way to enter data into a table.

A **database management system (DBMS)** is software that allows you to create and manage a computerized database and to create reports from stored data. Almost all business and organizations use database management systems to manage inventory records, scientific or marketing research data, and customer or client information. For example, a university collects data supplied by students during the course registration process and stores it in a database. To produce a roll for each class, the DBMS is instructed to locate and retrieve the names of students who registered for each course and to insert (in a specified order) the names in a report. The printed report is sent to the instructor.

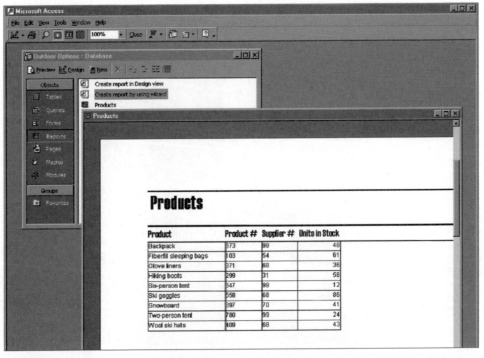

FIGURE 3-41: A report is a selection of data in a database. The user chooses which types of information should be included in the report, and the database automatically finds and organizes the data.

Businesses use database software in much the same way. For example, a business may store customer data in a database. Using a DBMS, instructions can be issued to create and print reports containing the names of customers in specific areas or territories. Using the report, each sales representative can contact the listed customers. Figure 3-41 shows an example of a report.

Although various types of database programs are available, the most popular type is the relational database model. A **relational database** is one in which various tables can be linked (or related) in a way that allows you to retrieve data from more than one table. Tables are linked through a common data field, such as a product number. Accessing a product number allows you to retrieve different kinds of information that may be stored in multiple tables in the database.

For example, suppose you visit an automobile dealer and express an interest in buying a blue Chevrolet Corsica. The dealer may have several Chevrolet cars in stock, but may not know if there is a blue Chevrolet Corsica among them. Using a computerized relational database, the dealer can quickly find the answer by querying (making an inquiry of) the database. Figure 3-42 illustrates the manner in which separate tables are linked (joined) to provide a response to a query.

Common Database Features

Features commonly found in database programs include the following:

- **Sort:** This feature allows the user to **sort**, or arrange, records in many different ways. For example, the records included in the table displayed in

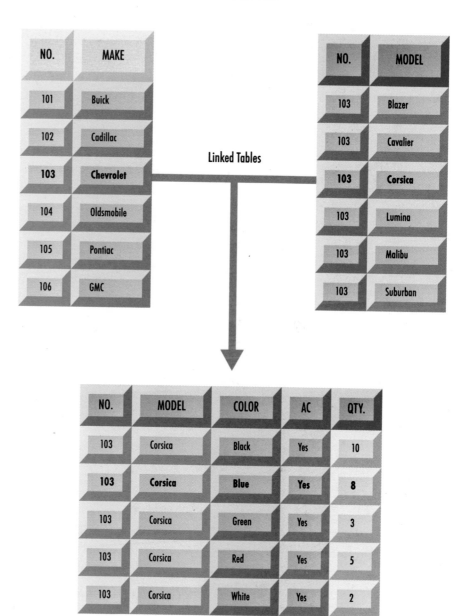

Relational databases frequently include multiple tables of data. This simplified illustration shows how tables may be linked. For example, suppose you visit an automobile dealer's showroom and inquire about Chevrolet Corsica automobiles. Using a computerized database, the salesperson can quickly access information from the three database tables shown in the illustration. A linkage of the tables shows that the dealership currently has eight blue Chevrolet Corsica automobiles in stock.

FIGURE 3-42: A relational database allows multiple tables to be linked so that the user can retrieve related data from more than one table.

Figure 3-43 could be sorted by city, by organization, or by any other field in the table.

- **Find:** The Find feature allows the user to locate specific information in a table by looking up a number or a particular type of text, such as a name or an address.
- **Query:** Databases typically allow the user to perform much more complicated searches than the Find command will allow. Such searches are accomplished by querying the database using **SQL (Structured Query Language)** or **QBE (Query by Example)**. Using one of these query methods, for instance, a user might search the table in Figure 3-43 for contacts in Zip Code 85889.
- **Links:** Relational database programs allow users to link tables in meaningful ways that make sense for a particular business. For example, a user might link the Clients table in Figure 3-43 to a Claims table and to a Policy List table.
- **Reports:** Relational database programs allow users to create reports that combine information from linked tables. For example, a user might link a Clients table with a Policy List table to produce invoices for clients.

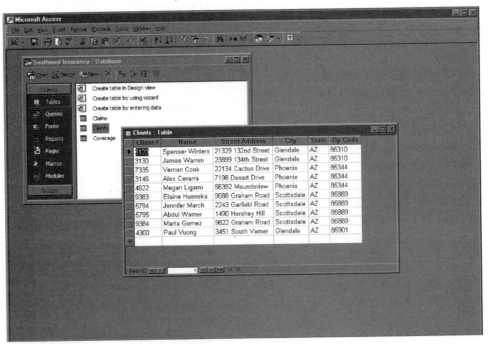

F I G U R E   3 - 4 3 : Records in the Clients table can be sorted in different ways and can be used to create a report that answers a specific query, or question.

PRESENTATION GRAPHICS SOFTWARE

If you've attended a group lecture or presentation, you probably know how boring they sometimes are. You can liven up your own presentations and hold an audience's attention by using a type of software called presentation graphics software.

Presentation graphics software allows a user to create computerized **slide shows** that combine text, numbers, graphics, sounds, and videos. Such programs are commonly used by sales representatives for pitching products to customers, by trainers and instructors for creating slide shows to accompany lectures, and by business people in general for delivering information and presenting strategies at meetings. Popular presentation software programs are Microsoft PowerPoint and Corel Presentations.

Presentation software allows a user to repurpose information, that is, change a presentation to suit different audiences. Other capabilities include being able to import files created in other programs such as word processors or spreadsheets and incorporate the material within one presentation. In addition to presenting a slide show via computer, the user can also output the presentation as 35mm **slides,** transparencies, or hard-copy handouts. A presentation run on a portable computer can be projected onto a screen using a multimedia projector (a self-contained projection unit with a plug-in for a computer) or an LCD panel (a semi-transparent projection device that attaches to the computer and sits on top of an overhead projector). Figure 3-44 shows the opening slide and lists the text for following slides in a presentation on telephone systems.

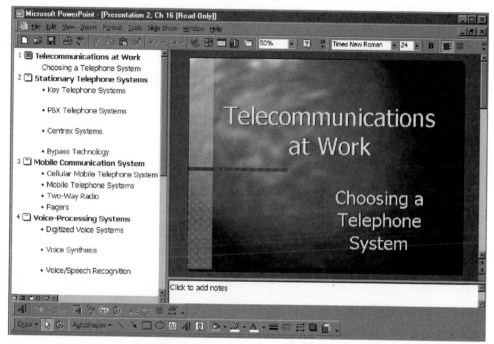

FIGURE 3-44: With Microsoft PowerPoint, the user can display a series of slides to check content and format.

Common Features of Presentation Software

Presentation applications typically include the following features:

- **Wizards:** Most presentation programs offer users a choice among presentation types. Once the user chooses a particular kind of presentation, the program provides a **wizard,** or miniprogram, to guide the user step by step through the creation of the slide show.
- **Templates:** Predesigned style formats, called **templates**, save time because they contain background colors, patterns, and other element selections that work well together. The user can select a built-in template or create a personalized template.
- **Handouts:** With Microsoft PowerPoint, creating handouts is as easy as selecting an option from the Print dialog box. Handouts can be outlines, notes, or reproductions of the screens from the presentation.
- **Clip art:** Powerful, attention-grabbing graphics can enliven a presentation and convey a message sometimes more effectively than text alone.

Presentation programs generally include collections of clip art, although users can also locate and import additional, higher-quality images.

COMMUNICATIONS SOFTWARE

In recent years, the ability to communicate quickly via computer or cellular phone has become increasingly important. Today, millions of users regularly send and receive e-mail messages, visit various Web sites, and search the Internet for information. Performing these tasks would be impossible without communications software, specifically Web browsers and search engines.

Communications software is software that allows your properly equipped computer (especially important is a modem) to communicate with other similarly equipped computers. You can send and receive electronic messages, visit Web sites, locate and

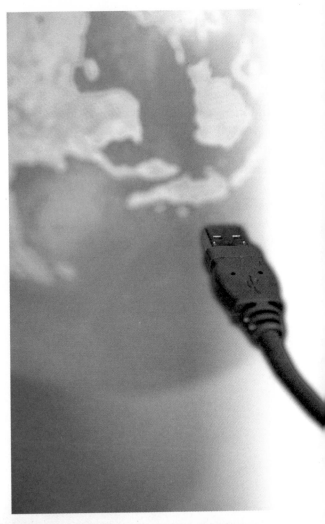

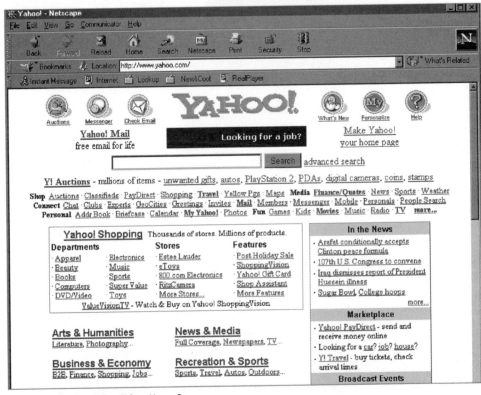

F I G U R E   3 - 4 5 : Yahoo Home Page

retrieve information stored on other computers, transmit large files, and much more.

Most users are already familiar with browsers and search engines. A **browser** is a type of communications software that allows you to visit various Web sites on the Internet and view information available at each site. Two popular browsers are Netscape Navigator and Microsoft Internet Explorer. A **search engine** is a software program that enables you to search for, locate, and retrieve specific information, such as information about polar bears. Among the more popular search engines are Yahoo!, AltaVista, HotBot, Excite, Lycos, Google, and Infoseek. Figure 3-45 shows the home page of Yahoo!

DESKTOP PUBLISHING SOFTWARE

Desktop publishing (DTP) software allows you to create impressive documents that include a combination of text, drawings, photographs, and various graphics elements in full color. Using DTP software, you can produce professional-quality publications. Indeed, textbooks such as the one you are now reading may be designed and laid out in pages with a desktop publishing application such as PageMaker or QuarkXPress. The completed files are sent to a commercial printer where they are output onto high-quality paper. Printed pages are then collated and bound into finished books. Using a page layout program requires quite extensive training, plus a background in graphics design.

Major word processors such as Microsoft Word offer a limited array of **desktop publishing** features, including the capability of drawing graphics, importing images, formatting text in special fonts and sizes, and laying out text in columns and tables. These features are suitable for creating simple newsletters, flyers, and brochures. Other desktop publishing applications include Microsoft Publisher, which is part of Microsoft's Office suite, and which can be used to create all types of publications.

Harald II Bluetooth, King of Denmark in the tenth century, is the namesake of the Bluetooth software technology.

Bluetooth

A promising new communications technology called "Bluetooth" is capturing the interest of computer professionals and portable device manufacturers around the world. The idea for Bluetooth technology was first conceived by the Swedish company Ericsson, although the technology was developed collaboratively by Ericsson, Nokia, IBM, Intel, and Toshiba. More recently, Motorola, Compaq, Dell, and Lucent have joined the alliance.

Named for Harald Bluetooth, a fearsome Viking king of tenth-century Denmark, Bluetooth is a wireless technology that provides low-cost, short-range radio links between mobile PCs, mobile phones, other portable devices, and even home appliances. According to developers, it will enable users to connect to a wide range of computing and telecommunications devices easily and simply, without cables.

A major goal of the alliance is to develop a short-range communications standard allowing wireless data communications at ranges of up to about 30 feet. Some companies, including Motorola, Ericsson, and Lucent, have already developed inexpensive computer chips for use with a variety of portable devices, including headsets and various communications devices.

Developers envision widespread use of Bluetooth technology in electronic commerce applications, such as electronically paying for parking, bus tickets, consumer goods, and movies. Also in the picture is a smart office, in which an employee with a Bluetooth device is automatically checked in when entering the building. The device also would simultaneously trigger a series of start-up actions, such as turning on lights and office computers.

Source: <http://www.bluetooth.com>.

Some software publishers bundle and sell a group of programs as a single package, called a **software suite**. Just as a hotel suite contains multiple rooms, a software suite contains multiple programs. A software suite may contain word processing, spreadsheet, database, and possibly other programs. Popular software suites include Microsoft Office, Lotus Development SmartSuite, and Corel WordPerfect Office.

Software suites offer certain advantages. Because the programs were developed using the same user interface, all programs in the suite work in a similar manner. Once you've learned one program, learning to use the others is easier because of the similarity of screen layouts, menus, buttons, icons, and toolbars. Another strong feature of suites is their *integration* capability, meaning files from one program can be imported seamlessly into another program. For example, information produced with a spreadsheet can be placed into a word processing document, or a database table can be imported into a slide-show presentation.

One method of moving information from one suite program to another is to copy and paste. Although quite easy, this method has some disadvantages. For example, if you created a PowerPoint slide show into which you copied an Excel spreadsheet file, you would need to recopy the file each time it is updated with new calculations.

A second method for incorporating files from one program to another within a suite of applications addresses the problem of information that may change. This method is called **object linking and embedding (OLE)**. It involves creating an object (a table, chart, picture, or text, for example) in one program and then sharing it with another program. Two types of sharing are possible: embedding and linking. Embedding is a type of copying, although it also allows the user to change the embedded file using the original program's editing features. However, the changes are not reflected in the original file. Using the example in the previous paragraph, a spreadsheet file embedded in the PowerPoint presentation could be edited, but the changes appear only in the PowerPoint presentation. Linking the file, however, ensures that any changes made in the original spreadsheet file will be reflected in the PowerPoint presentation also.

Onward Cyber Soldiers

The Information Age has led to a new development in warfare. Hackers and information guerrillas are fighting for their causes via the Internet, creating a battlefield that ignores international boundaries.

The Balkans, Russia, China, and most recently the Middle East have experienced the rise of hacktivism. In these infowars, Web sites are altered with messages advocating online attacks against the other side, sometimes even providing the software to do it. Supporters of a cause, even those on the other side of the planet, might find that their addresses and credit card numbers have been stolen and posted on the Internet. Information sites and libraries have been blocked and poisoned with viruses. Hackers have become experts in disinformation, planting false rumors and changing headlines.

As dependency on e-commerce and communication increases, so does the vulnerability of businesses and societies to such attacks. But there are some who see cyberwarfare as a good thing, wistfully hoping that this trend will eventually move all war away from the battlefield and into the virtual world.

Source: Schwartz, John. "New wrinkle in warfare: Point and click becomes point and shoot," *Minneapolis Star Tribune,* November 23, 2000.

PROPRIETARY SOFTWARE VS. FREEWARE/SHAREWARE

Commercial software products, particularly productivity applications, currently make up the bulk of software used by businesses and individuals. These products are considered **proprietary software**, meaning that a company or an individual owns them and expects users to purchase or lease them. Developers of proprietary software usually obtain legal copyright, making it illegal for others to make copies. The illegal copying or unauthorized use of copyrighted software is called **software piracy**.

An example of proprietary software is Microsoft Office. By completing and submitting the registration information that accompanies the product, a purchaser receives a license from Microsoft granting the user the right to use the software. In a network environment, a **site license** provides multiple-user rights. Registering the software provides the benefits of technical assistance and notification about software upgrades.

The second major segment of the software market includes freeware and shareware products, which are not sold through traditional commercial methods. Typically, users download these types of software from the Internet. A **freeware** program is software that can be copied or distributed at no cost, although the author retains the copyright and the program may not be sold or altered without permission. **Shareware** can also be copied or distributed liberally and copyright is retained by the author. Shareware differs from freeware in that the shareware agreement specifies a period of time after which, if the user wishes to continue using the product, he or she is obligated to send a small fee to the author. Sometimes the user receives an upgraded version when payment for the shareware is made.

WWW infolinks

software piracy:
www.spa.org (Software Information Industry Association)

shareware offerings:
www.shareware.com

Computers in Your Future?

Computer Security Engineer

Do you like staying one step ahead of the "bad guys"? The demand is growing for computer security engineers in businesses, universities, the government, and the military.

Computer security engineers use their skills to help organizations control access to their computer networks and protect the vital data they have stored. Responsibilities may include securing physical access to the computers; designing and implementing network control mechanisms; and providing application process controls to keep unauthorized users out of a particular program. Computer security engineers are responsible for building a defense against hackers and detecting when they have broken in.

This job takes a person to all levels of the organization. The computer security engineer first consults with management to develop a system that best suits the organization's computer use and security concerns. Then he works with all users in the organizations to familiarize them with the security measures. The computer security engineer is also responsible for keeping back-up files of important data.

The position requires training in a variety of networking technologies, computer programming, and risk management. The job has unpredictable hours, and the computer security engineer may be on-call to handle emergencies. There is a high level of responsibility and subsequent stress. However, the rewards for the secret service of cyber space are high. An independent consultant hired to fight hackers may command upwards of $250 per hour. An experienced professional can earn a salary of $100,000 or more.

Source: "Career Information Center: Computers, Business, and Office," 7th Edition, Visual Education Corp., Princeton, NJ, 1999.

ON THE HORIZON

Inspired by breakthroughs in processing technology as well as changing market needs, software developers are continually brainstorming new programs or improvements to existing software. Although trying to divine the path of software development is risky, some of today's leading-edge technologies provide clues to the future.

SPEECH RECOGNITION SOFTWARE

Several hardware devices and productivity applications currently incorporate speech recognition as an input mechanism. Although much improved from earlier attempts, the present speech recognition technologies have yet to meet the high accuracy standard demanded in transcription-intensive industries such as medical transcription. The exploding use of Web-enabled handheld computers probably means we'll see great leaps of improvement in speech recognition, simply because the market need is stronger than ever. IBM has developed a technology called

conversation speech biometrics, which may provide one of the significant advances. Suited particularly for identification and verification needs, such as those required during Internet purchases, the IBM technology compares a voice to a database of known speakers. The software is able to recognize the voice even though the database may not include the exact words spoken.

A related technology called **natural-language processing (NLP)** has advanced to the point where systems can understand the conversations of a five-year-old child. If NLP software can live up to its potential, imagine the possible applications, particularly the time saved in communicating with computers.

PATTERN RECOGNITION SOFTWARE

Pattern recognition software translates images, such as a customer's face, into digital information, filters out any unnecessary data, and then compares the result against a reference model. This type of software could be used for identification and verification. A version of it, called IBM DB2 Intelligent Miner for Data, is currently used to evaluate customers' responses and choices at Web sites, looking for buying patterns and using that information to try to sell new products to them.

ENHANCED ARTIFICIAL INTELLIGENCE

Synthetic characters similar to Ananova (www.ananova.com) may soon populate the Internet landscape as well as specific environments in the business world. Advancements in **artificial intelligence** also will result in more humanlike robots that can solve problems and even sense emotions. Experts caution, however, that robots or synthetic characters exhibiting intelligence on a par with humans is only a blip on the horizon. Enormous increases in computing power are required before artificial intelligence lives up to its name. When a piece of software can pass the Turing Test, say researchers, computers can be called intelligent.

Devised by British philosopher Alan Turing in 1937, the **Turing Test** involves placing a person at a computer terminal and having that person communicate with a computer in another room. If the person cannot determine if she's talking to a computer or to a human, the computer is intelligent.

To date, no computer has come even close to passing the Turing Test, but it is not outside the realm of possibility due to the development of sophisticated neural networks using "fuzzy logic." **Neural networks** imitate human thinking in that they can deal with ranges of possibilities ("almost done," "somewhere between 1 and 8"), whereas current computer processors deal only with on or off—yes or no. Molecular chips may enable the gargantuan processing power required to drive neural networks.

RENTABLE PRODUCTIVITY APPLICATIONS

Increasingly, companies are leasing productivity applications over the Internet from companies called **application service providers (ASPs)**. The ever-expanding capabilities of software coupled with the cost of continually upgrading to the new versions makes renting, rather than owning, software an attractive prospect.

Called **Webtops,** this new model of computing provides access to application suites through a Web browser. In the near future, a mobile user would therefore need to carry only a **Web appliance**, which costs far less than a laptop computer (see Figure 3-46). In the works are Webtop models expected to compete with Microsoft Office by offering a suite of productivity tools not tied to the Windows platform.

KEYTERMS

neural networks software programs that model the way neurons (nerve cells) are linked in the brain

Web appliance a simplified computer device that connects the user to the Internet, where programs and other applications are available at Web sites; Web appliances do not store and run programs themselves

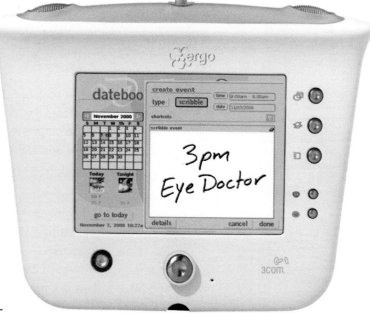

FIGURE 3-46: Audrey™, a Web appliance manufactured by 3Com Corporation, includes a built-in Web browser, a wireless keyboard, a serial port for Palm-compatible devices, two USB ports, and a 56 K built-in modem.

1959
More than 200 programming languages have been created to date

1960

1965
Professors John Kemeny and Thomas Kurtz create the BASIC programming language

1970

1975
The Altair 8800 personal computer runs a version of BASIC created by Bill Gates and Paul Allen

1976
Gary Kildall writes CP/M, a widely used operating system for early personal computers

1979
The first spreadsheet program, Visicalc, is created

1980
Bill Gates, co-founder of Microsoft Corporation, develops the MS-DOS operating system for the IBM PC

1980

1983
Lotus 1-2-3, a widely successful spreadsheet program, is developed by Lotus Corporation

1984
Apple's Macintosh PC, with its easy-to-use graphical user interface, is introduced

1989
Tim Berners-Lee develops a hypertext structure for sharing information worldwide; this technology is instrumental in the creation of the World Wide Web

1990

1992
Microsoft introduces Windows 3.1, which quickly sees sales of more than 3 million copies

1994
Linus Torvalds of Finland creates and freely distributes the Linux operating system

1995
Microsoft releases its Windows 95 operating system

1998
Microsoft releases Windows 98

1999
Microsoft releases Windows 2000

2000

CHAPTER SUMMARY

- **What Is Computer Software?** In the broadest sense, **software** is a set of programs that tell a computer what to do and how to manage the computer's resources, including all hardware devices. A **program** is a series of instructions that tells a computer the specific steps to process data into information. Along with the needed hardware, the right kinds of software enable a user to perform a variety of operations and applications that expand productivity for individuals, businesses, and organizations.

- **System Software** One of the major types of software, **system software** is essential to the operation of every computer. System software consists of a set of programs that control the operation of a computer system, including starting the computer, formatting disks, copying files, and enabling the productivity program you are using to work smoothly with your computer. Thus, system software serves as the **interface** between the user, the user's application software, and the user's computer hardware.

- **Operating Systems**, **Utility Programs, and Language Translators** These programs are the three main types of system software. An **operating system**, the most important type of system software, serves as a gateway between the application being used and the computer's hardware. An operating system performs many essential functions, including managing RAM, configuring and controlling devices, managing files, monitoring system performance, and providing a user interface.

- **Software User Interfaces** Every software program, including those for PCs, minicomputers, mainframes, and supercomputers, contains a set of instructions called a **user interface** that allows the software to communicate with the user and, in turn, the user to communicate with the software. The manner in which the user enters data and commands and in which information and processing options are presented is controlled by the program's interface. The operating system's user interface plus the processor type determine the computer's **platform**.

- **Graphical User Interfaces (GUIs)** A **graphical user interface (GUI)** is one that uses toolbars, menus, icons, and other visual elements to simplify the user's interaction. GUIs were made possible with the development of mouse technology and the introduction of more powerful computers and high-resolution graphics screens.

- **Graphical User Interface (GUI) Features** A graphical user interface offers menus of options for key features, icons that represent common commands, an on-screen desktop, document and program windows, dialog boxes, and an online help system. A **menu** provides an on-screen set of options from which a user selects by clicking with a mouse or by typing one or more keystrokes. An **icon** is a picture or symbol that represents an action to be taken. An **on-screen desktop** is a work area on which graphical elements such as icons, buttons, windows, links, and dialog boxes are displayed, similar to the way pens, folders, and tablets might be arranged on an office desk. A **window** is a rectangular area of the screen used to display a program, data, or information. A **dialog box** provides feature information or requests information from a user. **Online Help** is an indexed set of feature information files that provides the assistance a user requests.

- **Popular Operating Systems** Through the years, several operating systems have been developed for personal computers. Among the more popular operating systems are Windows 98, Windows NT, Windows 2000 Professional, Windows 2000 Server, Windows ME, Windows CE, Palm OS, Mac OS 9, OS/2, UNIX, and Linux.

- **Utilities and Translators** Two important kinds of system software are utility programs and language translators. A **utility program** performs a specific task, such as checking for viruses, uninstalling programs, and deleting data no longer needed. **Language translators** translate (convert) high-level language programs into machine-language programs so they can be executed by the computer. Two types of language-translating software are **interpreters** and **compilers**.

- **Productivity (Application) Software** The term **productivity software** refers to programs that allow users to perform specific tasks, such as creating documents, preparing income tax returns, managing finances, sending and receiving messages over the Internet, and designing new products. In short, productivity software enables a user to be more productive.

- **Categories of Productivity Software** Productivity programs are available for almost any task a user might need to do. Main categories include word processing, electronic spreadsheets, database management software, presentation graphics software, communications software, and desktop publishing software. Some software publishers bundle and sell a group of programs as single packages, called **software suites**.

KEYTERMS

Active Desktop, 20
applet, 29
application service provider (ASP), 49
artificial intelligence, 49
beta, 27
booting, 5
buffer, 5
button, 14
cell, 38
chart, 38
check box, 17
command-line interface, 8
communications software, 44
compiler, 32
context-sensitive, 18
conversation speech biometrics, 48
creating, 34
cross-platform OS, 28
database management system (DBMS), 40
default option, 11
desktop, 14
desktop publishing (DTP), 45
dialog box, 14
display window, 14
driver, 7
editing, 34
electronic spreadsheet, 37
field, 39
file compression program, 31
file manager, 7
footer, 35
form, 39
format, 35
formula, 37
freeware, 47
grammar checker, 34
header, 35

high-level language, 31
IBM OS/2, 27
icon, 10
interpreter, 32
Java™, 29
kerning, 35
language translator, 31
leading, 35
Linux, 28
Macintosh OS, 26
machine language, 31
macro, 38
menu, 10
menu bar, 10
multitasking, 6
multiuser OS, 28
natural-language processing (NLP), 48
neural network, 49
object linking and embedding (OLE), 46
open-source software, 28
option button, 17
Palm OS, 26
performance monitor, 8
platform, 19
presentation graphics software, 42
print spooler, 7
print spooling, 7
printing, 37
productivity (application) software, 32
prompt, 8
proprietary software, 47
pull-down menu, 10
QBE (Query by Example), 42
radio button, 17
record, 39

relational database, 41
run-time version, 29
saving, 37
scroll bar, 14
search engine, 45
shareware, 47
site license, 47
slide show, 42
software piracy, 47
software suite, 46
sort, 41
sort routine, 30
spelling checker, 34
SQL (Structured Query Language), 42
style sheet, 36
system software, 4
tab, 16
template, 34
text box, 18
time-sharing, 28
title bar, 14
toolbar, 13
Turing Test, 49
UNIX, 27
user interface, 8
utility program, 29
value, 37
Web appliance, 49
Webtop, 49
Windows CE, 26
Windows Me, 25
Windows 95, 20
Windows 98, 20
Windows NT, 22
Windows 2000 Professional, 23
Windows 2000 Server, 25
wizard, 34
word processing, 34

INTERNET

TUTORIAL 3

CONDUCTING AN ADVANCED SEARCH

The number of Web sites that an individual will see in a list as the result of a search request can be overwhelming. It is not uncommon to see thousands of hits result from searching by a few keywords. The challenge when searching for information on the Internet is to reduce the number of hits to the smallest possible number. Including a search operator with the keywords refines a search by limiting the sites that are displayed based on where or how the keywords are placed. Search operators vary between search engines so it is best to view the Advanced Search Help for a search engine prior to using operators.

In this topic you will find information on the Web by reading Advanced Search Help and then entering keywords with search operators.

Steps

1. Start Internet Explorer. If necessary, connect to your ISP and enter your username and password.

2. Key **www.lycos.com** in the Address text box and then press Enter.

Lycos, one of the oldest search engine companies, was developed in 1994 at Carnegie Mellon University. It is well known for its extensive categories, easy to use search page, and "Top 50" searches summarized and published each week.

3. Key **endangered species** in the Search for text box and then click Go Get It or press Enter.

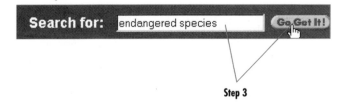

Step 3

In a few seconds a list of popular Web pages based on user selection history will be displayed and then farther down the screen the total number of sites found from searching the entire Lycos catalog are listed.

4. Scroll down the Results for endangered species page and read the titles of the Web pages found.

In the next steps you will refine the list to display only those pages that contain information about birds that are endangered.

5. Scroll to the top of the page and then click the Advanced Search button.

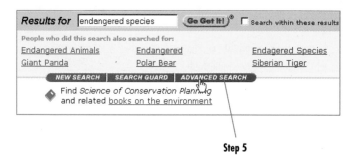

Step 5

6. Click Help. Scroll down the Advanced Search Help page and then read the information in the Building a Search Expression section.

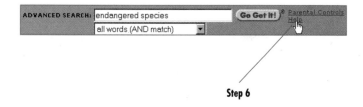

Step 6

The information on Boolean Operators is especially useful for narrowing search requests since these operators can be used in the primary search text box instead of using the Advanced Search page.

7. Click Back on the toolbar to return to the Advanced Search page.

8. Click in the Advanced Search text box after the text *endangered species,* press the space bar, key **+birds**, and then press Enter.

Key search +engines +review to find links to Web sites that review the popular search engines and provide helpful tips for effective searching.

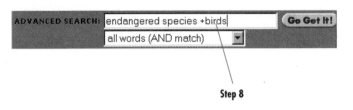

Step 8

9. Scroll down the results page. Notice the Web pages found contain all three words: *endangered, species,* and *birds.*

Yahoo provides an advanced search page that can be used to narrow a search based on search operators and the time period information has been published.

10. Key **www.yahoo.com** in the A̲ddress text box and then press Enter.

11. Click the advanced search link next to the Search text box.

12. Key **endangered species +birds** in the Search text box.

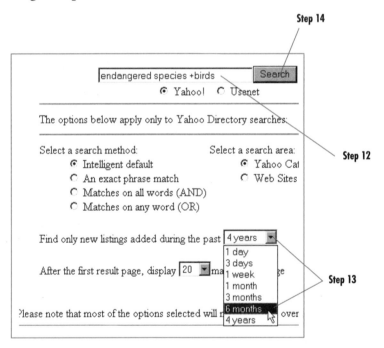

13. Click the down-pointing triangle next to Find only new listings added during the past [ ] and then click *6 months* in the drop-down list.

14. Click Search.

15. Scroll down the list of Web sites found.

16. Close Internet Explorer. If necessary, disconnect from your ISP.

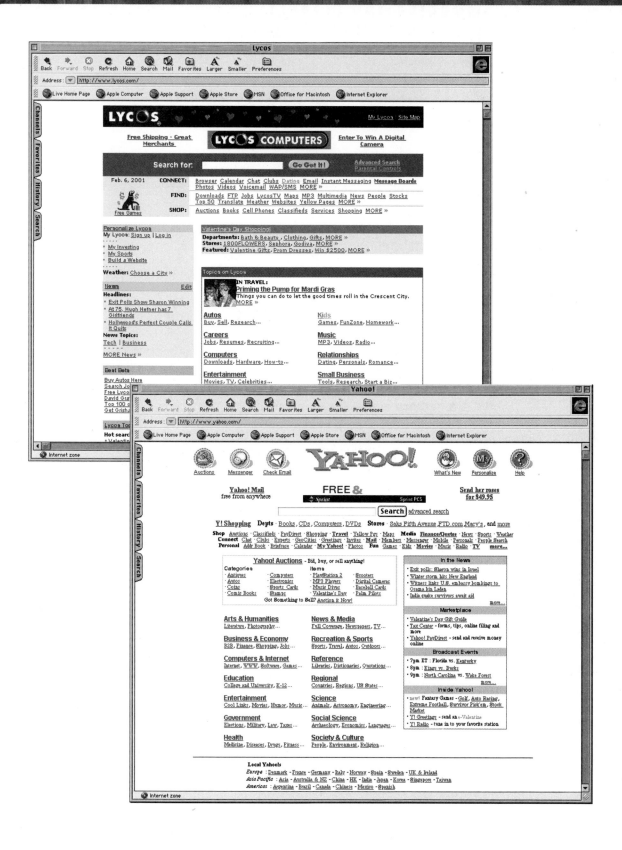

COMMUNICATING CLEARLY

Technology Terms: What do they mean?

a. on-screen desktop g. check box
b. display window   h. system software
c. software suite   i. graphical user interface (GUI)
d. utility   j. icon
e. software   k. menu bar
f. machine language l. productivity software

1. A set of programs that tells a computer what to do and how to manage the computer's resources.

2. An interface that uses menus, buttons, and symbols, thereby making it easier to work with text, graphics, and other elements.

3. A horizontal or vertical row display that shows the highest-level command options.

4. An on-screen work area on which graphical elements such as icons, buttons, windows, links, and dialog boxes are displayed.

5. A picture or symbol that represents an action such as opening, saving, or printing a file.

6. A rectangular area of the screen used to display a program, data, or information.

7. An element of a dialog box containing multiple options you can turn on or off.

8. A category of software that allows users to perform specific tasks, such as creating documents or preparing income tax returns.

9. A type of program that performs a specific task such as formatting a disk.

10. A group of productivity programs bundled and sold as a single package.

11. A special computer language consisting of zeros and ones.

12. A set of programs that control the operation of a computer system, including the computer and all components and devices connected to it.

Techno Literacy: How can new knowledge be used?

1. Is Windows Me for you?
   Visit the Web site of Microsoft Corporation at www.microsoft.com and locate information about Windows 2000 Me and Windows 2000 Professional. Prepare an oral or written report that compares the two operating systems. On what brands and models of computers are these operating systems preinstalled? Which OS would better suit your needs? Why?

2. Which program can improve my productivity?
   Visit a computer store in your area. Select a particular productivity program displayed in the store and read the product's description on the package. For which platform is the program written? What is the price? Will the program run on your computer? For what purpose(s) might you be able to use the program?

3. What's hot in applications software?
   Visit your school library and look through several computer magazines for one new and innovative productivity software program. Find an article that provides a detailed explanation of the program. Write a summary that describes the program's purpose, main features, and specifications, including the user interface, the amount of internal memory needed to run the program, and the amount of disk space required to store the program. Why is this an innovative program? What needs does this product meet? Are there competing products in the market? Will the product be a commercial success? Why, or why not?

4. Is a picture worth a thousand words?
   Ask your instructor (or another person) for the name of a business or organization in your area that regularly uses presentation graphics software to train sales reps or to provide information. Find out if you can attend one of the presentations. If you are able to attend, watch the slide show and then write an evaluation of the effectiveness of the presentation. List the technologies used (hardware and software) and describe the presentation features that impressed you most.

5. Is there a vaccine for this virus?
   With team members assigned by your instructor, investigate a computer virus that has infected large numbers of computers in recent years. What does the virus do? Where did it originate, and how does it spread? How widespread was the outbreak? How was the virus stopped?

CONNECTING WITH CONCEPTS
Technology Processes: What's right with this picture?

What process is illustrated in the drawing below? Identify the process and write a paragraph explaining it.

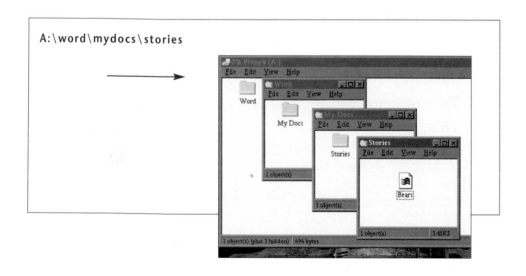

Key Principles: What's it all about?

1. An option that has been built into a software program under the assumption that it is the one most likely to be chosen is called a(n)

   a) default
   b) driver
   c) buffer
   d) algorithm

2. A rectangular area of the screen used to display a program, data, or information is a

   a) pane
   b) menu
   c) toolbar
   d) window

3. A box that provides information to the user or requests information from the user is called a(n)

   a) query box
   b) dialog box
   c) answer box
   d) data box

4. A section of memory used to hold information and data waiting to be transferred to or from an output device is a

   a) holding area
   b) cell
   c) buffer
   d) floppy disk

5. A small program that enables a computer to communicate with devices such as printers and/or a monitor is a

   a) driver
   b) graphical user interface
   c) speaker
   d) compiler

6. DOS stands for

   a) driver operating software
   b) disk ordering system
   c) density of software
   d) disk operating system

7. A type of software that converts an entire program into machine language is called a(n)

   a) coprocessor
   b) binary operator
   c) utility program
   d) compiler

8. Which of the following is **not** a function of an operating system?

   a) provide a user interface
   b) process data
   c) manage RAM
   d) configure and control peripheral devices

9. A productivity application used to analyze "what if" scenarios is a

   a) presentation program
   b) word processor
   c) spreadsheet program
   d) database manager

10. Which of the following features is not typically found in a GUI?

    a) pull-down menu
    b) dialog box
    c) icon
    d) directory command

MINING DATA

Conduct Internet searches to find information described in the activities below. Write a brief report that summarizes your research results. Be sure to document your sources using MLA format.

1. Research the advantages and disadvantages of open-source software programs such as Linux. Is there evidence to suggest that providing source code to developers has resulted in better programs over a shorter development time?

2. Speech recognition software has been a longtime dream of software developers. Research the current status of this technology, including possible next steps and the obstacles to overcome.

3. Biometric authentication is a growing field in software development. Using the key word "biometrics," research the meaning of the term and the possible applications of this technology in the field of education.

THINGS THAT THINK

1. Researchers at Massachusetts Institute of Technology (MIT) and elsewhere are developing robots and synthetic characters that not only think—for example, provide us with specific information based on the situation—but also display emotions. Scientists envision using these smart robots to diagnose patients' illnesses and, in a company's customer service department, to find exactly the product a customer needs. What are some other applications for this expanding technology?

2. Several companies are developing tracking devices that allow objects and people to be located over great distances via satellite and the Global Positioning System (GPS), a technology that uses satellite signals to determine the user's latitude and longitude. Projected applications include backpack devices that parents could use to track their children's whereabouts, cars that could send an alert if they've been stolen, and dog collar devices for locating lost pets. How else might the GPS technology be used?

PREDICTING NEXT STEPS

Microprocessors have evolved over the past quarter-century from the Intel 4044 chip to the powerful Pentium 4. The timeline below lists some major milestones in that development. Research this topic and fill in the gaps. Then predict the next major development (in terms of processor speed and/or power), along with a time frame. *(Check out Intel's Web site at www.intel.com for historical information. Also try the American Computer Museum at www.compustory.com.)*

1971   Intel Corporation releases the 4004 microprocessor, considered the first computer on a chip.

1985   Motorola produces a 32-bit 25 MHz microprocessor called the 68040.

2000   Intel announces the Pentium 4 chip, with processing speeds of up to 1.5 GHz.

SOLVING PROBLEMS

In groups or individually, brainstorm possible solutions to the issues presented.

1. In the software industry, companies dream of creating the next "killer app," a software program that is so useful and therefore becomes so popular that it drives new software and hardware development. The first killer app for the personal computer was Visicalc, which founded the electronic spreadsheet software industry and was instrumental in launching the widespread sales of the personal computer. Considering current market needs and trends, what is your candidate for the next great killer app?

2. In the Solving Problems section at the end of Chapter 2, you were asked to recommend an ideal computer system for the national sales manager of a mid-sized company. Given that person's computing needs, what kind of software purchases would you recommend if she wanted to be able to pre-pare slideshow presentations and other work-related documents at home? Assume that you have a budget of $800 for software purchases. Note that you will need to specify the type of computer system the national sales man-ager might have available at home.

EXAMINING ETHICAL ISSUES

Access the Computer Concepts Resource Center at EMC/Paradigm's Web site (www.emcp.com/college_division/ electronic_resource_center) and go to Computers: Exploring Concepts, then to Student Resources, then to the Ethical Issues page. Complete the activity for Chapter 3.

ANSWERS TO TECHNOLOGY TERMS AND KEY PRINCIPLES QUESTIONS

Technology Terms: 1 – e; 2 – i; 3 – k; 4 – a; 5 – j; 6 – b; 7 – g 8 – l; 9 – d; 10 – c; 11 – f; 12 – h

Key Principles: 1 – a; 2 – d; 3 – b; 4 – c; 5 – a; 6 – d; 7 – d; 8 – b; 9 – c; 10 – d

CHAPTER 4

CONNECTIVITY: TELECOMMUNICATIONS, NETWORKS, AND THE INTERNET

learning objectives

- Explain the role of telecommunications in the operations of networks and the Internet

- Differentiate the types of communications media and the kinds of communications protocols

- Classify networks based on architecture, users, and area of coverage

- Explain the differences among network topologies and identify their most effective uses

- Identify the major components of network hardware and software

- Describe the major uses of the Internet

- Summarize the principal tools used to access and navigate the Internet

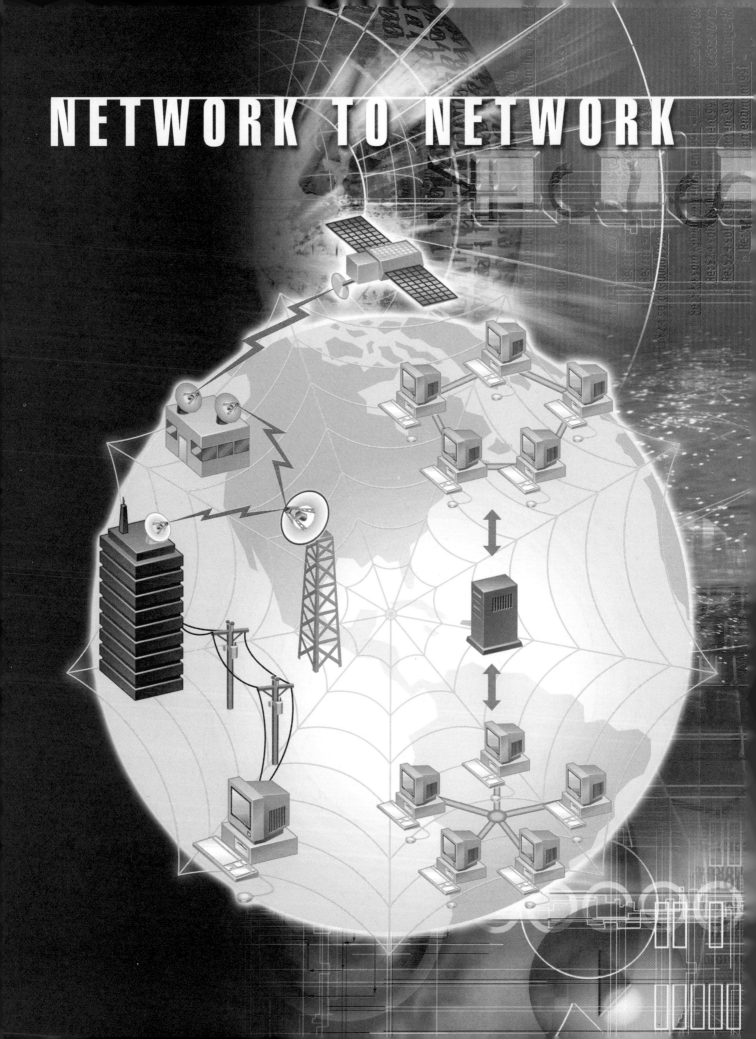

NETWORK TO NETWORK

CYBER SCENARIO

It's Monday, October 1, 2002. At the construction site of your new home, you stand before the wood-and-brick structure, picturing the completed product and imagining the excitement of moving day. Your dream house is halfway to becoming a reality—on time and, better yet, at a cost that is nearly 30 percent less than what was estimated by the house-planning software program you bought last year. What accounts for the extraordinary savings? Inaccurate data entered into the estimating program? A poorly programmed application? Sudden drops in the cost of materials and/or labor?

While any or all of the above factors are possible reasons, the truth is that the remarkable cost savings in constructing your new home are a direct result of the builder using a project management software application accessed over the Internet. This collaborative Web tool links the builder, the contractors, the materials manufacturers and dealers, and all vendors—plus the customer—at a central information site where the progress and vision of the project are apparent at all times.

Significant savings are achieved by using the collaborative project management software because the builder can order materials and have them delivered at precisely the right moment. She can also assign contractors to their jobs in the most timely manner, as related phases of the work are completed. For example, the heating and air conditioning systems installer is scheduled and called immediately after the carpenter finishes framing the house—not too soon and not a day too late. Traditionally, according to a report by the Banc of America Securities, some 33 percent spent in residential construction is lost because of backlogs, delays, and scheduling errors. A contractor might show up to complete the plumbing or heating project, for example, only to find that the site is not ready. Time equals money.

Other efficiencies afforded by the collaborative Web-based software include one-stop, online ordering of construction materials directly from manufacturers, a factor that further lowers the home-building expense. Instant messaging among all project partners means problems are addressed immediately. Team members confer with each other using all types of Web-enabled hardware, including desktop PCs, cell phones, and handheld Palm Pilots or Handspring Visors. Even vendors not officially part of the project can be granted access to the project management site on an as-needed basis.

NETWORKING OVER THE NET

Working together over the Web is a process that speaks to the value of networks and to the power and promise of the largest network in the world—the Internet. For years, companies have communicated and managed projects over their internal networks. However, expanding the process to include all of the different outside companies involved in a project is a major new direction prompted by the increased outsourcing of projects and enabled by the growth of the Internet.

Different types of online collaborative project management software are available, such as eRoom 5.0 by eRoom Technology Inc. of Concord, Massachusetts, which offers many of the features discussed in the preceding scenario. A more futuristic version of the technology is called CAVE (computer automatic virtual environment), a product that lets participants at different locations inhabit the same virtual space on the Internet. Rather than requiring user input, the software tracks each participant's actions and automatically and continually updates other project members on-screen. Moving this networking technology from leading-edge to mainstream status will require continuing improvements in hardware, in software, and in the speed of today's telecommunication systems.

TELECOMMUNICATIONS: CONNECTING NETWORKS TO THE INTERNET

Computers were originally designed as stand-alone devices. As such, a single computer was not capable of communicating with other computers. The development of special hardware devices and software in the 1970s and 1980s led to the creation of the first private networks in which connected computers could exchange data with each other. That data could take the form of a request for information, a reply to a request from another user's computer, or an instruction to run a program stored on the network. As demand for connecting to the Internet grew, companies turned to telecommunications systems to provide the means by which networks could link to other networks and eventually to the Internet, connecting users throughout the world.

Telecommunications originally referred to the sending and receiving of information over telephone lines. As telecommunications systems evolved in concert with computer hardware and software, the term was broadened to include other types of media over which computer data could be transmitted, including satellite systems, microwave towers, and wireless devices such as cell phones. Figure 4-1 illustrates the basic concept of telecommunications.

NETWORKING COMPONENTS

In chapter 1 you were introduced to the concept of computer networks as forming the skeletal framework of the Internet. Recall that a network consists of two or more computers, devices, and software, connected by means of one or more communications media, such as wires or telephone lines. These wires and telephone lines form the fundamental part of a network—the channel or **medium** through which data bits and bytes are transmitted. Because communications media are basic to networking, it is helpful to begin the study of networks by exploring the various types of media and the ways in which data are transmitted through them.

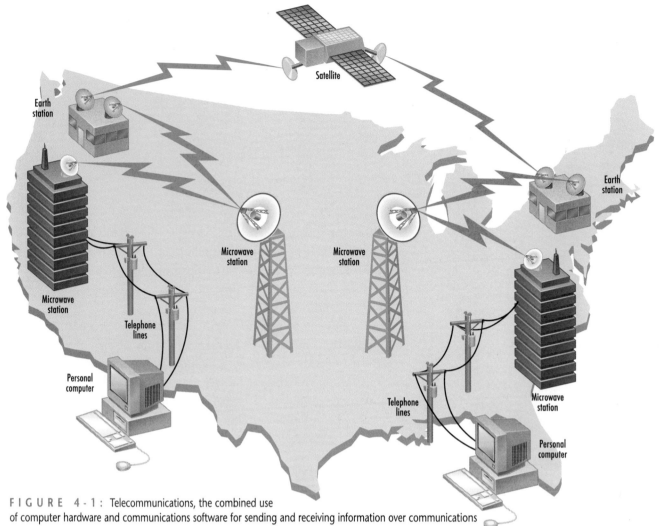

FIGURE 4-1: Telecommunications, the combined use of computer hardware and communications software for sending and receiving information over communications media, makes it possible for computer users throughout the world to communicate with each other.

CHARACTERISTICS OF DATA TRANSMISSION

The transmission of data over computer networks is described in terms of the following characteristics:

- bandwidth (rate of transmission)
- analog or digital (type of signal)
- serial or parallel (number and order of bits transmitted)

BANDWIDTH

Data is transferred from one computer to another in digital form—bits of 1's and 0's. In a network, the number of bits that can be transferred in a given second over a given medium is known as **bandwidth**. Bandwidth is measured in **bits per second (bps)**. Table 4-1 lists common measurements of bandwidth.

Bandwidths vary among different types of communications media. To understand bandwidth, consider the difference between the amount of traffic that can travel over a two-lane highway and a four-lane highway during a certain period of time, such as one hour. Obviously, the broader four-lane highway can handle a larger volume of traffic than a two-lane highway. A communications medium capable of carrying a large amount of data at faster speeds is referred to as a

All Together Now

Supercomputing can tackle some of the world's most complicated problems. Originally, the technology was used exclusively by the government research labs and industrial giants that could afford the enormously expensive custom-designed hardware. The tool became more affordable in the 1990s with the development of parallel systems, where smaller business computers were tied together to work as a supercomputer.

The newest tweak in supercomputing is using massive numbers of home and office computers linked together over the Internet. Net-based supercomputing, also called grid computing, takes advantage of the existence of more than 100 million computers around the globe, many of them doing nothing for large amounts of time.

Grid computing was first brought to the public's attention by SETA (Search for Extraterrestrial Intelligence), a nonprofit group that has signed up 2 million computer owners to help process data obtained by radio telescopes searching the heavens for evidence of other life. SETA's program averages more than 12 trillion calculations a day, making it one of the planet's busiest supercomputers.

Computer owners are lured to sign up with grid companies with offers of small payments, lottery chances, or contributions to charity. Anytime the volunteered computer sits idle, the grid program runs as a screen saver. By signing up thousands of computer owners, grid computer companies can provide clients with power equivalent to some of the world's top supercomputers.

Source: Feder, Barnaby J. "Supercomputing Takes Yet Another Turn," *New York Times,* November 20, 2000.

Abbreviation	Term	Meaning
54 Kbps	54 kilobits per second	54 thousand bits per second
30 Mbps	30 megabits per second	30 million bits per second
1 Gbps	1 gigabit per second	1 billion bits per second
1 Tbps	1 terabit per second	1 trillion bits per second

TABLE 4-1 Measurement of Bandwidth

broadband medium, whereas one capable of carrying a smaller amount of data at slower speeds is referred to as a **narrowband medium**. Fiber-optic cable is an example of a broadband medium; twisted-pair wire, commonly used in telephone lines, is an example of a narrowband medium.

Bandwidth can be an important factor in choosing a particular communications medium. When large amounts of data need to be transmitted quickly, such as with high-quality sound and video transmission, broadband media are more suitable. When only small amounts of data need to be transmitted and transmission time is less important—for example, simple text transmission—narrowband media may be suitable.

ANALOG VERSUS DIGITAL TRANSMISSION

Our telephone system was established to carry voice transmissions, a type of transmission signal known as analog. An **analog signal** is in the form of **continuous waves** transmitted over a medium at a certain **frequency range**. Changes in the wave transmissions reflect changes in voice and sound **pitch**, as shown in Figure 4-2.

Other forms of communication are also transmitted in analog form. Most cellular networks, cable television systems, and satellite dishes use analog communications media for carrying voice and sound transmissions, although newer technologies are making it possible for these kinds of transmissions to be made in digital form.

Modems

Whenever digital data is sent from a computing device to another computing device over an analog communications medium, such as a telephone line, both the sending device and receiving device must contain a modem to convert digital data into analog data, and vice versa. For example, data being sent from one computer to another computer across a telephone line is converted by the sending computer's modem into analog format so the data can travel across the telephone line. At the receiving end, it is converted back into digital format by the receiving computer's modem, as illustrated in Figure 4-3.

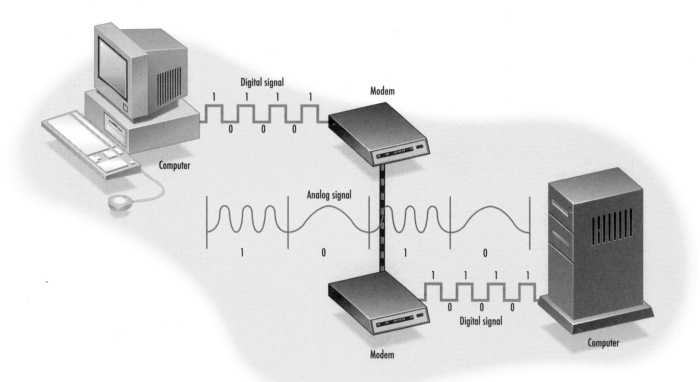

F I G U R E 4 - 2 : Analog (Wave) and Digital Signals

An analog signal takes the form of continuous waves transmitted over a medium at a certain frequency range. Changes in the wave transmissions reflect changes in voice and sound pitch. A digital signal consists of frequencies representing 0's and 1's.

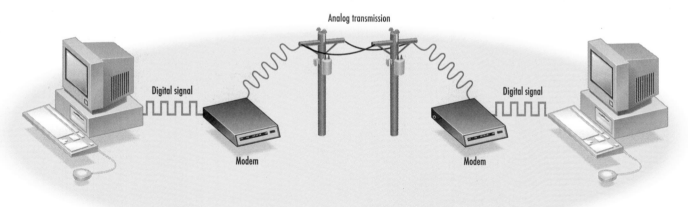

F I G U R E 4 - 3 : How a Modem Works

Whenever digital data is sent from a computing device to another computing device over an analog communications medium, such as a telephone line, both the sending device and receiving device must contain a modem to convert digital data into analog data, and vice versa.

Networks in which computers are located in close proximity, such as in the same building, often use newer media such as fiber-optic cables, which allow data to be sent in digital form. However, when data is to be sent over other media to computers or networks at distant locations, such as in another city, the sending computer or the network's host computer uses a modem to convert the data into analog form, which the medium can carry.

KEYTERMS

parity bit a bit added to ensure that the total number of 1-bits is always odd or always even

SERIAL VERSUS PARALLEL TRANSMISSION

Data travels across a communications medium in either serial or parallel form. In **serial transmission**, all of the bits (0's and 1's) that comprise the data are transmitted one bit after another in a continuous line. In **parallel transmission**, a group of 8 bits representing a single byte (plus 1 bit called a **parity bit**) are transmitted at the same time over nine separate paths. The accompanying parity bit ensures the correct number of 0- and 1-bits. Serial transmission and parallel transmission are illustrated and compared in Figure 4-4.

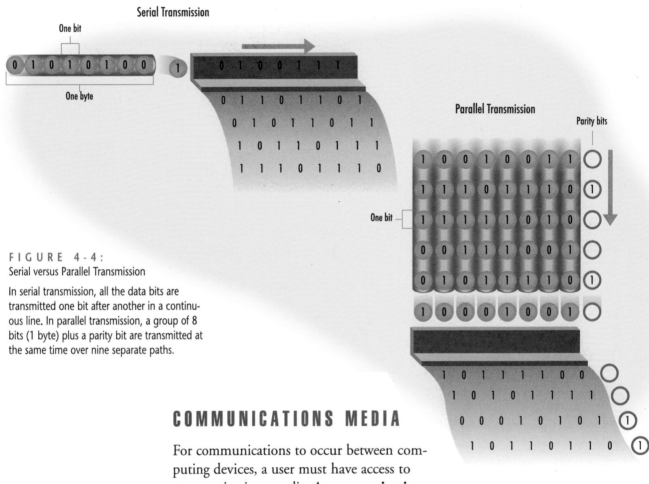

FIGURE 4-4:
Serial versus Parallel Transmission

In serial transmission, all the data bits are transmitted one bit after another in a continuous line. In parallel transmission, a group of 8 bits (1 byte) plus a parity bit are transmitted at the same time over nine separate paths.

COMMUNICATIONS MEDIA

For communications to occur between computing devices, a user must have access to communications media. A **communications medium** is a physical link (a connection) that allows a computer in one location to be connected to a computer in another location. When communications take place between computers located far apart, a combination of media may be used, some of which the user may never see. Communications media may be broadly classified as either wire or wireless.

WIRE VERSUS WIRELESS MEDIA

Many computers and networks today communicate with other computers and networks by means of wire media, meaning they are connected to each other using various kinds of wires. Some types of wire media, such as telephone lines, were originally developed for voice communications. However, they are now used for both voice and data communications. Newer communications media use fiber-optic cables consisting of optical fibers that allow data to be transmitted as light signals through tiny hairlike glass fibers.

Wireless systems allow information to be sent and received through the air in the form of radio waves. Infrared systems allow communications between computing devices, such as from a computer to a printer, by means of infrared signals.

The following sections explore types of commonly used communications media. The medium chosen for a particular network depends mainly on user requirements in terms of cost, speed, and other factors.

TYPES OF WIRE MEDIA

Twisted-Pair Cable

Twisted-pair cable, one of the older types of media, was originally developed for telephone networks. Early versions consisted of wires wrapped around one another. Today such cables typically consist of two parallel copper wires, each individually wrapped in plastic and bound together by another plastic casing. One of the wires carries the information while the other wire is grounded and absorbs any interference that may be present on the line (see Figure 4-5). The pairs are often bundled in packs of hundreds or thousands, buried in underground electrical conduits (pipes), and run to various locations such as buildings and rooms where they are connected to standard phone jacks.

Besides telephone systems, a main use of twisted-pair cable is to connect computers in networks and transmit data over relatively short distances. Millions of home computer owners use this medium with a modem because the cable is already in place for their telephones. Although relatively inexpensive, twisted-pair cable is susceptible to noise and interference. It also has a limited bandwidth (about 6 mbps) because the modem must translate the digital signals from a computer into the analog signals used by conventional telephone lines. To ensure more accurate transmissions, repeater stations are positioned along the way to refresh (strengthen) the communication signals.

ethics

Crossing the Digital Divide

Telephone service, computers, and Internet access—that is the technology people use to stay connected with the world today. Yet there is a great chasm in the United States dividing those who are connected and those who are not. In terms of Internet access, there is a definite gap between high- and low-income Americans; between urban and rural households; between whites and African Americans or Hispanics; and between college-educated and those with an elementary school education.

Why the concern about this digital divide? For one thing, a job in the technology sector pays 80 percent more than the average private sector wage. Other opportunities, including the ability to use the computer to start one's own business, to shop for lower-priced goods and services, to work or get an education from home, or to research health issues, are closed to those who are not wired to today's technology. To level the playing field, in April of 2000 President Clinton issued a "National Call to Action" to meet two goals: provide twenty-first-century learning tools for every child in school and to create digital opportunity for every American family and community.

Sources: Sly, Liz. "Mongolia's Nomads Roam World on Internet," *Chicago Tribune,* July 16, 2000; "The Clinton-Gore Administration: A National Call to Action to Close the Digital Divide," Office of the Press Secretary, The White House, April 4, 2000.

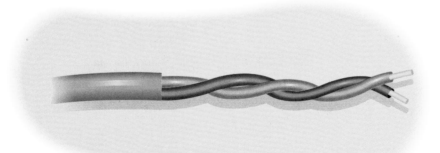

FIGURE 4-5: Twisted-Pair Cable

KEYTERMS

interference electrical signals such as static electricity that may disrupt the transmission of data; the signals may come from lightning or nearby electrical appliances or devices

Coaxial Cable

Coaxial cable is commonly used for VCR and cable television connections, in telephone networks, and in some computer networks. The cable consists of an insulated center wire grounded by a shield of braided wire (see Figure 4-6). Coaxial cable is more expensive than twisted-pair, but is less susceptible to interference and can carry much more data. **Baseband** coaxial cable, often used in computer networks, is about 3/8 inch thick and has a single channel that transmits digital signals at 10 to 80 mbps. **Broadband** coaxial cable has several channels that transmit a number of different analog signals at the same time. Broadband is used for cable television transmissions.

Millions of cable television subscribers already have cable installed in their homes and offices. By adding a special type of modem, called a **cable modem**, they can take advantage of this communications medium for their computers to provide much faster transmission speed than twisted-pair cable.

Cable Modem
Information Network:
www.cablemodem.net

Fiber-Optic Cable

Twisted-pair and coaxial cables both contain copper conductors and are used to transmit electrical signals—streams of electrons. Fiber-optic cable, on the other hand, is a string of glass used to transmit photons—beams of light. A **fiber-optic cable** typically consists of hundreds of clear fiberglass or plastic fibers (threads), each approximately the same thickness as a human hair. Data is converted into beams of light by a laser device and is transmitted as light pulses (Figure 4-7). Billions of bits can be transmitted per second. At the receiving end, optical detectors convert the transmitted light pulses into electrical pulses that can be read by computing devices. The advantages of using fiber-optic cable include the following:

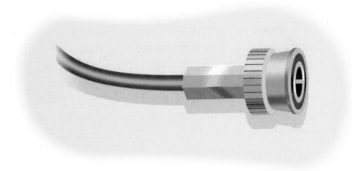

FIGURE 4-6:
Coaxial Cable

- faster transmission speed (up to 1 trillion bps)
- higher volume of data carried
- minimal interference
- greater security
- longer cable life

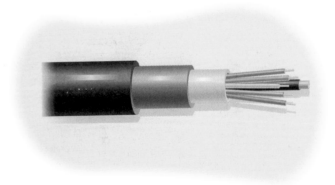

FIGURE 4-7:
Fiber-Optic Cable

Fiber-optic cable is expensive and difficult to work with, but the advantages of using the technology outweigh the disadvantages. The most important advantage of fiber-optic cables is that they are very high bandwidth, or broadband, media and therefore have become the medium of choice for many local area networks. Fiber-optic cable also connects the major servers that form the backbone of the Internet, and increasingly telephone companies are replacing worn-out telephone wires with fiber-optic cables. However, fiber-optic cables are still unavailable in some locations.

INTERNET SERVICES DIGITAL NETWORK (ISDN)

In some locations, special digital telephone lines, called **ISDN lines**, are available and can be used to dial into the Internet and transmit and receive information at very high speeds, ranging from 64 to 128 kbps. Using an ISDN line requires a special ISDN modem. Monthly fees for ISDN lines are higher than for regular phone lines, which adds to the user's communications costs. ISDN is not available in all locations. However, as phone companies upgrade their transmission capabilities, ISDN lines will become available in additional areas.

T LINES

Networks can be connected using T lines. A **T line** is a permanent connection between two geographically distant points set up by a telephone company and typically leased by a business. A leased T line is always active and dedicated for use only by the leasing business, which pays a monthly fee. These lines allow a business to connect its network to the Internet.

Two types of T lines are T1 and T3. A **T1 line** is a high-speed telephone line that allows for both voice and data transmission and can carry data at a speed of 1.544 mbps. A faster line is a **T3 line** capable of carrying data at speeds of up to 44.7 mbps. T1 lines are often used by businesses to connect to the Internet, whereas the Internet itself uses T3 lines for its backbone (its main communications media).

WIRELESS COMMUNICATIONS MEDIA

Wireless media transmit information as electromagnetic signals through the air or through empty space, much the way a battery-operated radio works. These media, which are growing in popularity as workers become more mobile, include the following technologies:

KEYTERMS

electromagnetic
referring to a force, or type of magnetism, created by electricity

- microwave systems
- satellite systems
- cellular technology
- infrared technology

MICROWAVE SYSTEMS

Microwave transmission involves the sending and receiving of information in the form of high-frequency radio signals. A **microwave system** transmits data through the atmosphere from one microwave station to another microwave station, or from a microwave station to a satellite and then back to earth to another microwave station, as shown in Figure 4-8. When data is sent from one microwave station to another, the stations must be positioned at relatively short line-of-sight intervals because radio signals do not bend around mountains and other objects. Therefore, there must be no visible obstructions between the sending microwave station and the receiving microwave station. The terrain determines the distance between microwave stations, but the distance is rarely more than 25 miles. Microwave stations are often placed on top of hills, mountains, or buildings to ensure unobstructed transmission routes.

DRIVERS

Larry Ellison, cofounder and CEO of Oracle Corporation, is one of the most flamboyant and outspoken entrepreneurs of this century. Ellison is one of the richest as well. With a net worth of $50 billion and a financially successful company, he has reached the pinnacle of corporate success.

Among some of his friends and peers, Ellison may be considered an eccentric. It has been rumored that he once tried to purchase a Russian MIG fighter plane, but U.S. customs would not allow the plane into the country. In another incident, Ellison reportedly upset San Jose airport officials by landing his private jet after an 11:00 p.m. curfew, an action resulting in a $10,000 fine. To many of his fellow business associates, however, he is a business genius, a marketing whiz, and an avid promoter of simplified computing machines and network computers.

Oracle is the world's leading supplier of information management software, and the world's second-largest independent software company, boasting annual revenues of more than $9.7 billion. The company's diverse product line includes database software products, applications servers, software information management tools, and software suites for electronic commerce applications. Oracle's database software is the most widely used corporate database worldwide, and the company's product line continues to expand at a rapid pace.

Source: <http://www.askmen.com>.

FIGURE 4.8: Microwave System

A microwave system transmits data through the atmosphere from one microwave station to another, or from a station to a satellite and then back to earth to another microwave station. The stations must be positioned at relatively short line-of-sight intervals because radio signals do not bend around objects, such as mountains.

SATELLITE SYSTEMS

A **communications satellite** is a solar-powered electronic device that contains several small, specialized radios called **transponders** that receive signals from transmission stations on the ground, called **earth stations**. Communications satellites are positioned thousands of miles above the earth. A satellite receives the transmitted signals, amplifies them, and then transmits the signals to the appropriate locations (see Figure 4-9). Satellites orbit the earth at the same speed as the earth's rotation, making them appear stationary when viewed from the ground. This is called a **geosynchronous orbit**. One of the benefits of satellite systems is the small number of satellites needed to transmit data over long distances. In fact, a small number of satellites properly positioned can receive and transmit information to any location on earth.

Communications satellites are capable of transmitting billions of bits per second, making them ideal for transmitting very large amounts of data. Because of the time it takes to send and receive data across such long distances, satellites are more appropriate for one-way communications (such as television and radio applications) than for interactive applications, such as telephone conversations or computer conferencing.

The expense involved in building a satellite, sending it into orbit, and maintaining it is very high. Because of the expense, companies have been formed to provide this fee-based technology to those who need it but are unable to bear the full cost of operating their own system.

ethics

The Internet Is the Water Cooler

Employees should know that the boss is probably looking over their shoulder when they communicate via company e-mail. Employers have a right to censor Internet use to weed out illegal activity that may cause a legal liability, and to make sure company time and money aren't being wasted. But the company's ability to censor *all* workplace communication, including talk critical of the company, is being challenged by workers citing the 1935 National Labor Relations Act (NLRA).

Nowadays, e-mail is the number-one mode of corporate communication, especially for telecommuters or those whose travel prevents them from griping in the break room. The NLRA gave workers the right to communicate with each other about their workplace, and the law extends to the technology of the Internet. Employers may be able to monitor and set policies on e-mail use, but their ability to define communication critical of the company as off-limits is on shaky legal ground.

Source: Yegyazarian, Anush. "Nosy Bosses Face Limits on E-Mail Spying—Workers Gain New Freedoms," *PC World,* September 2000.

Several satellites now in orbit handle domestic and international data, video, and voice communications for owners and subscribers. For instance, banks use satellites daily to transmit thousands of customer transactions to other banks. A bank in New York can transfer money from a customer's New York account to the customer's account at another bank in London, England, within a few seconds.

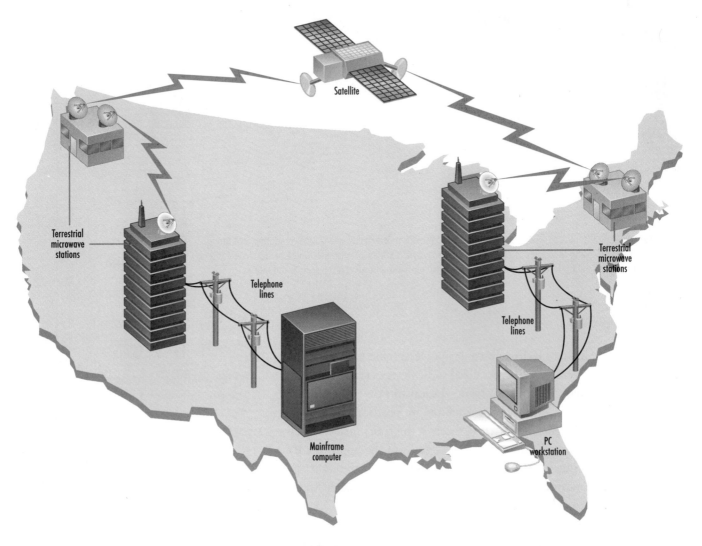

FIGURE 4-9: Satellite System

A communications satellite is a solar-powered electronic device containing small, specialized radios called transponders that receive signals from transmission stations on the ground. A satellite receives the transmitted signals, amplifies them, and then transmits the signals to the appropriate locations. Satellites orbit the earth at the same speed as the earth's rotation, making them appear stationary when viewed from the ground.

CELLULAR TECHNOLOGY

Using **cellular technology**, people can communicate wirelessly from and to nearly anywhere in the world. Cellular phones and devices work by maintaining contact with cellular antennae that resemble metal telephone towers or poles positioned throughout a cellular calling area. Each area, called a **cell**, has its own antenna and encompasses an area approximately 10–12 miles in diameter. As a user moves about from cell to cell, the antenna in which the user is located picks up the signal and relays it to the appropriate destination, as shown in Figure 4-10.

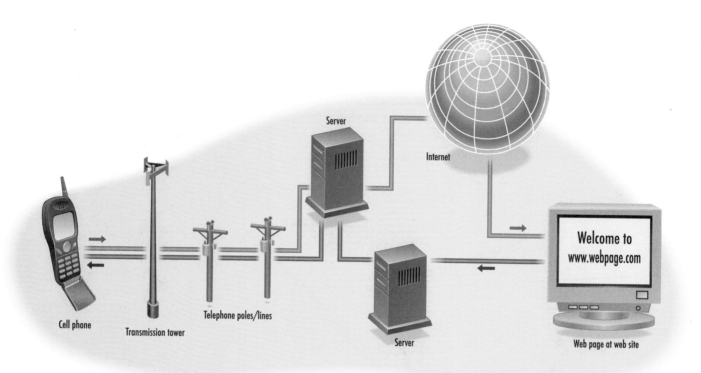

FIGURE 4-10: How a Cell Phone Works

Signals sent by cell phones are transmitted and received from cell to cell until they reach the intended destination.

Communications networks that support cellular communications also work well for handling business data. Using a portable computer with a cellular modem, a person can access Internet resources, including e-mail, along with information stored on the company's intranet databases. This can be especially important for users in some countries and in remote areas where communications facilities are crude or nonexistent.

Computers in Your Future?

Webmaster

Every major corporation, government entity, charitable foundation, and retail outlet has a Web site to market itself. Up until recently, Web sites tended to be managed by the person who fell into the job. Gradually, the position of Webmaster has evolved into a formal job title. A Webmaster is recognized as the person in charge of maintaining the contents of a Web site, keeping it up and running, and staying on top of new technologies, trends, and marketing ideas.

A Webmaster needs to have a clear vision of what the site can do now and in the future. The job requires programming skills, experience in building Web sites, and a basic knowledge of marketing. Effective communication abilities, a sense of creativity, and an eye for graphics are also essential.

Webmaster responsibilities include HTML coding, system administration, archive organization, and database management. The Webmaster must also make the site compatible with different browsers. In a large organization, a Webmaster may be a senior-level position within the marketing department.

The future looks strong for Webmasters, given the public's growing reliance on the Internet. Although beginning Webmasters may jump in at a salary of around $30,000, someone with considerable experience and skills can command pay in the $70,000–80,000 range.

Source: Pillai, Vidya. "A Cool Job in a Hot Industry," <www.siliconindia.com> 1999.

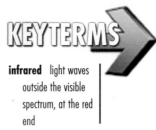

KEYTERMS

infrared light waves outside the visible spectrum, at the red end

INFRARED TECHNOLOGY

In recent years, infrared technology has become increasingly popular. **Infrared technology** provides wireless communication links between computers and their peripheral devices, such as keyboards and printers, or between handhelds and PCs. The same technology is used in a television remote control (see Figure 4-11).

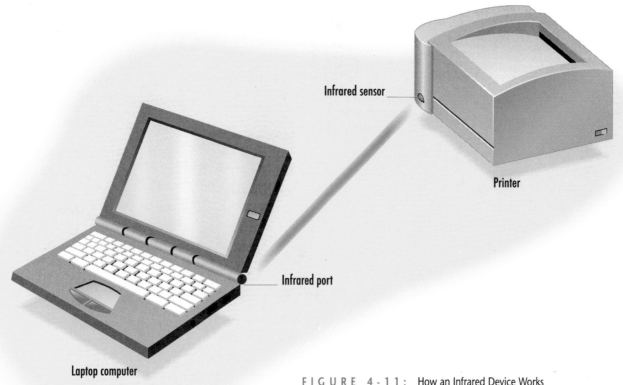

Infrared sensor

Printer

Infrared port

Laptop computer

FIGURE 4-11: How an Infrared Device Works

Data in the form of infrared light waves is transmitted from a special port in the laptop computer to an infrared sensor in the printer.

Infrared technology transmits data as light waves, instead of radio waves. One particular system uses a transmitter located at the rear of a keyboard to send typed data to a computer's CPU. A sensing device on the computer's infrared port reads the data and displays it on the monitor. Physical objects placed between the sending and receiving devices can interrupt transmissions because the light waves must follow a line-of-sight path between the devices.

In situations where data is sent and received over long distances, several different telecommunications systems may be used, including telephone lines, microwave towers, and satellite systems. Many companies with branch offices located throughout the United States often use combinations of media for sending and receiving data between locations.

NETWORK CLASSIFICATIONS

Networks vary enormously, from simple interoffice systems that connect a few personal computers and a printer to complex global systems that connect thousands of machines of different kinds. Networks can be classified in various ways: by their architecture, by the relative distances they cover, and by the users they are designed to support.

The term **network architecture** refers to the way a network is designed and built, just as the *architecture* of a building references its design. Two main architectural designs for networks are client/server and peer-to-peer.

Client/Server Architecture

In a **client/server architecture** (see Figure 4-12), a personal computer, workstation, or terminal (called a **client**) is used to send information or a request to another computer (called a **server**), which then relays the information back to the user's client computer, or to another computer (another client). For example, suppose you are using a PC in your school's computer lab and want to use Microsoft Word to write a letter to a friend. After starting your computer (the client), you issue a request to use Word, perhaps by simply clicking on the *Word* icon displayed in your monitor's screen. Your request goes to the network's main computer (the server) on which Microsoft Word is stored. The server prepares a copy of Microsoft Word and sends it to your computer (the client). Once the software is loaded, you can type and print the letter.

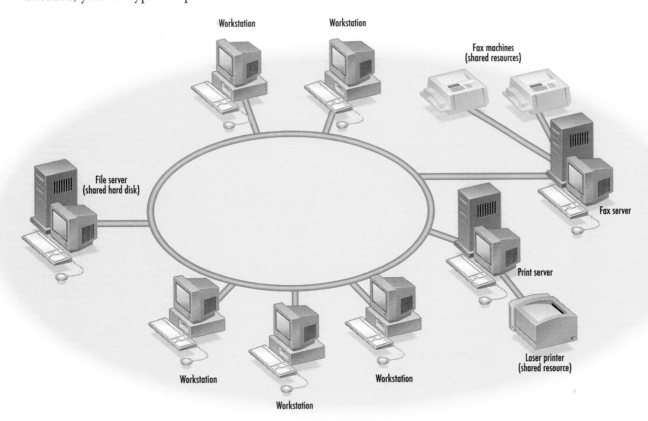

FIGURE 4-12: Client/Server Architecture

In a client/server architecture, a computer (the client) sends information or a request to another computer (the server), which then relays the information back to the client computer or to another client.

A major advantage of the client/server model is that application programs, such as Microsoft Office, can be stored on the server and accessed by multiple users. This eliminates having to install individual copies of programs on each computer within the network.

Peer-to-Peer Architecture

Peer-to-peer architecture (Figure 4-13) is a network design in which each computer comprising the network has equivalent capabilities and responsibilities. Every computer acts as both client and server. Peer-to-peer networks are usually simpler to install and maintain and are less expensive. However, they may not perform equally when operating under heavy workloads. Windows 98 and Windows 2000 Professional contain software to set up a peer-to-peer network.

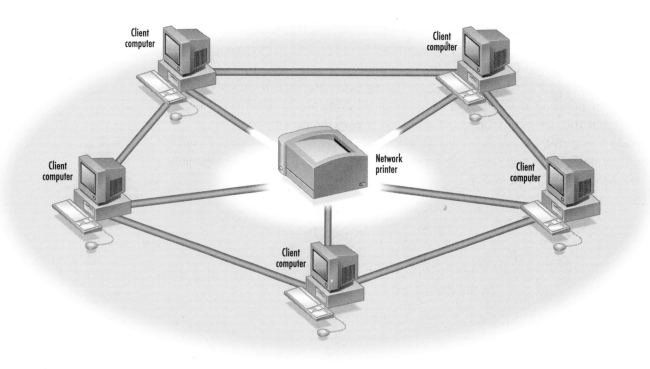

FIGURE 4-13: Peer-to-Peer Architecture

In a peer-to-peer architecture, each computer acts as both client and server.

NETWORKS CLASSIFIED BY COVERAGE

Small networks confined to a limited geographical area are called local area networks, while wide area networks are extensive and may span hundreds of miles.

Local Area Networks (LANs)

Local area networks (LANs) are private networks that serve the needs of businesses, organizations, or schools with computers located in the same building or in nearby buildings, such as those on a college campus. LANs make it convenient for multiple users to share programs, data, information, hardware, software, and other computing resources. LANs typically use a special computer, called a **file server,** which houses all of the resources. From the file server and a high-capacity hard disk, called a **disk server**, users can easily access programs and data. A **print server** allows multiple users to share the same printer. Sharing resources such as applications programs, hard disk capacity, and high-quality printers over networks saves companies money in hardware, software, and related costs. Figure 4-14 shows the arrangement of a local area network.

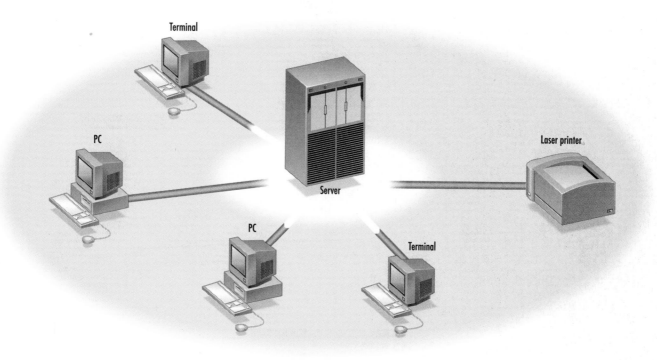

Terminal

PC

Server

Laser printer

PC

Terminal

FIGURE 4-14: Local Area Network

Local area networks (LANs) are private networks that serve the needs of businesses or organizations with computers located in the same building or in nearby buildings.

Wide Area Networks (WANs)

As the name suggests, a **wide area network (WAN)** is one that spans a large geographical area, connecting two or more LANs (see Figure 4-15). One example is a long-distance telephone network. Many telephone companies in the United States are linked together electronically and also are connected with international telephone companies. A business might use a WAN to communicate between a manufacturing facility in one part of a city and corporate headquarters in another.

Governments, universities, and large corporations use WANs to share data between separate networks. WANS typically make use of high-speed leased telephone lines, wireless satellite connections, or both.

GLOBE TROTTING

Connecting Native Americans

Computer technology and e-commerce may be driving a booming new economy, but Native Americans living on Indian reservations are being left behind. While 95 percent of the United States has access to phone service, the rate on some reservations is less than 20 percent. No phone connection means no access to all of the information and opportunities that the Internet offers.

The barriers to phone service for Native Americans are high: many reservation roads are unlabeled, and some tribal lands are so remote that laying cables is unfeasible. In addition, poverty precludes many tribe members from paying hook-up fees.

To bridge the digital divide, a dozen tribes formed the National Tribal Telecommunications Association in 1996 to gain a stronger voice and better representation in Washington. Additionally, six American Indian tribes in Arizona, New Mexico, and South Dakota have recently formed their own telecommunications companies. More should join them soon, aided by the $585 million the Federal Communications Commission has earmarked to expand phone access on Indian land. Thanks to the development of wireless technology, even the most remote reservation areas may soon have affordable telephone service—and Internet access.

Sources: Romero, Simon. "Tribes Seeking Phone Systems as Step to Web," *New York Times,* October 2, 2000; Bruno, Lee. "Wireless on the Reservations," *Red Herring,* October 2000.

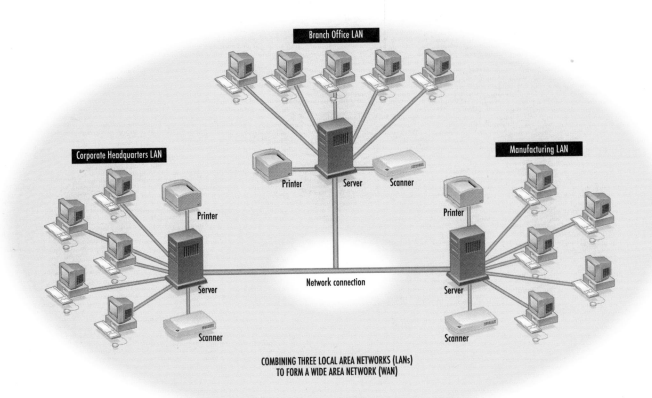

COMBINING THREE LOCAL AREA NETWORKS (LANs)
TO FORM A WIDE AREA NETWORK (WAN)

FIGURE 4-15: Wide Area Network

A wide area network (WAN) connects two or more LANs over a large geographical area.

There are various types of wide area networks. A **metropolitan area network (MAN)** is a wide area network limited to a specific area, such as a city or town. A **public access network (PAN)** is a wide area network operated and maintained by a large company, such as AT&T, MCI, or US Sprint, and which provides voice and data communications capabilities to customers for a fee. Businesses that use the facilities of large communications companies to provide subscribers with additional services are called **value added networks (VANs)**. Typical services offered include access to various network databases, electronic mail, and online advertising and shopping. America Online is an example of a VAN.

In recent years, a special type of Internet-based WAN has become increasingly popular among large businesses that need a cost-effective way to expand their networking options. This specialized WAN is called a **virtual private network (VPN).** Instead of leasing T1 lines to connect distant offices across the country, a company establishes a VPN by having each branch office set up a local Internet connection. Then, all company networking traffic gets routed through the Internet. Factors that make a VPN an attractive option are the cost savings (about $200–$300 per month for an Internet connection versus $1,200 or more per month for a T1 line) and the reliability, wide availability, and nearly unlimited bandwidth capacity of the Internet.

NETWORKS CLASSIFIED BY USERS

Networks can be classified by the groups of users they were designed to accommodate. This classification includes intranets and extranets.

Intranets

Networks that restrict access to authorized users are called intranets. An **intranet** is a network that is accessible only by a business's or organization's members, employees, or other authorized users. Access to an intranet's Web site is typically restricted by a **firewall**, which consists of special hardware and/or software that prevents or restricts access to and from the network (see Figure 4-16). All inquiries and messages entering or leaving the intranet pass through the firewall, which examines each inquiry or message and blocks those that do not meet the firewall's specified security criteria. Firewalls prevent unauthorized Internet users from accessing an intranet connected to the Internet.

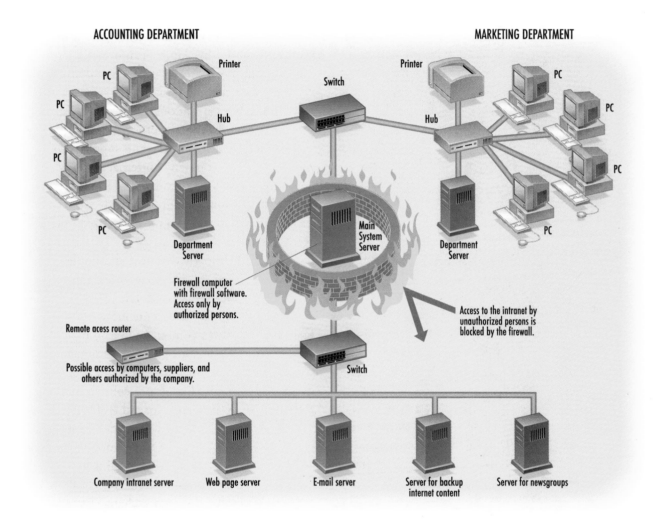

FIGURE 4-16: Intranet and Firewall

An intranet is accessible only by the business's or organization's employees or other authorized users. Access to an intranet's Web site is typically restricted by a firewall consisting of special hardware and/or software that limits usage to authorized users.

An intranet functions the same as a local area network that is *not* connected to other networks outside the organization. Stored information is available only to authorized users and certain kinds of information may be available only to specific persons, groups, or departments within the organization. For example, access to a company's new product designs may be restricted to employees in the research and design department who have special passwords. One of the largest intranets in the world is under development for the U.S. Navy and the Marine Corps. The awarding of the $7 billion contract to Electronic Data Systems Corporation in late fall of 2000 marks the first time a branch of the military has hired an outside company to set up and manage its network, which will link sailors and marines in the continental United States, Hawaii, Alaska, Puerto Rico, Guantanamo Bay, Cuba, and Iceland. Satellites will connect ships at sea. The system is anticipated to be fully operational by June 2003.

Extranets

An **extranet** (illustrated in Figure 4-17) is a network that makes certain kinds of information available to users within the organization and other kinds of information available to outsiders, such as companies doing business with the organization.

Many organizations have established extranets that allow authorized outside employees, customers, and suppliers to access the company's internal computerized applications and data via the Internet. The organization must provide passwords and/or User IDs to the authorized outside users.

A properly designed and implemented extranet may provide many useful services. Mobile workers can connect their notebooks or handheld computers to a company extranet via a communications medium such as a telephone line. Once connected, workers can send and receive e-mail messages. Managers can contact mobile workers carrying small pagers. Some newer pagers allow users to exchange e-mail messages with others having an e-mail connection. Extranets may also allow for the transmission of faxes.

Like intranets, extranets can be used for a variety of business activities. For example, an automobile manufacturer can post an advertisement for bids for raw materials such as engine parts, seat covers, and tires. An accompanying electronic bid form allows potential suppliers to submit a bid to supply these materials.

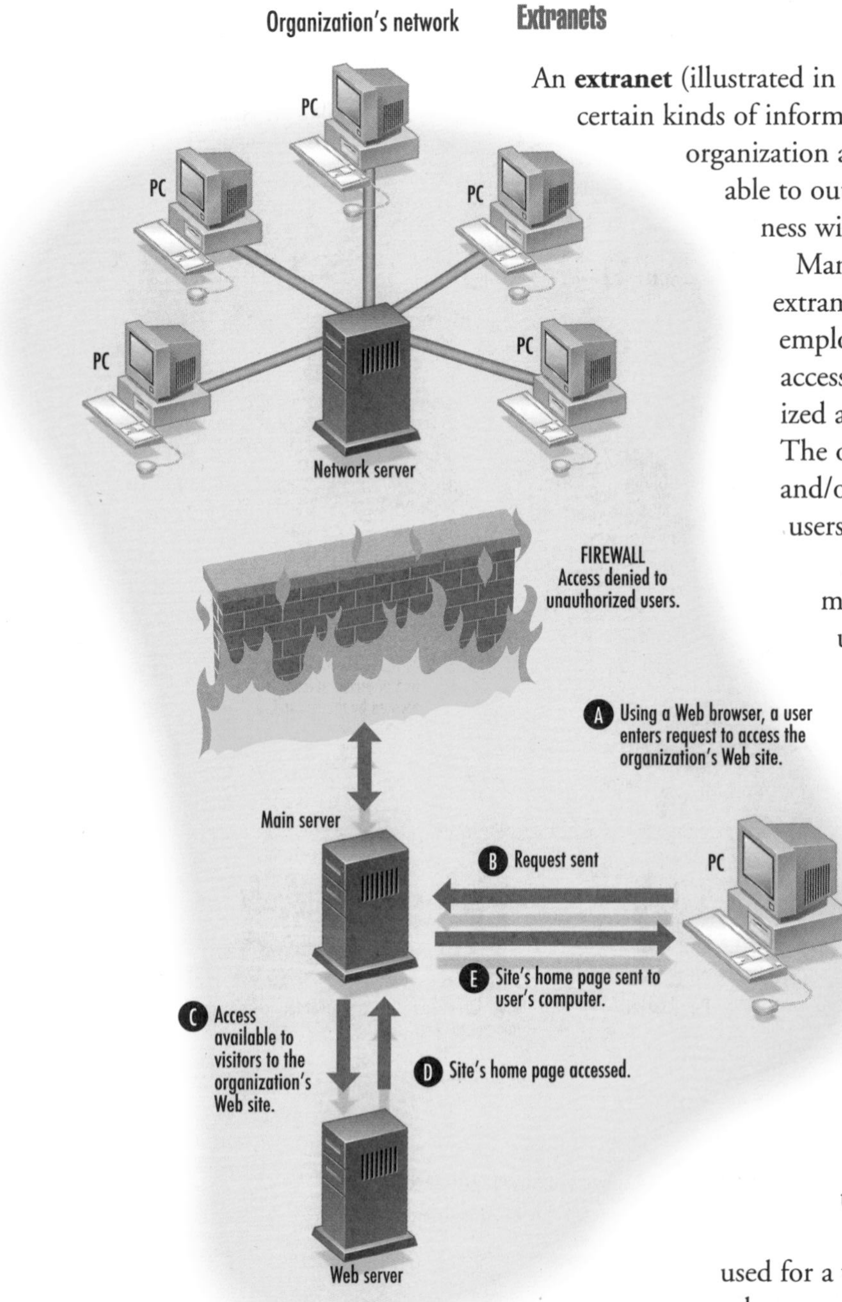

Organization's network

PC
PC
PC
PC
PC

Network server

FIREWALL
Access denied to unauthorized users.

Ⓐ Using a Web browser, a user enters request to access the organization's Web site.

Main server

Ⓑ Request sent

PC

Ⓔ Site's home page sent to user's computer.

Ⓒ Access available to visitors to the organization's Web site.

Ⓓ Site's home page accessed.

Web server

FIGURE 4-17: Extranet
An extranet makes certain kinds of information available to internal users and other kinds of information available to external users.

Some extranets are used for recruiting new employees. A business can post job openings and application forms, along with links to other documents providing information about area housing, transportation, medical facilities, schools, and recreation. Employee insurance claim forms can be posted, as well as forms for filing employee grievances and complaints.

NETWORK TOPOLOGIES (LAYOUTS)

Network topology, or layout, is the abstract pattern by which the network is organized. Topology should not be confused with the actual wiring path of a network, which is determined by the physical layout of walls and floors and other environmental factors.

One way to think of a topology is to picture a map showing roads, rivers, railroads, and other items such as cities and mountains. Looking down at the map, you can view the relationship of various physical locations. A diagram of a network's topology is much like a map. This allows a viewer to locate each network component, or **node**. The common network topologies are bus, star, and ring.

BUS TOPOLOGIES

In a **bus topology** all computers (nodes) are linked by means of a single line of cable with two endpoints. The cable connection is called a **bus**. All communications travel the length of the bus. Each computer has a network card with a **transceiver**, a device that sends messages along the bus in either direction. A given message contains data, error checking code, the address of the node sending the message, and the address of the node that is to receive the message. As the communication passes, each computer's network card checks to see if it is the assigned destination point. If the computer finds its address in the message, it then reads the data, checks for errors in the transmission, and sends a message to the sender of the data acknowledging that it was received. If the computer's network card does not find its address, it ignores the message. Figure 4-18 (on page D-25) shows the layout of a bus topology.

Wearable PCs

Xybernaut Corporation, located in Fairfax, Virginia, has led the way in the research, development, and sales of wearable computer systems since 1990, and the company's efforts have resulted in the development and production of some remarkable new wearable computer systems. An impressive new system, the MA4-TC, was introduced at the November 2000 Comdex show at Las Vegas.

According to company officials, the MA4-TC wearable computer is a fully functioning, networked computer for mobile business applications. The MA4-TC weighs slightly less than 900 grams and is about the size of a clock radio. Powered by a 400 MHz Intel Pentium III microprocessor, it is capable of running all standard operating systems including Windows 95/98/2000 and Windows NT, UNIX, and Linux. The MA4-TC displays on a headset-mounted, full-color video console comparable to a 15-inch monitor when viewed at a distance of 18 inches.

According to a company official, the MA4-TC is a full-function computer system capable of running any application a laptop or desktop will run with almost no change. The system is completely mobile, allowing users to perform their day-to-day work hands-free, while having immediate access to information essential to their work performance. For example, work crews can connect to the corporate network to upload large, graphics-rich files rather than having to wait for a wireless download. In the field they can access needed data or the Internet anywhere wireless communication is available. The voice-activated system allows wearers to contact supervisors and quickly download needed information without having to use their hands.

By 2002, Xybernaut plans to add a wireless Bluetooth-linked headset and speech-recognition technology plus a foreign-language translator to the device.

Sources: "Wearable PC Goes to Work." *InfoWorld*, November 20, 2000; <http://www.xybernet.com>.

Upstarts

Avner Ronen can count on his experience from five years in the Israeli Defense Forces to keep him cool and steady in his battle with America Online. In January of 2000, Ronen founded Odigo, which specializes in instant-messaging technology. With his wife, Maskit, who was his computer instructor in the military and is now one of Odigo's software engineers, Avner has opened an American office in New York's Silicon Alley.

Instant messaging allows messages sent over the Internet to appear in the computer screen without opening any files, permitting real-time conversations between users. With innumerable personal and business applications, instant messaging is now used by almost 200 million people. Odigo's vision is for all instant messaging users to be able to communicate freely, in the same way that telephone users can easily contact each other, regardless of who their service providers are.

AOL, which controls 90 percent of the instant-message market, clearly does not share that vision. Odigo and others, including Yahoo! and Microsoft Network, continue to try to maintain a link with AOL's instant-messaging network, and AOL keeps blocking the effort.

Odigo is growing by approximately 10,000 users a day. The company's business plan, however, is to earn most of its revenues from licensing its technologies. Odigo already boasts of 84 corporate clients in 28 countries, and it recently logged its one-millionth user.

Source: Sella, Marshall. "Immigrants with an I.P.O.," *New York Times Magazine,* September 17, 2000.

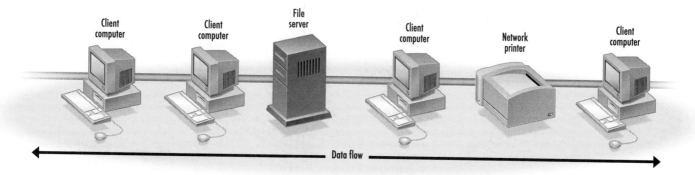

FIGURE 4-18: Bus Topology

In a bus topology, all computers are linked by one cable, the bus. All communications travel the full length of the bus, with each computer's networking transceiver checking the message for its intended destination site.

A problem can occur if two or more computers send messages at the same time. This creates an interference pattern, and when one of the computers detects this pattern, it jams the network, stopping all transmissions. Computers that are sending messages then wait and resend, a process that is repeated until a message gets through without being blocked. Another problem with a linear bus topology is that a broken connection along the bus can bring down the whole network.

Bus topologies commonly use coaxial or fiber-optic cables. The bus topology is less expensive than some other network layouts, but may be less efficient.

STAR TOPOLOGIES

In a **star topology**, multiple computers and peripheral devices are linked to a central computer, called a **host**, in a point-to-point configuration resembling a star, as shown in Figure 4-19. Typically, the host computer is a more powerful minicomputer or mainframe computer. The host acts as a switching station, reading the addresses of messages sent by the nodes and routing the messages accordingly. Companies with multiple departments needing centralized access to databases and files often prefer this topology.

A main disadvantage of the star topology is its dependence on the host computer. Because all communications must go through the host, the network becomes inoperable if the host fails to function properly. On the other hand, the hub can prevent the data collisions that may occur with bus topologies, and the rest of the network can remain operational when a given node's connection is broken.

RING TOPOLOGIES

In a **ring topology**, there is no host computer and each computer or workstation is connected to two other computers in a circular path (see Figure 4-20). Communications are passed in one direction from the source computer to the destination. If one computer isn't working, that computer is bypassed. A potential problem with ring topologies, however, is that if two computers are trying to send communications at the same time, one or both of the messages may become garbled.

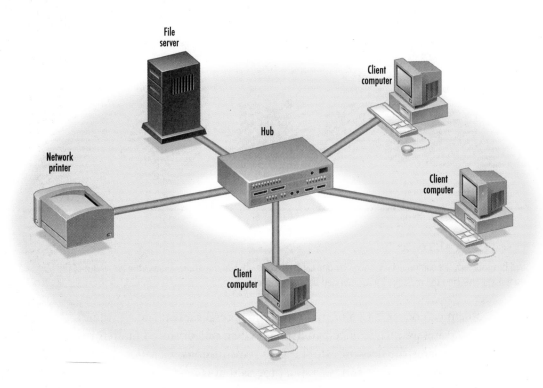

FIGURE 4-19: Star Topology

In a star topology, all computers are linked to a central host computer, through which all communications travel.

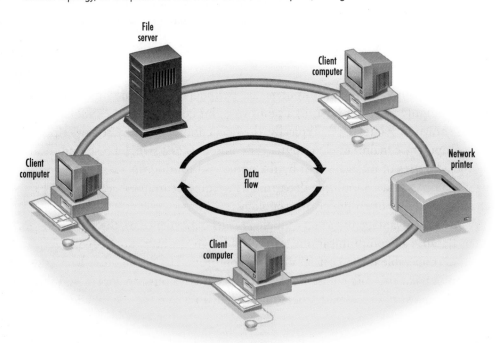

FIGURE 4-20: Ring Topology

In a ring topology, each computer is connected to two other computers in a circular path.

HYBRID TOPOLOGIES

Some businesses prefer using one kind of network layout throughout the organization, while others set up a variety of different topologies, which are considered **hybrid topologies**. Indeed, the more common practice is for companies to combine network layout types to suit their particular situation. For example, a company's plant in Akron, Ohio, may use a token ring topology while another plant in Charlotte, North Carolina, may set up a bus topology.

NETWORKING AND COMMUNICATIONS HARDWARE

Setting up a computer network generally requires special hardware to link all of the computers and to facilitate communication. Certain hardware devices are used with wide area networks, whereas other pieces of equipment are designed for local area networks.

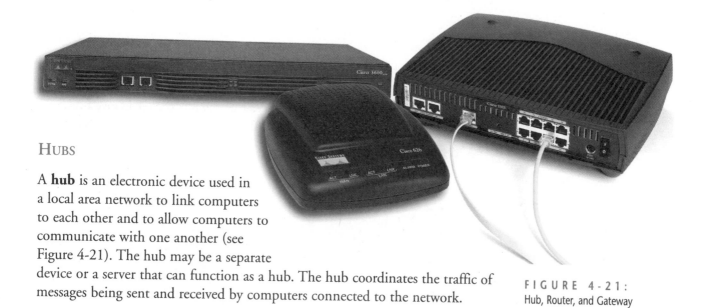

HUBS

A **hub** is an electronic device used in a local area network to link computers to each other and to allow computers to communicate with one another (see Figure 4-21). The hub may be a separate device or a server that can function as a hub. The hub coordinates the traffic of messages being sent and received by computers connected to the network.

FIGURE 4-21:
Hub, Router, and Gateway

REPEATERS

Also called *amplifiers*, **repeaters** are specially designed electronic devices that receive signals along a network, increase the strength of the signals, and send the amplified signals along the network's communications path. A repeater works similarly to an amplifier in a home stereo system. Figure 4-22 shows examples of repeaters.

Information often must travel long distances. However, the wires and cables may not be designed to carry the messages the full distance. Repeaters are designed to rectify this problem. A network spread over wide distances may use several repeaters along the way.

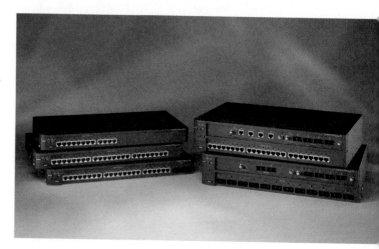

FIGURE 4-22: Network Repeaters

ROUTERS

A **router** is a unique electronic device typically used in large networks, including the Internet, to ensure that messages are sent to their intended destinations (see Figure 4-21). As is true with repeaters, a large network covering several miles may use several routers. When a router along a message's destination receives a message, it sends the message along the path to the next router, and so on, until the message reaches its final destination.

Routers are designed and programmed to work together. If a part of the network is not working properly, a router can choose an alternate path by sending a message through a different router so the message will arrive at its final destination.

BRIDGES

A **bridge** consists of hardware and/or software that allows for communication between two networks that are *similar*. If the investment broker in the previous example wants to retrieve information stored on the same kind of network the other broker is using, a bridge between the two networks allows communications to occur between the networks. Figure 4-23 illustrates the difference between a bridge and a gateway.

GATEWAYS

A **gateway** (Figure 4-21) consists of hardware and/or software that allows communication between *dissimilar* networks. For example, a gateway is needed if an investment broker using a ring network wants to retrieve information stored on a star network.

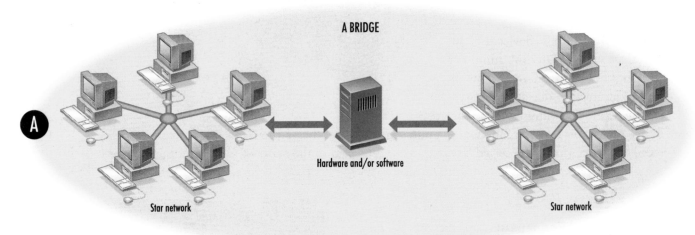

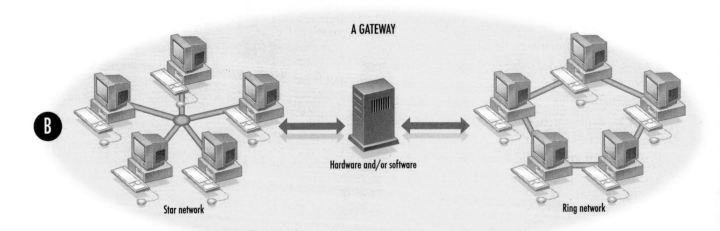

FIGURE 4-23: Bridge (A) and Gateway (B)

A bridge is a combination of hardware and software that enables devices on one LAN to communicate with devices on another similar LAN. A gateway is a combination of hardware and software that allows dissimilar networks to communicate.

MULTIPLEXERS

A **multiplexer** is an electronic device that increases the efficiency of a network system by allowing 8, 16, 32, or more low-speed devices to share simultaneously a single high-speed communications medium. When used to connect devices with the host computer, the multiplexer accepts data from several devices, combines or *multiplexes* it, and sends it immediately across a single high-speed medium to a second multiplexer that divides, or *demultiplexes* the data and then transmits it to the host computer. Figure 4-24 shows an example of a multiplexer.

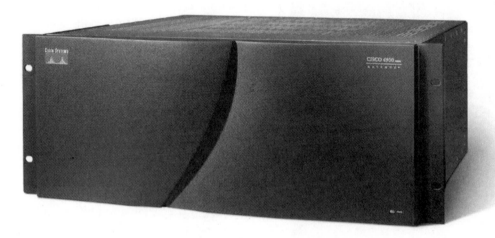

FIGURE 4-24: Network multiplexer

CONCENTRATORS

With a **concentrator**, data is transmitted from only one device at a time over the channel. The data is then multiplexed with other data and stored until there is enough data to make transferring it over an expensive communications medium more cost effective. Using a concentrator assumes that not all terminals will be ready to send or to receive data at the same time. A minicomputer with memory functions that allow for the storage and forwarding of transmissions can function as a concentrator.

COMMUNICATIONS SOFTWARE AND PROTOCOLS

Communications software is a type of utility software that allows computers to "talk" with each other. Combined with the appropriate hardware, communications utilities allow you to connect your computer to another computer, such as a network server, and to access and use resources on a LAN or WAN, including stored programs, data, and information. Communications software also allows you to dial a modem so you can send an e-mail message, access the Internet, surf the Web, and more.

Newer PCs containing a modem often come equipped with communications software. If not, you can purchase the software from a variety of sources. Users who subscribe to an Internet service provider are typically provided with communications software that can be installed.

FEATURES OF COMMUNICATIONS UTILITIES

Communications software programs contain a variety of useful features. Most programs allow you to:

- access and use the services of an ISP or online service, such as America Online or Microsoft Network
- send information to, and receive information from, other computers
- access other computers around the world
- send and receive electronic mail messages
- send and receive faxes

Numerous types of communications software are available, including e-mail, Web browsers, and groupware. **E-mail software** allows a user to create, send, receive, print, store, forward, and delete e-mail messages and to attach files to messages being sent. A Web browser allows a user to access and view Web pages. **Groupware** is communications software that allows groups of people on a network to share information and to collaborate on various projects, such as designing a new product or preparing employee manuals. For a given network, the software must adhere to a particular network protocol, or standard for network communications.

COMMUNICATIONS PROTOCOLS

A **protocol** is a set of rules and procedures for exchanging information among computers on a network. To avoid transmission errors, the computers involved in the communication must have the same settings and follow the same standards. Over the years, numerous protocols have been developed. Table 4-2 shows a sample of communications protocols now being used.

COMMUNICATIONS PROTOCOLS	
Type of Protocol	**Purpose/Use**
Hypertext Transfer Protocol (HTTP)	Define how Web pages are transmitted
Simple Mail Transfer Protocol (SMTP)	Send e-mail messages between servers
Post Office Protocol (POP)	Retrieve e-mail from a mail server; newest version is POP3
Internet Message Access Protocol (IMAP)	Retrieve e-mail from a mail server; newer than POP and has replaced POP on some e-mail servers; newest version is IMAP4
Transmission Control Protocol/Internet Protocol (TCP/IP)	Connect host computers on the Internet
File Transfer Protocol (FTP)	Allow large files to be transmitted and received over the Internet

TABLE 4-2: Examples of Communications Protocols

Efforts are currently under way to simplify protocols by establishing standards that all computer and communications equipment manufacturers will adopt and follow. Toward that end, the International Standards Organization, based in Geneva, Switzerland, has defined a set of communications protocols called the **Open Systems Interconnection (OSI) model**. The United Nations has adopted the OSI model. However, unless and until all manufacturers adopt OSI, a variety of protocols will remain in use.

Directional Protocols

Almost all communications use directional protocols that determine the directional flow of transmissions among devices. Three possible directions are simplex, half-duplex, and full-duplex, as illustrated in Figure 4-25.

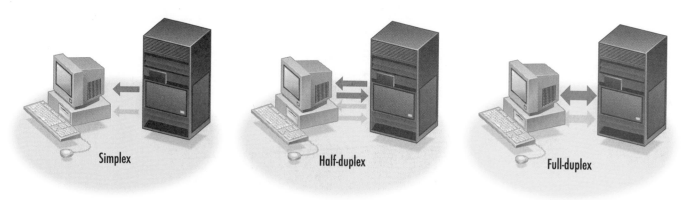

FIGURE 4-25: Simplex, Half-Duplex, and Full-Duplex Transmissions

With simplex transmission, transmissions flow in only one direction. With half-duplex transmission, transmissions can flow in either direction, but in only one direction at a time. With full-duplex transmission, transmissions can flow in both directions at the same time.

Simplex Transmission: With **simplex transmission**, communications flow in only one direction. This direction can be compared to a public announcement system at a football game. The PA announcer makes announcements to the audience, but cannot receive messages from the audience. Likewise, a computer that transmits data via a simplex channel can either send or receive data, but cannot do both.

Half-Duplex Transmission: With **half-duplex transmission**, communications can flow in both directions but not at the same time. A walkie-talkie system is an example of half-duplex transmission. Two people can communicate, but only one person at a time can transmit while the other listens. When used over long distances, half-duplex transmission often results in delays. Thus, half-duplex transmission is typically used with a central computer system and the terminals connected to it. In these systems, the user usually needs to wait for a response from the main computer before continuing, making simultaneous transmission unnecessary.

Full-Duplex Transmission: Simultaneous transmission in both directions is achieved through **full-duplex transmission,** which can be compared to two people communicating via telephone. Both can speak and hear at the same time. Full-duplex transmission eliminates delays due to response time, which can be an important advantage when large amounts of data are transmitted between minicomputers, mainframe computers, and supercomputers.

Asynchronous versus Synchronous Transmission

Earlier you learned that data is sent over communications media in serial form, that is, one bit after another bit until the complete message is transmitted. Since the bits in serial transmission are sent out one at a time, transmission protocols have been developed to alert the receiving device as to where characters (bytes) begin and end. These protocols, called asynchronous and synchronous transmission, are illustrated in Figure 4-26.

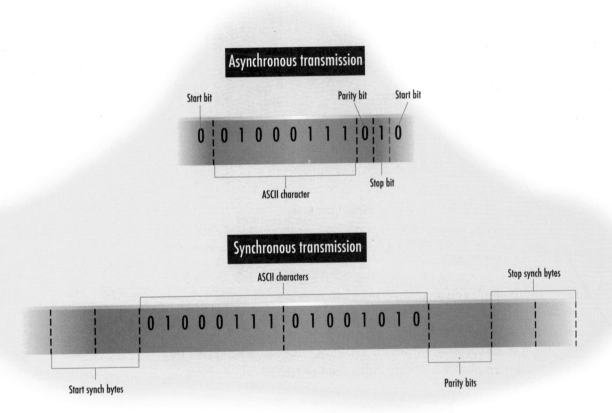

FIGURE 4-26: Asynchronous and Synchronous Transmissions

With asynchronous transmission, control bits surround each byte of data. An extra bit is added at the front and end of each character to signal its beginning (start) and ending (stop). The parity bit checks for errors. Synchronous transmission provides a fast and efficient way of sending data. Blocks of bytes are wrapped in start and stop bytes called synch bytes.

When communications are sent by **asynchronous transmission**, each byte of data is surrounded by control bits. An extra bit is added at the front of the character and another bit at the end. The front bit, called a **start bit**, signals the beginning of a character. The bit at the end, called a **stop bit**, signals the end of that character. There is also the error checking bit called a **parity bit**. Data sent by asynchronous transmission is transmitted at irregular intervals, and a modem is usually involved.

Synchronous transmission provides a faster and more efficient way of sending data. With **synchronous transmission**, blocks of bytes are wrapped in start and stop bytes called **synch bytes**. Large computer systems often use synchronous transmission due to faster transmission speeds. PC users wanting to retrieve data from large computer systems can buy add-in boards that provide synchronous transmission.

The sending and receiving computers must use the same transmission method. If the sending computer uses the asynchronous method to send data and the receiving computer has chosen the synchronous method to receive the data, the receiving computer will be unable to receive the data.

Some protocols exist exclusively for local area networks, while others operate in wide area networks. The following sections discuss protocols for both types of networks, along with other useful protocols.

PROTOCOLS FOR LOCAL AREA NETWORKS (LANs)

Protocols that govern data transmissions vary among local area networks with different topologies and different PCs or workstations. Many LANs of the bus topology type are set up using network software called Ethernet, which includes a group of Ethernet protocols. These protocols specify how the network is to be set up, how the network devices communicate with each other, how problems are identified and corrected, how components are connected, and more. Ethernet provides for fast and efficient communications.

Ring and star topology networks use a **token ring protocol** that sends an electronic signal, a **token**, around the ring quickly. The token is capable of carrying both an address and a message. As the token passes a workstation, the workstation checks to see if the token is addressed for that workstation. If the token is free with no address, the workstation can latch onto the token, thereby changing the token's status from free to busy. The workstation then adds an address and message to the token. The receiving station receives the message and changes the token to free. The token then continues around the ring.

PROTOCOLS FOR WIDE AREA NETWORKS (WANs)

Specific protocols have been developed for use with wide area networks. A widely used networking program called **Systems Network Architecture (SNA)** uses a **polling protocol** for transmitting data. Workstations are asked one by one if they have a message to transmit. If a polled workstation replies "yes," the protocol transmits the message and then questions (polls) the next device.

A newer type of network software for ring networks dispersed over a large area and connected by fiber-optic cables is called **Fiber Distributed Data Interface (FDDI)**. The software links the dispersed networks together using a protocol that passes a token over long distances. FDDI may be used to connect various university campuses wanting to share information among them.

INTERNET AND WEB PROTOCOLS

The Internet and the Web require specific protocols to communicate with computers around the world. Earlier you learned that the Internet uses a transmission technique called packet switching, in which data is divided into small blocks, or packets, which are sent along the Internet to their destinations. A protocol called **Transmission Control Protocol/Internet Protocol (TCP/IP)** governs how packets are constructed and sent to their destinations.

The World Wide Web uses a protocol called **Hypertext Transfer Protocol (HTTP)** to transfer Web pages over the Web to computers requesting them. Most Web addresses, or URLs, begin with the letters "HTTP" to indicate the protocol being used.

ELECTRONIC MAIL PROTOCOLS

Most ISPs and online services provide an electronic mail service using a computer designated as a **mail server** to facilitate the sending and receiving of e-mail messages. A message being sent is transmitted according to a communications protocol called **Simple Mail Transfer Protocol (SMTP)**. SMTP, installed on the ISP's or online service's mail server, determines how each message is to be routed through the Internet and then sends the message.

Upon arrival at the recipient's mail server, the message is transferred to another server, called a **POP server**. A protocol in the recipient's communications software, called **Post Office Protocol (POP)**, allows the recipient to retrieve the message. Figure 4-27 illustrates how electronic mail is sent and received with SMTP and POP.

WIRELESS APPLICATION PROTOCOLS

A need for a new Internet protocol has emerged from the expanding use of handhelds, including cell phones, pagers, and PDAs. Businesses need to be able to deliver their Web content to wireless devices, but the current technology only accommodates simple text, and no single protocol has emerged as the standard. Many experts think that the Wireless Application Protocol will fill that need.

Cell phones and their networks have a low bandwidth, which slows down the Web page transmission process and makes the display of graphics nearly impossible. The **Wireless Application Protocol (WAP)** includes a standardized language called **Wireless Markup Language (WML)**. Special software on a wireless-enabled Web site converts the HTML-coded page to WML, removing the graphics, and then sends the text to the wireless device where it is displayed on the screen. Future versions of WAP may enable graphics to be transmitted also, or this protocol may be replaced by an entirely new set of standards.

THE INTERNET: A WORLDWIDE NETWORK

The Internet is the largest network in the world. Technically, its design most closely resembles a client/server model in that groups of networks act as clients, and ISPs act as servers (see Figure 4-28). Since the inception of the Internet in the early 1970s, this enormous invisible structure has grown to connect more than 170 million users worldwide through a vast system of networked computers and telecommunications systems. Many social philosophers consider the Internet the most significant technical development of the twentieth century for the simple reason that it can potentially connect every person on earth and it can allow the sharing of all collected knowledge to date, as well as all new information as it develops.

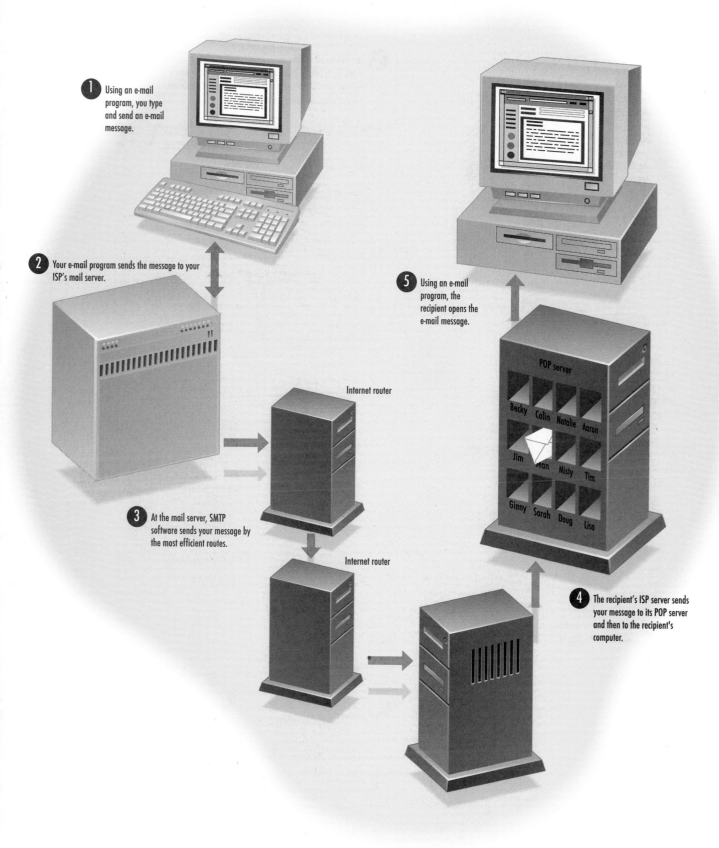

1 Using an e-mail program, you type and send an e-mail message.

2 Your e-mail program sends the message to your ISP's mail server.

3 At the mail server, SMTP software sends your message by the most efficient routes.

Internet router

Internet router

5 Using an e-mail program, the recipient opens the e-mail message.

POP server

Becky Colin Natalie Aaron

Jim Dean Misty Tim

Ginny Sarah Doug Lisa

4 The recipient's ISP server sends your message to its POP server and then to the recipient's computer.

F I G U R E 4 - 2 7 : Electronic Mail POP Servers

Most electronic mail systems use a computer designated as a mail server that receives incoming e-mail messages. The messages are then sent to, and stored on, the ISP's POP server, from which the recipient can retrieve the messages.

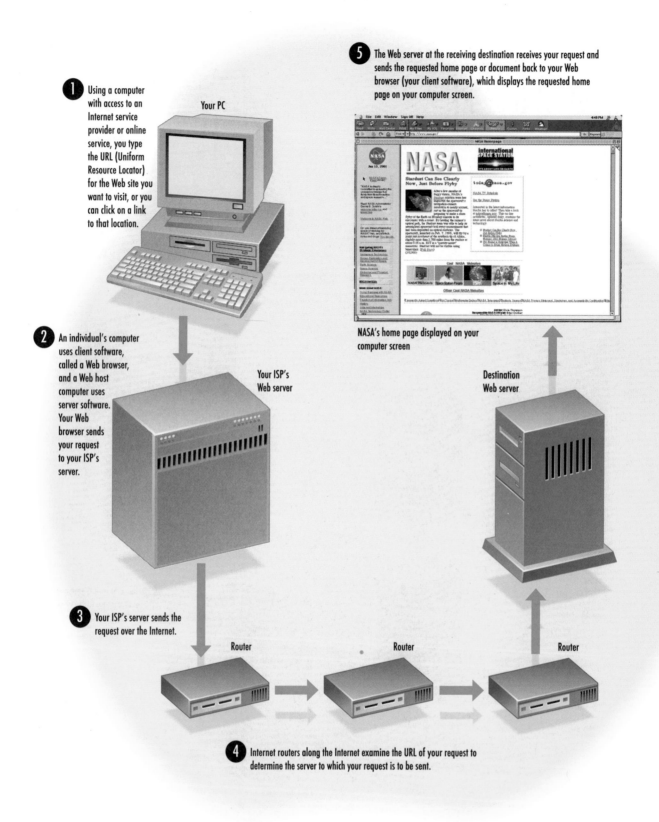

5 The Web server at the receiving destination receives your request and sends the requested home page or document back to your Web browser (your client software), which displays the requested home page on your computer screen.

1 Using a computer with access to an Internet service provider or online service, you type the URL (Uniform Resource Locator) for the Web site you want to visit, or you can click on a link to that location.

Your PC

NASA's home page displayed on your computer screen

2 An individual's computer uses client software, called a Web browser, and a Web host computer uses server software. Your Web browser sends your request to your ISP's server.

Your ISP's Web server

Destination Web server

3 Your ISP's server sends the request over the Internet.

Router

Router

Router

4 Internet routers along the Internet examine the URL of your request to determine the server to which your request is to be sent.

F I G U R E   4 - 2 8 : Using the Web

The following applications, introduced in chapter 1, represent the main ways people use the Internet today:

- communicate through e-mail
- retrieve information
- transfer files of information
- discuss topics online
- provide entertainment
- shop for goods and services
- learn new skills
- sell, purchase, and distribute products
- post messages to electronic bulletin boards
- telecommute to jobs

ELECTRONIC MAIL (E-MAIL)

Electronic mail (e-mail), the process of sending, receiving, storing, and forwarding messages in electronic form, is the most widely used Internet application. It is a fast and inexpensive way to communicate.

Each e-mail user has a unique electronic address, which is made available by his Internet service provider or online service. To send an e-mail message, the sender needs to specify the recipient's e-mail address, the sender's address, and a message subject, then type the message and click a *Send* button. Files can be attached to, or sent along with, the e-mail message. In Microsoft Outlook, the attachment feature is called *Insert File*, and it is accessible via the paperclip icon in the Toolbar. Figure 4-29 shows the e-mail screen of Microsoft Outlook.

Computer industry research firm IDC estimates that the number of e-mail mailboxes in North America has grown from about 70 million in 1995 to more than 300 million in 2001. By 2005, according to IDC, North Americans will send 18 billion e-mails every day.

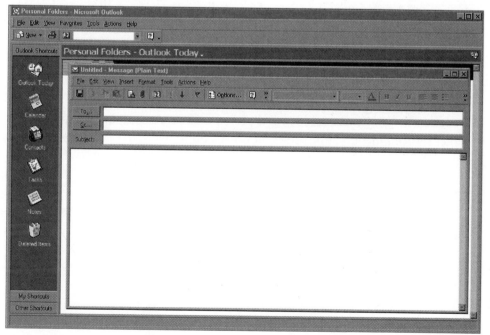

FIGURE 4-29: Microsoft Outlook includes e-mail capabilities. Files can be attached to e-mail messages by clicking the paperclip icon.

INFORMATION RETRIEVAL

Many universities, libraries, and government agencies make their large databases available to Internet users. Aided by increasingly sophisticated software, a user can research any kind of topic, from anacondas to Zen Buddhism. Information retrieval has become an important application for students, writers, historians, scientists, and others engaged in research.

FILE TRANSFER

Literally millions of files, including text documents, pictures, images, music, and more, are available to Web users. Using a protocol called **File Transfer Protocol (FTP)**, a person can send and receive large files, such as reports. For example, a company accountant can send a multiple-page employee report to the U.S. Department of Labor, or receive a complete copy of the newest tax laws from the IRS over the Internet.

CHAT ROOMS

A **chat room** is an application that allows users to talk with each other in **real time** (live, at the moment) via the computer monitor about topics of mutual interest. Online services provide chat rooms, along with news, travel reservations capability, and electronic magazines. Users can sign up to participate in a chat room on almost any topic. For example, an environmentally conscious user can participate in a chat room discussing global warming. User comments and opinions, often frank and uncensored, can be exchanged freely and anonymously with other online participants.

ENTERTAINMENT

Entertainment is a popular activity among Internet users of all ages, and particularly among young people. A variety of free online games are available, including *Bejeweled*, *Backgammon*, checkers, and bridge. Retail games requiring the user to own the software are popular as well, including such hits as *Age of Empires II* and *Rainbow Six*. A user can select an individual game or one requiring two or more players. To attract new users, some Web sites offer prizes to the winner of a multiplayer game.

Music also can be downloaded and played on a user's computer from various Internet sources, including Napster and others. Some Web sites charge a small fee for the service.

ONLINE SHOPPING

Online shoppers spend millions of dollars annually on a variety of products and services ranging from travel tickets to children's toys. In the month of July 2000 alone, consumers spent some $2.7 billion dollars in online purchases, according to *InfoWorld* magazine.

Many sellers post online catalogs from which a user can make selections. A selected item is added to a "shopping cart" and shopping continues. After the user has finished shopping, he pays for his purchases by entering a credit card number, and the purchased items are shipped to the customer's address.

DISTANCE LEARNING

Some colleges and textbook publishers offer online courses and programs of study over the Internet. This relatively new Internet application is referred to as distance learning. **Distance learning** may be defined as the electronic transfer of information from a college or publisher's host computer system to a student's computer and the transmission of required responses from the student's computer to the college or publisher's computer. A course presented in this manner is called an **online course**. Perhaps you are taking an online course right now, using the computer concepts course available with this text. Figure 4-30 shows the opening screen of EMC/Paradigm's Introduction to Computers Web course.

F I G U R E   4 - 3 0 :   EMC/Paradigm's Introduction to Computers Web Course

Distance learning is becoming increasingly popular among students of all ages and among those with interests that may not be included in a standard college curriculum or at the school closest to the user. It also has proved an attractive learning alternative for students whose schedules or careers make it difficult to attend regular classes. For them, distance learning offers an opportunity to pursue or continue their education. An early and well known college provider of online courses is the University of Phoenix, whose home page is shown in Figure 4-31.

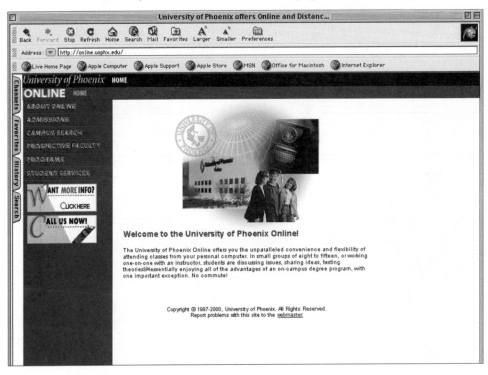

FIGURE 4-31: University of Phoenix Home Page

ELECTRONIC COMMERCE (E-COMMERCE)

e-commerce:
www.ebizchronicle.com

Online shopping is a part of a broader Internet application, called electronic commerce. **Electronic commerce (e-commerce)** refers to modern business Internet technologies in which business information, products, services, and payments are exchanged between sellers and customers (called B2C) and between businesses (called B2B). Airline tickets, hotel reservations, and computer hardware typically rank as the top three categories of sales.

In addition to selling products and services, businesses are using the Internet to advertise products, order inventories from manufacturers and wholesalers, order raw materials, recruit employees, file government reports, and more.

ELECTRONIC BULLETIN BOARDS

Similar in use to bulletin boards found in classrooms and dormitories, an **electronic bulletin board system (BBS)** is an electronically stored list of messages that can be accessed and read by anyone having access to the bulletin board. A user can post messages, read existing messages, or delete messages. The Internet provides a channel to hundreds of bulletin boards around the world. Figure 4-32 shows an example of an electronic bulletin board.

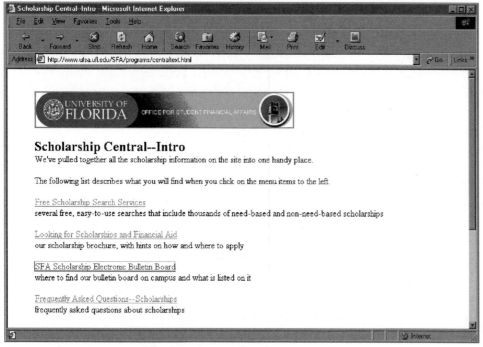

F I G U R E 4 - 3 2 : An Electronic Bulletin Board System

TELECOMMUTING

Millions of workers are now performing their work activities at home instead of at the workplace by using their computers, a modem, and a telephone line. This activity is known as **telecommuting**. Some employers have discovered that allowing employees to telecommute offers some important advantages. Among the advantages are increased employee productivity, an opportunity to employ highly productive but disabled workers, and savings on travel costs to and from the workplace.

KEYTERMS

productivity In business, a measure of goods and services produced (output) per unit of input (worker hours)

CONNECTING TO THE INTERNET

To connect to the Internet, most users require the following equipment and software:

- a computer, a personal digital assistant (PDA), or a Web phone
- a modem or cable modem
- a telephone line or cable connection
- telecommunications software, usually provided by an ISP (see below)
- a Web browser (available as a free download or as part of an application suite)
- an account with an Internet service provider (ISP) or with an online service, such as America Online (AOL), CompuServe, or the Microsoft Network, that provides Internet connections and other materials (the ISP may be a cable company)

TYPES OF INTERNET CONNECTIONS

Internet service providers and online services provide customers with access to the Internet. An **Internet service provider (ISP)** is a company that has a permanent connection to the Internet and that provides Internet access to individuals and others for free or for a fee (for example, $20 per month). ISPs are available at local, regional, and national levels. A **local ISP** typically provides users with one or more telephone numbers they can use to dial-up the ISP's network computer. **Regional ISPs** serve one or more states, and a **national ISP** is a larger ISP that provides telephone numbers in most major cities. Their larger size allows the national ISP to provide more services and technical support for users than local ISPs can provide. Communications traveling across wide distances often pass through national ISPs.

An **online service** also provides users with Internet access, but additionally offers special features such as online news, weather reports, financial news, and sporting news. Examples of online services include America Online and Microsoft Network.

When connecting to the Internet from a home or while traveling, users often use an Internet connection method called dial-up access. **Dial-up access** allows a person to connect to the Internet using a computer and a modem to dial into an ISP or online service over a standard telephone line. Dial-up access is a feature typically included with the software provided by a user's ISP or online service. Once the software is installed on a user's computer, a dial-up access icon may be placed on the user's computer desktop. A user can automatically dial into the ISP or online service's computer by simply clicking on the dial-up icon, as shown in Figure 4-33.

FIGURE 4-33: Windows Desktop with ISP Icon

ALTERNATIVES TO THE TELEPHONE/MODEM CONNECTION

Telephone modems are usually the slowest telecommunications medium for Internet users setting up an individual Internet account. Faster options include the following systems:

- ISDN (integrated services digital network)
- satellite
- cable modem
- DSL (digital subscriber line)

ISDN (Integrated Services Digital Network)

Some telephone carriers offer ISDN service and will provide a modem when the customer signs a contract. ISDN lines are twice as fast as telephone modems, although Internet connection speed drops when the user surfs the Net while talking on the phone. Typical charges are $25 or more per month.

Satellite

To use a satellite connection, a person needs a satellite dish, a modem built into the PC or handheld, and an Internet account. Costs are $20 to $100 per month for the service, plus $350 for a dish, modem, and installation. Downloading Web files is quick via satellite, but the user cannot talk on the phone and surf the Web simultaneously.

Cable Modem

Cable TV companies can provide a special modem and software for high-speed Internet access. The cost is about $20 to $60 monthly, plus an installation fee of about $100. Cable modems offer the advantage of simultaneous Web access and telephone calls, but the service is not available nationally. In addition, as more subscribers sign up in a particular area, the service slows down.

DSL (Digital Subscriber Line)

A DSL provides access to the Internet through the user's existing phone lines, with the phone carrier or Internet Service Provider providing the DSL modem and the network card. DSL service costs $30 to $180 monthly, and some carriers include the Internet service account in the monthly fee. DSL service is as fast as cable modems and provides simultaneous Web access and telephone use, but the service is usually available only to users within three miles of the telephone carrier's central switching office.

DSL service:
www.adsl.com

USING A BROWSER

To access and move about the Web, an activity called *browsing* or *surfing*, a user must have a special piece of software called a browser installed on her computer or on the network she uses. A **browser** is a program that finds Web pages and displays the pages on the user's screen. Two popular browsers are Netscape Navigator from Netscape Communications Corporation and Internet Explorer from Microsoft Corporation. Both work in a similar manner.

When a user first accesses a Web site, the first page displayed is that site's **home page**. A home page often contains hyperlinks coded in a special Web language that connects the user to other pages at that site or to other Web sites.

Web Languages

Recall from chapter 1 that most Web pages are created using **hypertext markup language (HTML),** as shown in Figure 4-34. HTML gives developers wide latitude in determining the appearance, or design, of the pages. Most Web browsers, including Microsoft's *Internet Explorer* and Netscape's *Navigator,* can display Web pages in HTML format.

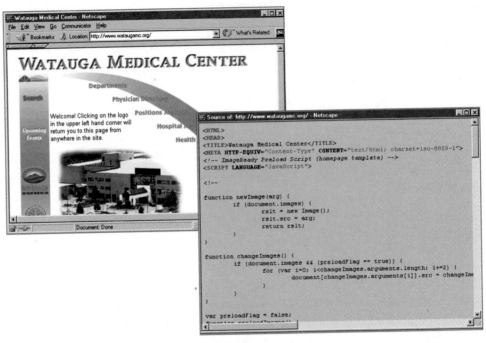

FIGURE 4-34: Web Page and Its HTML Code

A new and improved Web language, called **eXtensible Markup Language (XML)**, is becoming increasingly popular. Whereas HTML only defines the content of a Web page, XML also describes how the content looks when the page is displayed on a computer screen. The enormous potential of XML lies in its ability to organize data so that computers can communicate directly without human direction. For example, suppliers and manufacturers could turn their computers loose in the market, letting them find, purchase, and sell products and services without human help. Medical researchers could allow their computers to search the databases of other research centers to identify possible new applications of scientific breakthroughs. Several producers of software applications, including Microsoft Corporation, are now using XML in developing some of their applications.

Web Addresses

After activating a browser, the user issues a request to visit a specific Web site or page by typing an address, called a **uniform resource locator (URL)** for the site, for example:

http://www.emcp.com

A URL has several parts separated by a colon (:), slashes (/), and dots (.). The first part of a URL—in this case, *http*—identifies the communications protocol to be used. The material immediately following the protocol in a URL is format information, such as *www* for World Wide Web pages.

The next part of the address is the **domain name**, which identifies the person, organization, server, or topic (*emcp*, for EMC/Paradigm in the example above). Next, following a dot, comes the **domain suffix**, which identifies the type of organization. In the example above, *com* stands for company. Table 4-3 lists the additional domain suffixes commonly used. The entire URL constitutes a **path-name** describing where the particular information can be found.

T A B L E 4 - 3 :
Common Domain Suffixes Used in URLs

Domain Suffixes for Institutions and Organizations	
.com	company or commercial institution (Ford, Intel)
.edu	educational institution (Harvard, Washington University)
.gov	governmental site (NASA, IRS)
.int	international treaty organization, Internet database (NATO)
.mil	military site (U.S. Department of Defense)
.net	administrative site for the Internet or ISPs
.org	nonprofit or private organization or society (Red Cross)

In the fall of 2000, the Internet Corporation for Assigned Names and Numbers (ICANN), an organization created in 1998 by the U.S. Commerce Department to expand the list of existing domain suffixes, approved the new suffixes listed in Table 4-4.

Domain Suffixes Identifying Countries					
.af	Afghanistan	.fi	Finland	.pl	Poland
.at	Austria	.fr	France	.ru	Russia
.au	Australia	.il	Israel	.se	Sweden
.be	Belgium	.it	Italy	.tw	Taiwan
.br	Brazil	.jp	Japan	.uk	United Kingdom
.ca	Canada	.kr	Republic of Korea	.us	United States
.ch	Switzerland	.mx	Mexico	.yu	Yugoslavia
.de	Germany	.nl	Netherlands	.za	South Africa
.dk	Denmark	.no	Norway	.zw	Zimbabwe
.es	Spain				

New Domain Suffixes	
.info	general use
.biz	general use
.pro	professionals
.name	personal Web sites
.museum	museums
.aero	airline groups
.coop	business cooperatives

T A B L E 4 - 4 :
New Domain Suffixes

The last major part of the address, which is optional, is the file specification. The **file specification** is the name of a specific file or file folder. At some Web sites a vast amount of information is available on the server. If you know the name of the particular file or page you are seeking, or the name of the folder containing the information, accessing the information is easier and faster. The following URL includes a file specification (mars):

http://www.nasa.gov/mars

The Path of a Web Site Request

After the user types a site's URL, the request is sent to the Internet where routers examine the request to identify the specific Web site address (URL) server and then send the request to the appropriate Web server. The Web server receives the request and uses the *http* communications protocol to determine which page, file, or object is being requested. Upon finding the requested page, file, or object, the server sends it back to the user's computer where it is displayed on the user's screen.

Metabrowsers

A new Web technology called metabrowsers has been developed to provide more efficient Internet surfing. A **metabrowser** allows the user to put all her favorite sites onto one page and thus reduce the number of clicks it takes to check those favorite Web pages daily. Using the software, a person can create "views" that organize favorite sites by category—for example, a view for finances, a news view, and an entertainment view. You simply enter the URLs, and all of the sites appear on the same page. Scrolling down allows you to view one after the other. Some of the popular metabrowsers are Octopus.com, Quickbrowse, OnePage, and Hodlee.com.

USING SEARCH ENGINES

At present, more than one billion pages are available on the Web. A user can search for, and retrieve, specific kinds of information from these pages by using a search engine. A **search engine** is a software program that allows a user to hunt for, locate, and retrieve information on the World Wide Web. Unlike a browser in which an address is entered to access a specific Web site, a search engine allows a user to find specific kinds of information by entering search criteria in the engine's search box. For example, assume you want to find information about the *Battle of Vicksburg* for a report you are writing for a history class. You can use a search engine to retrieve a list of sites offering articles on this topic by typing your search criteria—in this case the words "Battle of Vicksburg"—in the search box and clicking on the *Search* button. A list of articles, hyperlinked to their respective Web sites, will appear in your screen. You can select and read a listed article by clicking on the article title. Popular search engines include AltaVista, Yahoo!, Google, Excite, Lycos, Infoseek, and HotBot. Figure 4-35 shows the home page of Google.

FIGURE 4-35: Google Home Page

NETWORKING AND INTERNET CONCERNS

Several technical and legal issues are influencing the direction of the development of networks and the Internet. Among the more significant technical issues facing companies and individuals are the need for standard protocols and sufficient transmission bandwidths. For consumers particularly, the privacy and security of Internet communications and transactions are of paramount concern. How to protect original content using existing or revised copyright laws is another dilemma. And for every Internet user, the threat of viruses being transmitted over the Internet is a daily worry.

STANDARD PROTOCOLS AND ADEQUATE BANDWIDTH

Developers are using a variety of communications standards as they write new software programs that interact with networks. For example, there is disagreement by developers of wireless communications devices concerning acceptable wireless communications standards. The Wireless Application Protocol (WAP) seems to be gaining acceptance, but the final verdict is not in. Additionally, bandwidths now available with some communications media result in relatively slow transmission speeds, particularly with huge multimedia files. The result is growing frustration among Internet users, particularly given the industry estimate that Internet traffic is doubling every three months, as of late 2000.

PRIVACY ISSUES

A major concern among many users is the issue of privacy, primarily with e-mail communications and e-commerce transactions. Almost everyone is aware that e-mail messages can be intercepted and read by others. There is the real possibility that an employee's e-mail messages may be read by the employee's supervisor. Indeed, according to current law, employers have a right to do just that. This practice may have become more common as businesses have discovered that some employees spend considerable time surfing the Internet for personal reasons instead of performing their work.

consumer information:
www.pueblo.gsa.gov

online auction security:
www.shoppingspot.com

Many e-commerce Web sites use special software that tracks purchasers' buying habits and any other individual information that can be gleaned from customers' visits to the site. Certain corporate Web sites follow the same practice, without the surfer's knowledge. Recently, the World Wide Web Consortium (W3C), a Web advisory group, has developed a browser specification to address the concern of keeping Web users' personal data private. Called P3P for Platform for Privacy Preference, the standard would alert Web surfers about how a corporate Web site would use information collected on that individual. Additional testing is under way before the specification can be implemented.

SECURITY PROTECTIONS

Security is a major concern, especially in electronic commerce transactions. Businesses selling products and services over the Internet have discovered that many potential customers are reluctant to use a credit card for payment. Stories abound in which hackers have penetrated computer systems and stolen credit card numbers. Major retail companies, however, have instituted sophisticated security encryption systems that protect customers' financial information.

COPYRIGHT INFRINGEMENT

Internet-related crimes:
www.cybercrime.gov

cyberspace law:
www.abanet.org

The violation of **copyright** laws is a frequent occurrence on the Internet. Much of the information posted on the Web, including printed information and music, is copyrighted. Copying these materials is illegal and punishable by law, and most Web sites include a copyright notice that spells out general guidelines as to how the site's content may be used (see Figure 4-36). Nevertheless, copyright laws are frequently ignored, and the involved parties end up in court.

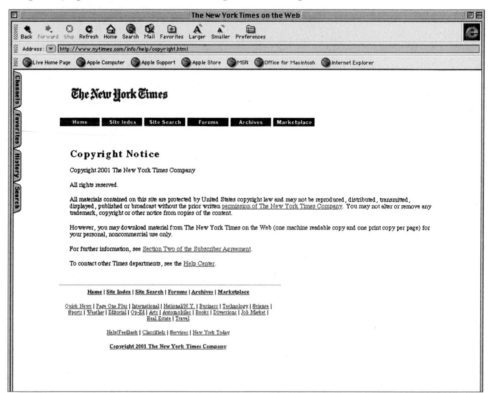

FIGURE 4-36: Copyright Notice on *The New York Times* Home Page

Because existing copyright laws were written with printed materials in mind, Congress passed a new law in 1998 that addressed the major issues related to protecting digital content on the Internet. Called the **Digital Millennium Copyright Act of 1998**, the law generally prohibits people from taking action to break down software encryption programs and other safeguards that copyright holders have established to control access to their works, including DVDs, software, and digitized books and music. Entertainment companies, for example, have tried to protect their movies on DVD by including a security code. But hackers and other computer experts have developed programs capable of cracking those codes. A key provision of the Digital Millennium Copyright Act of 1998 makes the use and distribution of the security-cracking codes illegal and imposes civil court damages ranging from $200 to $2,500. Repeat offenders face criminal penalties of up to $1 million in fines or 10 years in jail.

computer virus myths:
www.Vmyths.com

Computer viruses represent a significant threat to all computer systems. A virus is a chunk of computer code that can damage or destroy valuable programs and data. Some viruses make innumerable copies of themselves, clogging and choking storage devices. Some erase everything on a storage device. Some display messages or graphics, and some simply corrupt programs or operating systems and cause them to crash. To date, tens of thousands of viruses have infiltrated the PC world at one time or another. New viruses appear regularly and are frequently sent over the Internet via e-mail, causing frustration at a minimum and, more important, serious losses of data and money. The "I Love You" virus of 2000, for example, cost U.S. businesses an estimated $11 billion. The possibility of virus transmission over wireless devices and the Internet is a special recent concern, since the technology is quite new and is changing rapidly. Industry observers note that as the operating systems of handhelds climb in power—some models now have the computing capability of a desktop—so will the potential for virus invasions.

Virus scanning software is widely available. However, virus scanners can only detect current, known viruses, and the security measures implemented on handhelds tend to be limited or nonexistent. What's needed in the industry is new technology that can detect possible viruses when they're first created and launched. What's needed for users is to be fully aware of how viruses are transmitted and to be on guard for unusual e-mail attachments from unknown, anonymous senders.

Computers in Your Future?

Computer Network Technician

As the number of companies and institutions establishing their own computer networks grows, so will the demand for computer network technicians. These technicians build and maintain the networks that link workers' computers, allowing them to send e-mail and to share data and computer applications.

A computer network technician plans and implements his or her employer's network, troubleshooting as problems arise. Responsibilities include determining the needs, analyzing costs, and selecting equipment and network protocols. Once needs are determined, the computer network technician configures and installs hardware and resolves any conflicts in the system.

Personal skills needed include the patience to spend long hours at a keyboard debugging a program, as well as the dexterity to untangle and reweave a multitude of wires. Because the technician also assists nontechnical workers using the hardware and software, a good candidate must possess excellent communication skills, both oral and written. Formal training in computer science and a B.A. in computer science, electrical engineering, or a related field are usually required. Certification in a number of networking specialties is also valuable.

A novice computer network technician can expect to earn up to $45,000, and the salary increases with additional certifications, training, and experience. Senior technicians can earn more than $100,000 annually. Because the demand for computer network technicians is growing, incentives and competitive benefits are often part of the package.

Source: "Career Information Center: Computers, Business, and Office," 7th Edition, Visual Education Corp., Princeton, NJ, 1999.

ON THE HORIZON

The future holds tremendous promise for the Internet and Web. New Internet hardware, software, and media are appearing that will help solve some of the problems identified above. Education about the Internet and its applications will result in users being more knowledgeable and better informed.

OPTICAL NETWORKS: SHINING LIGHT OF THE FUTURE

Perhaps the most fundamental trend affecting the future of the Internet is the trend toward an optical, or fiber-optic, medium that will serve as the transmission channel for all exchanges of data over the Net. Currently, the backbone of the Internet is fiber-optic-based, but expanding the optical medium nation-wide—and eventually worldwide—will increase transmission speed and capacity by what will seem like light-years compared to today's capabilities. This stunning potential is based on recent developments in optical technology that allow "a single strand of fiber thinner than a human hair to carry every phone call, e-mail, and Web page used by every person in the world."[1] Equally important, the cost of moving information over long distances is projected to be 0.006 percent of the 1996 price.

Companies are expected to adopt the new technology in four significant ways:

- Long-distance carriers will spend billions on the latest optical equipment, upping network capacity by 80 to 160 times.
- Telephone companies will update the optical "rings" that carry voice traffic around a region of cities. The result? Data transmission will jump to 10 GB per second, some 10 times faster than the speed of the current technology.[2]
- Telephone companies also will upgrade the switches in local phone networks from electrical switches to optical switches, which in some situations are thousands of times faster.
- Businesses will replace their Ethernet connections with optical connections supplied by large communications firms at a relatively low cost. Downloads will take seconds instead of hours.

ANOTHER INTERNET?

In the future, using the Internet may become as universally accepted as the telephone. But the continual increase in traffic is clogging the Information Highway.

1. "At the Speed of Light," *Business Week*, October 2000.
2. *Ibid.*

Vast improvements in bandwidth and transmission speed anticipated from the evolving optical network represent a major solution. Another remedy is a revolutionary new type of Internet, called **Internet2**, currently under development. When fully operational, Internet2 will enable large research universities in the United States to collaborate and share huge amounts of complex scientific information at amazing speeds. Led by over 170 universities working in partnership with industry and government, the Internet2 consortium is developing and deploying advanced network technologies and applications. The primary goals of Internet2 are to:

- create a leading-edge network capability for the national research community
- enable revolutionary Internet applications
- ensure the rapid transfer of new network services and applications to the broader Internet community

Internet2 is a testing-ground network for universities to work together and develop advanced Internet technologies such as telemedicine, digital libraries, and virtual laboratories. An example of their collaboration is the *Informedia Digital Video Library (IDVL)* project. Once implemented, IDVL will offer a combination of speech recognition, image understanding, and natural language processing technology to automatically transcribe, segment, and index video segments, enabling intelligent searching and navigation, along with selective retrieval of information.

Internet2 universities will be connected to an ultra-high-speed network called the Abilene backbone. Each university will use state-of-the-art equipment to take advantage of transfer speeds provided by the network.

Partners in industry, government, and other countries are now working with Internet2 universities to develop and test the new technologies that will form tomorrow's Internet. You can learn more about Internet2 by visiting the project's Web site at www.internet2.edu. Figure 4-37 shows the home page of Internet2.

FIGURE 4-37: Internet2 Project's Home Page

CHAPTER SUMMARY

- **Telecommunications. Telecommunications** refers to the combined use of computer hardware and communications software for sending and receiving information over communications media, including phone lines and other types of media. Telecommunications makes it possible for computer users throughout the world to communicate with each other.

- **Characteristics of Data Transmission.** Data can travel over communications media in a variety of ways. An **analog transmission** takes the form of **continuous waves** transmitted over a medium at a certain **frequency range**. Changes in the wave transmissions reflect changes in voice and sound **pitch**. A **digital transmission** sends data in the form of bits (0's and 1's). In **serial transmission**, all of the data bits are transmitted one bit after another in a continuous line. In **parallel transmission**, a group of 8 bits representing a single byte (plus 1 bit called a **parity bit**) are transmitted at the same time over nine separate paths. The accompanying check bit indicates the end of the 8-bit byte. .

- **Communications Media.** A **communications medium** is a physical link (a connection) that allows a computer in one location to be connected to a computer in another location. **Twisted-pair cable** consists of two independently insulated wires twisted around one another. One of the wires carries the information while the other wire is grounded and absorbs any interference. **Coaxial cable** consists of an insulated center wire that is grounded by a shield of braided wire. A **fiber-optic cable** consists of hundreds of clear fiberglass or plastic fibers (threads). An **ISDN line** is a special digital telephone line that transmits and receives information at very high speeds, ranging from 64 kbps (64,000 bits per second) to 128 kbps. A **T line** is a permanent connection between two points set up by a telephone company and typically leased by a business to connect geographically distant offices. A **microwave system** transmits data via high-frequency radio signals through the atmosphere from one microwave station to another, or from a microwave station to a satellite and then back to earth to another microwave station. With a **satellite system**, a satellite receives the transmitted signals, amplifies them, and then transmits the signals to the appropriate locations. **Cellular technology** uses antennae resembling telephone towers to pick up signals within a specific area (cell). **Infrared technology** transmits data as infrared light waves from one device to another, providing wireless links between PCs and peripherals such as keyboards and printers.

- **Network Architectures.** The term **network architecture** refers to the way a network is designed and built. A **client/server architecture** uses a personal computer, workstation, or terminal (called a **client**) to send information or a request to another computer (called a **server**), which then relays the information back to the user's client computer, or to another computer (another client). In a **peer-to-peer architecture**, each PC or workstation has equivalent capabilities and responsibilities.

1969
ARPANet is created to link supercomputers at research sites

1973
Robert Metcalfe invents Ethernet; TELENET markets a private packet-switched network

1974
Xerox Corporation's Alto personal computer is created, making use of a LAN

1979
Tim Berners-Lee conceives of the World Wide Web

1980

1982
The term "Internet" makes its first appearance

1983
Mosaic Web browser is produced by the National Center for Supercomputing Applications

1986
NSFNet is created by the National Science Foundation; Number of Internet hosts surpasses 5,000

1990

1996
US Communications Decency Act (CDA) is signed into law

1997
Most of provisions in CDA are ruled unconstitutional

1998
Digital Millennium Copyright Law of 1998 is approved

1999
Palm Computing launches Wireless Palm VII with Internet access

2000
Number of Internet users worldwide exceeds 170 million

2000

- **Network Topologies (Layouts). Network topology,** or layout, refers to the way computers and peripherals are configured to form networks. In a **bus topology** all computers are linked by a single line of cable (a **bus**). All communications travel the length of the bus. In a **star topology**, multiple computers and peripheral devices are linked to a central computer, called a **host**, in a point-to-point configuration. In a **ring topology**, there is no host computer and each computer or workstation is connected to two other computers, with the entire network forming a circle. A **hybrid topology** combines different kinds of network layouts into one.

- **WANS and LANS.** A **wide area network (WAN)** spans a large geographical area. There are various types, including **metropolitan area networks**, **public access networks**, **value added networks**, and **virtual private networks**.

  Local area networks (LANs) are private networks that connect PCs or workstations located in the same building or in nearby buildings. LANs make it convenient for multiple users to share programs, data, information, hardware, software and other computing resources. Software applications and other resources are typically stored on a special computer called a **file server**. With a file server and a high-capacity hard disk, called a **disk server**, users can access programs, data, and other resources just as easily as if the resources were stored on their individual computers. A **print server** allows multiple users to share the same printer.

  An **intranet** is a network that is accessible only by the business or organization's members, employees, or other authorized users. Access to an intranet's Web site is restricted by a **firewall** that limits usage to authorized users. An **extranet** is a network that makes certain kinds of information available to users within the organization and other kinds of information available to outsiders, such as companies doing business with the organization.

- **Network and Communications Hardware.** A **hub** is an electronic device used in a local area network to link groups of computers and to allow them to communicate with one another. **Repeaters,** also called **amplifiers,** are electronic devices that receive signals along a network, amplify the signals, and send the amplified signals along the network. A **router** is a unique electronic device typically used in large networks, including the Internet, to ensure that messages are sent to their intended destinations. A **gateway** consists of hardware and/or software that allows communication between *dissimilar* networks. A **bridge** consists of hardware and/or software that allows for communication between two *similar* networks. A **multiplexer** is an electronic device that increases the efficiency of a network system by allowing 8, 16, 32, or more low-speed devices to share simultaneously a single high-speed communications medium. With a **concentrator**, data is transmitted from only one device at a time over the channel.

- **Communications Software. Communications software**, together with appropriate hardware equipment, allows you to connect your computer to another computer and to access and use network resources. **E-mail software** allows a user to create, send, receive, print, store, forward, and delete e-mail

messages and to attach files to messages being sent. A **Web browser** allows a user to access and view Web pages. **Groupware** allows groups of people on a network to share information and to collaborate on various projects.

- **Communications Protocols.** A **protocol** is a set of rules and procedures for exchanging information between network devices and computers. Protocols are built into communications software. **Communications protocols** consist of standards (rules) that govern the transfer of information among computers on a network and those using telecommunications. **Directional protocols** determine the directional flow of transmissions among devices. Three possible directions are **simplex**, **half-duplex**, and **full-duplex**.

  Asynchronous transmission and synchronous transmission define the method of sending bytes of data. With **asynchronous transmission,** characters are transmitted singly. Control bits surround each byte, and an extra bit is added at the front and end of the character to signal its beginning and ending. With **synchronous transmission**, blocks of bytes are wrapped in start and stop bytes called **synch bytes**. Synchronous transmission is faster, although most computers use asynchronous transmission.

  An Internet protocol called **Transmission Control Protocol/Internet Protocol (TCP/IP)** governs how packets are constructed and sent to their destinations. The World Wide Web uses **Hypertext Transfer Protocol (HTTP)** to transfer Web pages to computers requesting them. A message being sent is transmitted according to a communications protocol called **Simple Mail Transfer Protocol (SMTP)**. Upon arrival at the recipient's **mail server**, the message is transferred to another server, called a **POP server**. A protocol called **Post Office Protocol (POP)** allows the recipient to retrieve the message.

- **Telecommunications and the Internet.** Telecommunications plays an essential role in allowing computer users, including individuals, businesses, and organizations, to communicate with other computers around the world and to engage in Internet applications, such as electronic mail (e-mail), information retrieval, file transfer, chat rooms, entertainment, online shopping, distance learning, electronic commerce (e-commerce), electronic bulletin boards, and telecommuting.

- **Internet Service Providers and Online Services.** An **Internet service provider (ISP)** is an organization that maintains a permanent connection to the Internet and provides dial-up access to users for free or for a monthly fee. Upon signing up for service with a **local ISP**, a customer receives one or more telephone numbers to dial-up the ISP's network computer. **Regional ISPs** service one or several states. A **national ISP** provides telephone numbers in most major cities. An **online service** provides Internet access as well as special features such as online news, weather reports, financial news, and sporting news.

- **Accessing and Using the Internet and Web.** To access and move about the Web, an activity called **browsing** or **surfing**, a user must have a special program, called a browser, installed on the user's computer or network. A **browser** enables a user to find Web pages and display them in the screen.

Most Web pages are created in **Hypertext Markup Language (HTML)**, which adds links to other Web pages. A new and improved Web language called **eXtensible Markup Language (XML)** allows computers to surf Web sites and locate information without the intervention of the user.

After activating a browser, the user can visit a specific Web site by typing its **uniform resource locator (URL)**. The Web uses a communications protocol called **Hypertext Transfer Protocol (HTTP)** for transferring data from the Web site's computer to the user's computer. A user can find specific kinds of information using a **search engine**, a software program that searches, locates, and retrieves information on the World Wide Web.

- **Internet Problems and Concerns.** Major concerns for computer users are maintaining **privacy** and keeping personal information **secure**, especially in electronic commerce transactions. Adequate **bandwidths** are of special importance to users who frequently transmit and receive large files, such as videos, graphics, and/or sound. The **violation of copyright laws** is a frequent occurrence, and computer **viruses** represent a significant threat to all computer systems.

- **Future Trends.** A significant change to watch is the evolution of a totally **fiber-optic Internet**, resulting in extremely high transmission speeds and bandwidth capacity. Another major development under way is **Internet2**, a new type of Internet that, when fully operational, will enable large research universities in the United States to collaborate and share huge amounts of complex scientific information at amazing speeds.

KEYTERMS

analog signal, 6
asynchronous transmission, 32
bandwidth, 5
baseband, 10
bits per second (bps), 5
bridge, 28
broadband, 10
broadband medium, 6
browser, 43
bus, 23
bus topology, 23
cable modem, 10
cell, 14
cellular technology, 14
chat room, 38
client, 17
client/server architecture, 17
coaxial cable, 10
communications medium, 8
communications satellite, 13
concentrator, 29
continuous waves, 6
copyright, 48
dial-up access, 42
Digital Millennium Copyright Act of 1998, 48
disk server, 18
distance learning, 39
domain name, 44
domain suffix, 44
earth station, 13
electromagnetic, 11
electronic bulletin board system (BBS), 40
electronic commerce (e-commerce), 40
electronic mail (e-mail), 37
e-mail software, 30
eXtensible Markup Language (XML), 44
extranet, 22
Fiber Distributed Data Interface (FDDI), 33
fiber-optic cable, 10
file server, 18
file specification, 45
File Transfer Protocol (FTP), 38
firewall, 21
frequency range, 6

full-duplex transmission, 31
gateway, 28
geosynchronous orbit, 13
groupware, 30
half-duplex transmission, 31
home page, 43
host, 25
hub, 27
hybrid topology, 26
Hypertext Markup Language (HTML), 43
Hypertext Transfer Protocol (HTTP), 34
infrared technology, 16
interference, 9
Internet service provider (ISP), 41
Internet2, 51
intranet, 21
ISDN line, 11
local area network (LAN), 18
local ISP, 42
mail server, 34
medium, 4
metabrowser, 45
metropolitan area network (MAN), 20
microwave system, 11
multiplexer, 29
narrowband medium, 6
national ISP, 42
network architecture, 17
network topology, 23
node, 23
online course, 39
online service, 42
Open Systems Interconnection (OSI) model, 31
parallel transmission, 8
parity bit, 7
pathname, 45
peer-to-peer architecture, 18
pitch, 6
polling protocol, 33
POP server, 34
Post Office Protocol (POP), 34
print server, 18
productivity, 41
protocol, 30

public access network (PAN), 20
real time, 38
regional ISP, 42
repeater, 27
ring topology, 25
router, 27
search engine, 46
serial transmission, 8
server, 17
Simple Mail Transfer Protocol (SMTP), 34
simplex transmission, 31
star topology, 25
start bit, 32
stop bit, 32
synch bite, 33
synchronous transmission, 33
Systems Network Architecture (SNA), 33
telecommunications, 4
telecommuting, 41
T line, 11
T1 line, 11
T3 line, 11
token, 33
token ring protocol, 33
transceiver, 23
Transmission Control Protocol/Internet Protocol (TCP/IP), 34
transponder, 13
twisted-pair cable, 9
uniform resource locator (URL), 44
value added network (VAN), 20
virtual private network (VPN), 20
wide area network (WAN), 19
Wireless Application Protocol (WAP), 34
Wireless Markup Language (WML), 34

INTERNET

TUTORIAL 4

CREATING A WEB PAGE IN WORD

Creating a document that can be viewed from a Web site involves storing it in hypertext markup language (HTML). Software programs such as Microsoft FrontPage are dedicated to creating and managing Web sites. Most software applications released in the past few years include a conversion feature that will save the current document on the screen as a Web page. Prior to these conversion utilities, users had to know how to insert HTML "tags" into documents. These tags were the codes that instructed browsers how to display the text. Microsoft Word 2000 includes Web Page wizards, Web Layout view, and several Web formatting options for creating Web pages.

In this topic you will create a Web page in Microsoft Word using the Web Page wizard.

Steps

1. Click the Start button, point to Programs, and then click *Microsoft Word.*

If necessary, check with your instructor if the steps to open Microsoft Word 2000 on the computer you are using are different than those in step 1.

2. At the blank document screen, click File and then click New.

3. Click the Web Pages tab in the New dialog box and then double-click the Web Page Wizard icon in the list box.

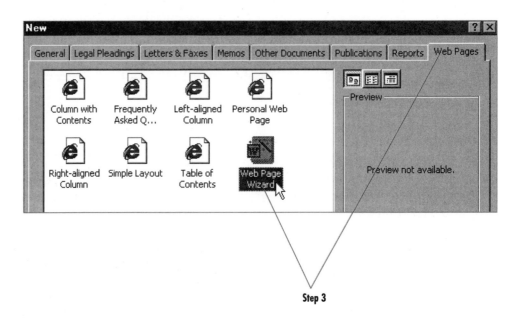

Step 3

CONNECTIVITY: Telecommunications, Networks, and the Internet

4. Click <u>N</u>ext> at the first Web Page Wizard dialog box that describes what the wizard will do.

5. Key **Student Name** (substitute your first and last names for Student Name) in the Web site <u>t</u>itle text box, and then press Tab to move to the Web site <u>l</u>ocation text box.

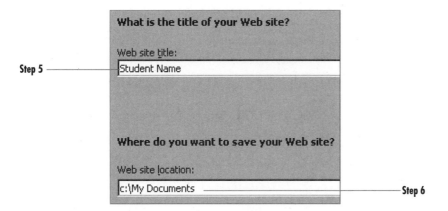

6. Key **C:\My Documents** or **A:** in the Web site <u>l</u>ocation text box and then click <u>N</u>ext>. Check with your instructor to see where you should save the Web page if you are not sure.

7. Click <u>N</u>ext> at the Navigation page in the Web Page Wizard.

When a Web site is created, the navigation links are usually displayed in a horizontal or vertical frame. Since our Web site is only one page, we do not need to be concerned with navigation links.

8. With *Blank Page 2* already selected in the <u>C</u>urrent pages in Web site list box in the Add Pages page of the Web Page Wizard, click <u>R</u>emove Page. Click *Personal Web Page*, click <u>R</u>emove Page, and then click <u>N</u>ext>.

This will leave only one page, *Blank Page 1,* in the Current pages in Web site list box.

Most ISPs include space on their Web server for clients to publish personal Web pages. If you want to publish to a Web server, check with your ISP for the correct address to key in the Web site location text box.

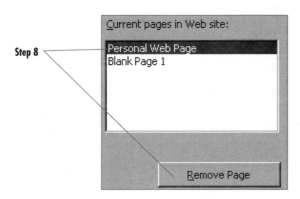

9. Click Next> at the Organize Pages page in the Web Page Wizard.

If there were multiple pages that we were building for the Web site, we would use the Move Up and Move Down buttons with a Web page selected to move the page to the desired position in the Web site.

10. Click Browse Themes in the Visual Theme page of the Web Page Wizard.

11. Scroll up or down the Choose a Theme list box and then click *Clearday*. (If *Clearday* is unavailable, choose another theme.)

A preview of the colors, fonts, bullet style, and horizontal line style for the Clearday theme displays in the Sample preview box. Microsoft Word includes several predefined themes that can be used to create Web pages with a professional appearance. Explore other themes in the dialog box by clicking the theme name and previewing it before continuing.

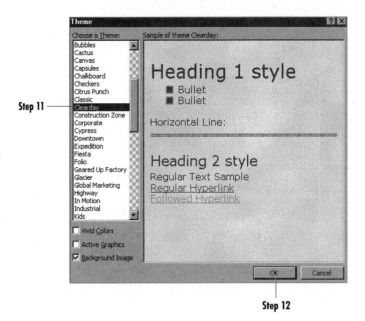

12. Click OK to accept the Clearday theme for the Web Page, and then click Next> in the Visual Theme page of the Web Page Wizard.

13. Click Finish at the last page in the Web Page Wizard. Click No when the message appears that your Web site contains only one Web page and asks if you still want to include navigation features.

In a few seconds, a Web page will appear in the Clearday theme with the text *This Web Page is Blank Page 1* at the top left of the document. Microsoft Word is automatically switched to Web Layout view. At this point you would start keying the content for your Web page. Notice the title bar displays the document name *Blank Page 1.htm*.

14. Select the text *This Web Page is Blank Page 1* and then press Delete.

15. Key your first and last names and press Enter. Key your student identification number and press Enter. Key your e-mail address and then press Enter twice.

16. Experiment with formatting options such as styles, center, bold, font colors, or bullets by selecting text and then clicking buttons on the Formatting toolbar.

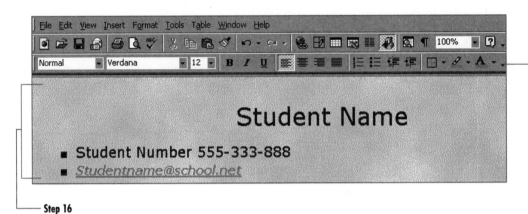

Select text and then click options from the Formatting toolbar to change the style, alignment, colors, or add bullets.

Step 16

17. Click the Save button on the toolbar, and then click <u>F</u>ile and E<u>x</u>it to close Microsoft Word.

Insert Clipart in a Web page in the same manner you would a Word document. Click the Insert Clip Art button on the Drawing toolbar, or click <u>I</u>nsert, point to <u>P</u>icture, and then click <u>C</u>lip Art.)

COMMUNICATING CLEARLY
Technology Terms: What do they mean?

a. router	f. simplex	k. communications satellite
b. protocol	g. HTML	l. electronic commerce
c. broadband medium	h. gateway	m. communications medium
d. electronic mail	i. search engine	n. telecommunications
e. star network	j. browser	o. network topology

1. A solar-powered electronic device that contains a number of small, specialized radios, called transponders, that receive signals from transmission stations on the ground, called earth stations.

2. A communications medium capable of carrying a large amount of data at fast speeds.

3. The way computers and peripherals are configured to form networks.

4. Modern business Internet technologies in which business information, products, services, and payments are exchanged between sellers and customers and between businesses.

5. A set of rules and procedures for exchanging information between network devices and computers.

6. An electronic device typically used with large networks, including the Internet, to ensure that messages are sent to their intended destinations.

7. Hardware and/or software that allows communications between two dissimilar networks.

8. A physical link that allows a computer in one location to be connected to a computer in another location.

9. A transmission method in which information can flow in only one direction.

10. A program that enables a user to find Web pages and to display the pages in the user's computer screen.

11. A program that allows a user to search for, locate, and retrieve information on the World Wide Web.

12. A language used to create most Web pages.

13. The combined use of computer hardware and communications software for sending and receiving information over communications media.

14. The process of sending, receiving, storing, and forwarding messages in electronic form over communications facilities.

15. A network in which multiple computers and peripheral devices are linked to a central, or host, computer.

Techno Literacy: How can new knowledge be used?

1. What kinds of networks are used in your local area?
   Investigate the types of networks that local organizations are using. Begin your research with your school. Then call or visit three businesses. Ask all parties for the same information: type of network, network topology, number of computers on the network, and the communications media (including whether wire or wireless) used. Write a summary explaining why each organization established its particular setup. What were their primary needs, and how does the network meet those needs?

2. How can networks improve efficiency?
   Choose a situation that you know well in which a number of people use personal computers. Possibilities include homes, businesses, school media centers, and dormitories. Make a detailed list of functions that people in such situations carry out using computers. Then explain how these functions might be performed more efficiently by means of networking.

3. Which ISP would (or currently *does*) best meet your needs for providing Internet access?
   Find out which ISPs are available to you. If you do not have access to a computer at home, assume you are researching this information for your school. For each ISP, identify the services offered and the cost, the equipment (type of server[s] used), and the software. Then create a chart in Excel or Word that compares the ISPs on those factors. Select the ISP that would best meet your needs and present the information to your class using a PowerPoint slide show.

4. Which Web sites are your favorites?
   Imagine that you have a new metabrowser, Octopus.com, installed on your computer and you are about to set up your favorite Web pages. Which views would you set up and which sites would you include in each view? Create a table that lists the views and the URLs to be placed in each view.

CONNECTING WITH CONCEPTS
Technology Processes: What's right with this picture?

What process is illustrated in the drawing below? Write a paragraph explaining how the process works, step by step.

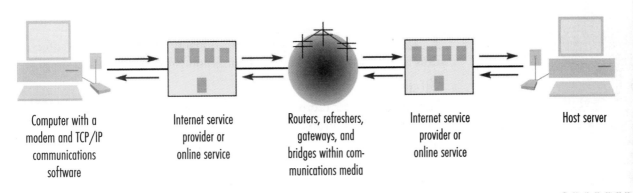

| Computer with a modem and TCP/IP communications software | Internet service provider or online service | Routers, refreshers, gateways, and bridges within communications media | Internet service provider or online service | Host server |

Key Principles: What's it all about?

1. _____ is a type of transmission signal in which information is sent in the form of continuous waves over a medium at a certain frequency range.

    a) analog   c) serial
    b) digital   d) bandwidth

2. The term _____ refers to the amount of data that can travel over an analog medium.

    a) synchronous   c) serial
    b) digital   d) bandwidth

3. _____ is an older type of communications medium originally developed for use by telephone networks.

    a) fiber-optic cable   c) twisted-pair cable
    b) satellite systems   d) coaxial cable

4. _____ is a type of wire that consists of an insulated center wire grounded by a shield of braided wire.

    a) fiber-optic cable   c) twisted-pair cable
    b) satellite systems   d) coaxial cable

5. _____ is an increasingly popular communications medium that requires no phone lines or cables.

    a) coaxial cable   c) twisted-pair cable
    b) cellular technology   d) fiber-optics

6. A _____ is an electronic device used in a local area network that links groups of computers to one another and allows computers to communicate with one another.

    a) gateway   c) repeater
    b) router   d) hub

7. Standards (rules) that govern the transfer of information among computers on a network and those using telecommunications are called

    a) parallel transmissions
    b) serial transmissions
    c) communications protocols
    d) Web languages

8. _____ is a type of directional protocol that allows information to be sent in both directions, but in only one direction at a time.

    a) half-duplex
    b) Hypertext Transfer Protocol
    c) Operating System Protocol
    d) transponder

9. The method of transmission in which blocks of bytes are wrapped in start and stop bytes is called

   a) asynchronous transmission
   b) synchronous transmission
   c) parallel transmission
   d) security transmission

10. Which of the following is a network architecture that uses a central, or host, computer through which all transmissions pass?

    a) client/server architecture
    b) peer-to-peer architecture
    c) computer architecture
    d) layout architecture

MINING DATA

Conduct Internet searches to find information described in the activities below. Write a brief report that summarizes your research results. Be sure to document your sources, using MLA format.

1. Data mining is a technology that businesses use to glean new information from the data stored in their databases. The technology uses relational tables similar to the way they are used in relational databases. For example, an auto dealership could use data mining to identify past customers who paid their car loans on time and then send those customers new product offerings. A comparable tool called *text mining* is being developed by large companies such as IBM and SAS to facilitate the analysis of thousands of textual documents that may be stored on a company's file server. Using the search techniques you have learned throughout the Internet tutorials in this text, locate information that explains text mining. Write a summary of what it is and how it could be used. Try IBM's Web site as a first source: www.ibm.com.

2. In the future, you can expect to do more and more of your Web browsing and other communications activities via a wireless handheld computer. Experts predict that business workers will probably be able to access their company's productivity applications from any location in the world by using a Web top on a Web appliance. Using advanced Internet search techniques, locate Web sites that define and discuss Web tops and Web appliances. Write a one-page report explaining your findings. What advantages do these new technologies offer?

3. How to provide increased bandwidth for Internet transmissions in the fastest and most economical way is an urgent issue facing telecommunications companies. Research this issue to define the problem, identify possible obstacles, and propose viable solutions.

CHAPTER 4

CONNECTIVITY: Telecommunications, Networks, and the Internet • D-63

MANAGING CHANGE

THINGS THAT THINK

1. Distributed computing is a concept that involves tapping the processing power of thousands of PCs attached to the Internet to perform complex calculations that otherwise would require a supercomputer. One such project in the Netherlands runs computer simulations of how immune systems react to flu infections and vaccinations. Derrick Smith, a computer scientist leading the project, has invited Internet users with a connection that's always on to download the program and thus join in the research effort. The program launches its work whenever the computer is idle, activating a screen saver that tracks the number of tasks completed on the computer daily. This report is then sent to Smith. What other kinds of problems could be solved using distributed computing? Create a list and prioritize the projects.

2. A new protocol called the *common names resolution protocol (CNRP)* was released by a task force of the Internet Society for beta testing in the fall of 2000. This technology allows users to access Internet sites using brief names that are easy to remember instead of the sometimes lengthy URLs currently required. This development will be particularly helpful for users of hand-held computers, which have small display screens. One major hurdle remains before the software can be completed: how to deal with international domain names in various languages. Can you think of ways to overcome the language barrier problem?

PREDICTING NEXT STEPS

Review the timeline below, which summarizes major benchmarks in the development of the Internet. Based on your knowledge and any research you might conduct, predict the next important steps in the life of the Internet. Think of three changes that may occur over the next 10 years.

1957	With the Soviet Union's launch of *Sputnik,* the United States forms the Advanced Research Projects Agency (ARPA)
1966	ARPA introduces its plan for a national network
1973	First international connections are made to the ARPAnet
1986	NSFNET is created
1991	World Wide Web is launched
1999	First full-service, Internet-only bank is opened

SOLVING PROBLEMS

In groups or individually, brainstorm possible solutions to the issues presented.

1. The year 2000 saw several copyright infringement lawsuits brought against Web sites such as Napster.com and MP3.com, which provided for the downloading of music free of charge. Where do you stand on this issue? Research current copyright law. Then develop your own guidelines about the extent to which copyrighted material can be downloaded from the Web. Under what circumstances, if any, should the downloading of copyrighted content be allowed?

2. Since the Internet and e-mail are used so frequently in the workplace, many companies worry that their employees use these services for nonbusiness-related activities. How can a company ensure the productivity and good attitude of workers while maintaining their privacy?

EXAMINING ETHICAL ISSUES

Access the Computer Concepts Resource Center at EMC/Paradigm's Web site (www.emcp.com/college_division/ electronic_resource_center) and go to Computers: Exploring Concepts, then to Student Resources, then to the Ethical Issues page. Complete the activity for chapter 4.

ANSWERS TO TECHNOLOGY TERMS AND KEY PRINCIPLES QUESTIONS

Technology Terms: 1 – k; 2 – c; 3 – o; 4 – l; 5 – b; 6 – a; 7 – h 8 – m; 9 – f; 10 – j; 11 – i; 12 – g; 13 – n; 14 – d

Key Principles: 1 – a; 2 – d; 3 – c; 4 – c; 5 – b; 6 – d; 7 – c; 8 – a; 9 – a; 10 – a

address A specific location in memory where an instruction or data is stored. The computer assigns an address to each location so the instruction or data can be quickly located and retrieved when needed

Advanced Research Projects Agency (ARPA) A government agency created by President Eisenhower to fund and coordinate defense-related research

American Standard Code for Information Interchange (ASCII) A coding scheme used on most computers, including personal computers, to represent data. ASCII makes it possible for data in this form to be transferred from one computer to another computer.

analog Continuous, not broken into bits; said of telephone signals, sound waves, temperatures, and all other signals that are not discrete

applet A small application program, generally one created using the Java programming language, that performs specific functions; applets are used to extend the capabilities of Web pages

application service provider (ASP) A private company that leases applications software to customers over the Internet

application software Programs that enable a user to perform specific tasks. Examples of application software include word processors, database programs, spreadsheets, and desktop publishing.

arithmetic/logic unit (ALU) The part of the CPU that carries out the instructions and performs the actual arithmetic and logical operations on the data. Arithmetic operations the ALU can perform are addition, subtraction, multiplication, and division. The ALU can also compare data items.

ARPANet A wide area network (WAN) created in 1969 that enabled research institutes and universities engaged in government research projects to collaborate by sharing information

artificial intelligence The science of using computers to simulate intelligent mental activities or physical behaviors such as problem solving, learning, and natural language processing

asynchronous transmission A data transmission method in which control bits surround each byte of data. An extra bit is added at the front of the character and another bit at the end. The front bit, called a start bit, signals the beginning of a character. The bit at the end, called a stop bit, signals the end of that character. There is also the error checking bit called a parity bit.

audio input The process of entering (recording) speech, music, and/or sound effects into a computer

backward compatibility Being able to work with earlier versions of a program or earlier models of computers

bandwidth The amount of data that can travel over an analog medium

bar code reader An electronic device that uses photo technology to "read" the lines in a bar code. The lines and spaces contain symbols that the computer translates into information.

beta A prerelease version of a piece of software distributed so that users can test it to evaluate features and to identify any existing bugs

binary system A number system with a base of 2. Unlike the familiar base 10 decimal system, the binary system uses only two numbers (0 and 1)

BIOS (basic input/output system) A program that boots (starts) a computer when it is turned on and controls communications with the keyboard, disk drives, and other components

biotechnology The application of computer processing or technical processes to the science of living organisms

bit (binary digit) The smallest unit of data a computer can understand and act on

bitmap A storage technique in which scanned text or a photo is stored as a matrix of rows and columns of dots

bits per second (bps) The number of bits (the fundamental digital unit, which can be either a 0 or a 1) that can be transmitted in a second's time; the usual measure of bandwidth

bridge Hardware and/or software that allows for communication between two networks that are *similar*

broadband medium A communications medium capable of carrying a large amount of data at fast speeds

browser A software application that enables a person to access sites on the World Wide Web that may include an e-mail or newsgroup program

buffer A temporary storage place to which part of data to be displayed, printed, or transmitted is written

bus A collection of tiny wires through which data, in the form of "0s" and "1s," is transmitted from one part of the computer to another

bus bandwidth A term that refers to the amount of data (as 0s and 1s) that can travel along a bus (a tiny collection of wires) from one part of the computer to another

bus topology A type of network topology in which all computers are linked by means of a single line of cable, called a bus, with two endpoints. All communications travel the length of the bus. As they pass, each computer checks to see if it is the assigned destination point.

button A graphical element that, when selected, causes a particular action to occur. For example, clicking on the Windows Start button in the lower left corner of the screen displays a menu of options from which you can choose. When a button is selected, the button may appear as though it has been pressed by a user's finger.

byte A combination of eight bits (0's and 1's) that represents a letter of the alphabet, a number, or a special character inside a computer. There are enough different combinations of bits (0's and 1's) in an eight-bit byte to represent 256 different characters.

cable modem A special type of modem that provides fast transmission speeds

cache memory A dedicated holding area in RAM in which the data and instructions most recently called from RAM by the processor are temporarily stored

carpal tunnel syndrome The condition of weakness, pain, or numbness resulting from pressure on the median nerve in the wrist; the syndrome is associated with repetitive motion, such as typing or using the mouse

CD-R (compact disk, recordable) A disk technology that allows a user to write data onto a compact disk. The disk can be written on only once, cannot be erased, but can be read from an unlimited number of times.

CD-ROM (compact disk, read-only memory) A disk technology in which data is permanently recorded on an optical disk and can be read many times, but the data cannot be changed

CD-RW (compact disk, rewritable) A newer type of optical disk storage technology that uses an erasable disk on which a user can write multiple times

cell In a spreadsheet or database grid, the intersection of one row and one column or of one field and one record, into which text, numbers, formulas, links, or other elements may be entered

cellular technology An increasingly popular technology that allows people to communicate without having to be connected via wired phone lines or cables. Using cellular technologies, communication can occur between people almost anywhere in the world

central processing unit (CPU) The part of a computer that interprets and carries out instructions that operate the computer and manages the computer's devices and resources. The CPU consists of components, each of which performs specific functions.

chart A visual representation of data that often makes the data easier to read and understand. A chart displays data in graphical rather than numerical form.

chat room (chat group) An online area, provided by an online service or an Internet host, where people can meet, exchange ideas and information, and interact socially

check box A box containing multiple options you can turn on or off. You can activate a particular option in the box by clicking on the option. When an option is activated, a check mark appears beside the option. Unlike option buttons where you can select only one option, check boxes allow you to choose multiple options.

chip A thin wafer of silicon containing electronic circuitry that performs various functions, such as mathematical calculations, storage, or controlling computer devices

client/server architecture A type of network architecture in which a personal computer, workstation, or terminal (called a *client*) is used to send information or a request to another computer (called a *server*) which then relays the information back to the user's client computer, or to another computer (another *client*)

clock cycle The time between two ticks of a computer's system clock. A typical personal computer goes through millions or even billions of clock cycles per second.

clock speed The pace of the microprocessor's internal clock, which determines how fast operations are processed within the CPU; clock speed is measured in megahertz (MHz)

cluster A group of two or more sectors on a disk which is the smallest unit of storage space used to store data

coaxial cable A type of wire that consists of an insulated center wire and grounded by a shield of braided wire

cold boot Process of starting a computer by turning on the unit's power switch

command-line interface A user interface, like the one created by the DOS operating system that makes use of typed commands

communications medium A medium, such a telephone line, used for carrying data or information between computers and networks

communications satellite A solar-powered electronic device that contains a number of small, specialized radios called *transponders* that receive signals from transmission stations on the ground called earth stations, amplifies the signals, and then transmits the signals to the appropriate locations

communications software Software that allows your properly equipped computer to communicate with other similarly equipped computers. You can send and receive electronic messages, visit various Web sites, locate and retrieve information stored on other com-

puters, electronically transmit large files, and much more. For example, thousands of businesses send daily reports to their home offices.

compiler A type of language-translating software that translates an entire program into machine language before the program will run. Each language has its own unique compiler.

computer An electronic device capable of interpreting and executing program instructions and data and performing the required operations to produce the desired results

computer programmer Person whose profession is to write sets of coded instructions that direct a computer's operations

computer virus A bit of programming code, created as a prank or as a malicious action, that secretly affects other programs and causes unintended consequences

concentrator A communications device that enables data to be transmitted from only one device at a time over a communications medium

control unit The part of the CPU that directs and coordinates the overall operation of the computer system. It acts as a traffic officer, signaling to other parts of the computer system what they are to do. It interprets each program instruction in a program, and then initiates the action needed to carry out the instruction.

conversion speech biometrics A technology developed by IBM capable of recognizing a person's voice even though the database may not include the exact words spoken

coprocessor A special type of dedicated processor designed to perform certain kinds of processing, such as processing large amounts of numerical data

copyright The legal protection of an individual's or business's original work, such as applications software, music, and books, that prohibits others from duplicating or illegally using such work or products

creating The development of a document, such as a letter or memo, by entering text and numbers, inserting graphical images, and performing other actions using one or more input devices, such as a keyboard or mouse

cross-platform OS An operating system capable of being used on more than one type of computer

D

data Raw, unprocessed information

data register A reserved location in main memory for storing data being processed or being used in a specific processing application

database A computer application in which data is organized and stored in a way that allows for specific data to be accessed, retrieved, and used

database management system (DBMS) Software that allows a user to create and manage a computerized database, and to create reports from stored data

decoding The activity of translating or determining the meaning of coded instructions

default option An option that has been programmed into a program by the software publisher under the assumption that that option is the one most likely to be chosen

desktop computer A personal computer system designed to fit on the top of a desk

desktop publishing (DTP) A computer application that allows you to use your PC and DTP software to create and produce impressive documents that include a combination of text, graphics, photographs, and objects in a variety of colors

desktop publishing (DTP) software A type of software that enables a user to produce documents that closely resemble those done by printing companies

desktop The primary screen created by a graphical user interface; in Windows 95, this screen contains, among other items, a menu bar, a taskbar, the Start button and its menus, a recycle bin, and an icon called "My Computer"

dialog box A common type of graphical user interface feature that displays a rectangular box that provides information to a user and/or requests information from a user. Usually, a dialog box is displayed temporarily and disappears once the user has entered the requested information.

dial-up access A method for accessing the Internet in which a user can connect to the Internet using a computer and a modem to dial into an ISP or online service over a standard telephone line

digital Composed of discrete bits—1s and 0s—understood by computers

digital camera A type of camera that record and store images, including people, scenery, documents, and products in a digitized form that can be entered into and stored by a computer

Digital Millenium Copyright Act of 1998 A law that generally prohibits people from taking action to break down software encryption programs and other safeguards that copyright holders have established to control access to their works, including DVDs, software, and digitized books and music

digitizing pen An electronic pen device, resembling a standard writing pen, used with a drawing tablet to simulate drawing on paper

disk drive A storage device that houses a secondary storage medium such as a floppy or hard disk

disk pack A vertically aligned group of hard disks mounted inside a disk drive on a large computer system. When activated, electromagnetic read/write heads record information and/or read stored data by moving inward and outward between the disks.

disk server A type of server that enables users to access programs, data, and other resources just as easily as if the resources were stored on their individual user computers

display The screen, or monitor, of a personal computer

display goggles A type of monitor presently used for computer games that may become a standard feature of some of the new mobile computer devices such as belt-top computers or other systems worn on the body

display window A rectangular area of the screen used to display a program, data, or information

distance learning The electronic transfer of information from a college or publisher's host computer system to a student's computer at a remote site and the transmission of required responses from the student's computer to the host computer system. A course presented in this manner is called an *online course*.

DNA sequence An arrangement of DNA (deoxyribonucleic acid) molecules that make up the human cell

docking station A laptop computer accessory that provides additional ports plus (typically) a charger for the laptop's battery, extra disk drives, and other peripherals

dot-matrix printer An impact printer that forms and prints characters in a manner similar to the way numbers appear on a football scoreboard

dots per inch (dpi) A measurement in which resolution (text and image quality) is measured and expressed as the number of dots occupying one square inch

download To transmit data, such as a digitized text file, sound, or picture, from a remote site to one's own computer via a network

drawing tablet A tablet with wires under the surface that, when used with a digitizing pen, allows the user to create and capture drawings that can be entered and stored on a computer

driver A small program that enables the computer to communicate with devices connected to it, such as a keyboard or a monitor

dumb scanner A scanner that can only capture and input a scanned image. Once entered into a computer, the image cannot be edited or altered

dumb terminal A terminal that has no processor of its own and that is used for input and output, often to and from a mainframe or minicomputer

DVD-ROM (digital video disk-ROM) An extremely high capacity disk capable of holding several gigabytes of data, such as a movie or the entire contents of a telephone book listing every resident in the United States.

editing The process of altering the content of an existing document. You are editing a document anytime you insert, delete, cut, copy and paste items into a document. A document can be edited until the user is satisfied with the content of the final document.

electronic bulletin board system (BBS) An Internet application in which an electronically stored list of messages that can be accessed and read by anyone having access to the bulletin board. A user having access can post messages, read existing messages, or delete messages

electronic commerce (e-commerce) Refers to modern business Internet technologies in which business information, products, services, and payments are exchanged between sellers and customers and between businesses

electronic mail (e-mail) A text, voice, or video message sent or received remotely, over a computer network or the system by which such a message is sent

electronic spreadsheet A productivity program that provides a user with a means of organizing, calculating, and presenting financial, statistical, and other numeric information. Spreadsheets are used to manipulate numbers electronically instead of using a pencil and paper.

e-mail software Software that allows a user to create, send, receive, print, store, forward, and delete e-mail messages and to attach files to messages being sent

executing The CPU process of performing an operation specified in a program instruction

execution time (E-time) The time required for the arithmetic/logic unit to decode and execute an instruction

expansion board (add-on board or add-in board) An electronic circuit board that can be inserted onto the motherboard inside a computer to add new capa-bilities to a computer. Examples include sound boards, video boards, graphics boards, and boards that allow you to capture and enter photos into your computer.

expansion slot An opening in a computer motherboard where an expansion board can be inserted (installed)

Extended Binary Coded Decimal Interchange Code (EBCDIC) A coding scheme used mainly on mainframe computers

eXtensible Markup Language (XML) A new and improved Web language that not only defines the content of a Web page but also describes how the content looks when the page is displayed on a computer screen

extranet A network that makes certain kinds of information available to users within the organization and other kinds of information available to outsiders, such as companies doing business with the organization

fetching The CPU process of retrieving instructions or data from memory for execution

Fiber Distributed Data Interface (FDDI) A type of network software for ring networks dispersed over a large area and connected by fiber optic cables is called Fiber Distributed Data Interface (FDDI). The software links the dispersed networks together using a protocol that passes a token over long distances.

fiber-optic cable A cable consisting of optical fibers that allows data to be transmitted through tiny hair-like glass fibers as light signals

field In a table created by a database management system application, a column into which one kind of information about an entity, such as name or address, is entered

file compression program A utility program that greatly reduces the size of a file, and thus, the space needed to store the file and the time that it takes to transfer the file over the Internet

file manager An operating system function that performs basic file management functions, including keeping track of used and unused disk storage space and allowing a user to view stored files and to format, copy, rename, delete, and sort stored files

file server A special type of computer that allows other computers to share its resources

File Transfer Protocol (FTP) A protocol that enables a user can send and receive large files, such as reports, over the Internet

firewall Special hardware and/or software that prevents or restricts access to, or from, a network.

Firewalls are frequently used to prevent unauthorized Internet users from accessing a network connected to the Internet

flat-panel display A type of display that uses a technology that allows display units to be smaller, thinner, and lighter so they can be used with small computers, such as notebook computers, personal digital assistants (PDAs), and other devices

floppy disk (diskette or **disk)** A secondary storage medium consisting of a thin, circular mylar wafer, sandwiched between two sheets of cleaning tissue inside a rigid plastic case

floppy disk drive A secondary storage device capable of recording information to, and reading information from, a small disk placed inside the device

foot mouse A mouse that allows a user with carpal tunnel syndrome or other hand or wrist injuries to use a computer

footer In word processing, a line or more of repeated text such as a page number and a document's title that appears at the bottom of the document's pages

form In a database management system, a document used for entering information to be stored in one or more linked records

format (Noun) The appearance of a document, for example, page margins, the spacing between lines, and text alignment between the margins; (verb) to change the appearance of a document

formatting The procedure of preparing a disk for use during which the disk surface is arranged into tracks, sectors, and clusters

formula Any mathematical equation or an equation entered into a cell in a spreadsheet or database

freeware A computer program that is provided free to users by its creator but for which the creator usually retains the copyright

full-duplex transmission The simultaneous transmission of information of data in both directions at the same time

gateway Hardware and/or software that allows communication between *dissimilar* networks

gigabyte Unit of memory equal to 1,073,741,824 bytes

gigahertz A frequency of one billion times a second

grammar checker A part of a program or a stand-alone application that automatically searches for errors in grammar, usage, capitalization, or punctuation and suggests correct alternatives

graphical user interface (GUI) A computer interface that enables a user to control the computer and launch commands by pointing and clicking at graphical objects such as windows, icons, and menu items

graphics Still or moving images, including photos, illustrations, and symbols

graphics card An add-on card that enables a computer to capture and display graphical images

graphics tablet A flat tablet used together with a penlike stylus or a crosshair cursor. To capture an image, the user grasps a stylus or crosshair cursor and traces an image or drawing placed on the tablet surface.

groupware Communications software that allows groups of people on a network to share information and to collaborate on various projects, such as designing a new product or preparing employee manuals

half-duplex transmission A transmission method in which transmissions can flow in both directions but not at the same time

handheld computer A personal computer small enough to fit into a person's hand

handheld scanner A small scanner used for scanning small or curved areas

hard copy A permanent version of output, such as a letter printed on paper

hard disk A secondary storage medium consisting of one or more rigid metal platters (disks) mounted on a metal shaft and sealed in a container, called a disk drive, that contains an access mechanism used to write and read data

hard disk drive A device for reading and writing to the magnetic storage medium known as a hard disk

hardware All physical components that comprise the system unit and other devices connected to it, such as a keyboard or monitor. These connected devices are collectively referred to as *peripheral devices* because they are outside, or peripheral to, the computer itself.

header In word processing, a line or more of repeated text such as a page number and a document's title that appears at the top of the document's pages

hertz A unit of measure that refers to the number of cycles per second

High-Capacity FD (HiFD) disk drive A high capacity floppy disk capable of holding large amounts of data

high-level language An English-like computer language used for writing application programs

home page The first page usually displayed when a user accesses a Web site. A home page often contains links to other pages at that site or to other Web sites

hub An electronic device used in a local area network that links groups of computers to one another and allows computers to communicate with one another. A hub coordinates the traffic of messages being sent and received by computers connected to the network.

hybrid topology A combination of networks having different topologies, such as a star network and a ring network

Hypertext Markup Language (HTML) A set of codes used to create pages for the World Wide Web; codes specify typefaces, images, and links within text

Hypertext Transfer Protocol (HTTP) The communications standard used to transfer documents on the World Wide Web

IBM OS/2 A graphical user interface operating system developed by IBM that can run application programs native to it and also application programs written for DOS and Windows systems

icon A graphic symbol that represents a software program, a command, or a feature

impact printer A printer that prints much like a typewriter, by striking an inked ribbon against the paper

information Data that has been processed and so rendered usable or intelligible

information processing cycle A cycle during which information is entered, processed, outputted, and/or stored by a computer

infrared A type of radiation similar to light with a wavelength outside the visible spectrum; used in TV remote controls and in wireless handheld computers to send data

infrared technology A communications technology that provides for wireless links between PCs and other computing devices, such as keyboards and printers

ink-jet printer A nonimpact printer that forms images by spraying thousands of tiny droplets of electrically charged ink onto a page. The printed images are in dot-matrix format, but of a higher quality than images printed by dot-matrix printers.

input Data that is read into a computer or other device or the act of reading in such data

input device Any hardware component that enables a computer user to enter data and programs into a computer system. Keyboards, point-and-click devices, and scanners are among the more popular input devices, and a desktop or laptop computer system may include one or more input devices.

instruction register A memory location (register) where instructions being used for processing are stored

instruction time (I-time) The amount of time required to fetch an instruction from a register

intelligent scanner A scanner that uses optical character recognition (OCR) software that allows a captured image to be manipulated (edited or altered) with a word processor or other application program

interface The connection between a user and software, between two hardware devices, or between two applications

Internet (Net) A worldwide network of computers linked together via communications software and media for the purpose of sharing information. It is the largest and best-known network in the world.

Internet service provider (ISP) An organization that has a permanent connection to the Internet and provides temporary access to individuals and others for free or for a fee

Internet2 A revolutionary new type of Internet currently being planned and developed that, when fully operational, will enable large research universities in the U.S. to collaborate and share huge amounts of complex scientific information at amazing speeds

interpreter A type of language-translating software that reads, translates, and executes one instruction at a time

intranet A network normally belonging to a large business or organization that is accessible only by the business or organization's members, employees, or other authorized users

ISDN line A special digital telephone line that can be used to dial into the Internet and transmit and receive information at very high speeds, ranging from 64 kbps (64,000 bits per second) to 128 kbps. An ISDN line requires the use of a special ISDN modem.

Java A third-generation programming language used to write full-scale applications and small applications, known as applets, for use on the World Wide Web

GLOSSARY

Jaz® cartridge A removable hard disk manufactured by Iomega Corporation that offers 1GB of storage

joystick An input device (named after the control lever used to fly older fighter planes) consisting of a small box that contains a vertical lever that, when pushed in a certain direction, moves the graphics cursor correspondingly on the screen. It is often used for computer games.

kerning In word processing and page layout programs, the space between the letters of a word

keyboard An electronically controlled hardware component used to enter alphanumeric data (letters, numbers, and special characters). The keys on most keyboards are arranged similarly to those on a typewriter.

kilobyte Unit of memory equal to 1,024 bytes

language translator A special type of program needed to translate (convert) high-level language programs into machine-language programs so they can be executed by the computer

laptop computer A computer small enough to be placed on a lap or carried by its user from place to place

laser printer A nonimpact printer that produces output of exceptional quality using a technology similar to that of photocopy machines

leading In word processing and page layout programs, the space between lines of type

Linux An operating system based on AT&T's UNIX and one of the newest operating systems developed by a Finnish programmer named Linus Torvalds. Unlike most other operating systems, the original version is a nonproprietary operating system and is available for free to the public.

local area network (LAN) A computer network physically confined to a relatively small geographical area, such as a single building or a college campus

local ISP An Internet service provider that typically provides users with one or more telephone numbers they can use to dial-up the ISP's network computer

machine cycle A cycle used by a computer during which four basic operations are performed. These operations are (1) fetching an instruction, (2) decoding the instruction, (3) executing the instruction, and (4) storing the result.

machine language A program consists entirely of zeroes and ones that a computer can understand and execute quickly

Macintosh OS The first profitable graphical user interface released with Apple's Macintosh computers in 1984. With its impressive graphics and ease of use, it quickly became the model for other GUIs.

macro A sequence of instructions designed to accomplish a specific task and generally executed by issuing a single command

magnetic storage device A storage device that works by applying electrical charges to iron filings on magnetic storage media, orienting each filing in one direction or another to represent a "0" or a "1." Data are stored and retrieved, or accessed, either sequentially or directly.

magnetic tape storage A type of secondary storage for large computer systems that uses removable reels of magnetic tape. The tape contains tracks that extend the full length of the tape. Each track contains metallic particles that are magnetized, or not magnetized, to represent 0 and 1 bits.

mail server A computer used to facilitate the sending and receiving of electronic mail messages

main memory Addressable storage locations directly controlled by the central processing unit (CPU) used to store programs while they are being executed and data while it is being processed

mainframe computer A large, powerful, expensive computer system capable of accommodating hundreds of users doing different computing tasks

math coprocessor A special type of coprocessor dedicated to processing numerical data

matrix A rectangular arrangement of elements into rows and columns

megabyte Unit of memory equal to 1,048,576 bytes

megahertz Millions of cycles per second, a unit used for measuring clock speed in computers

memory A place for storage, temporary or permanent, of data, programs, or instructions

menu An on-screen set of options from which a user can make selections by clicking on an option using a mouse or by typing one or more keystrokes. When a selection is made the desired action, such as saving a document, occurs. Many software programs display a menu bar, also called main menu, at the top or side of the screen when the program is activated.

menu bar A horizontal or vertical bar that shows the highest-level command options

metabrowser A Web browser that allows the user to put all of her favorite sites onto one page and thus reduce the number of clicks it takes to check those favorite sites daily

metropolitan area network (MAN) A wide-area network limited to a specific geographical area, such as a city or town

microprocessor (processor or CPU [central processing unit]) chip A single integrated circuit chip containing millions of electrical transistors, packed onto a surface smaller than a postage stamp, that processes data in a computer.

microwave system A communications technology that transmits data in the form of high-frequency radio signals through the atmosphere from one microwave station to another microwave station, or from a microwave station to a satellite and then back to earth to another microwave station

minicomputer A large and powerful computer capable of accommodating hundreds of users at the same time. Users can access a minicomputer by using a terminal or a personal computer. A *terminal* contains only a monitor and keyboard, but no processing capability of its own. Because it must rely on the processing power of a minicomputer, these terminals are often referred to as *dumb terminals*. It can also function as a server in a network environment.

modem A hardware device that translates signals from digital to analog and from analog to digital; making it possible for digital computers to communicate over analog telephone lines

molecular storage A type of storage in which programs and data are represented by tiny molecules

monitor The screen, or display, on which computer output appears

Moore's law Not really a law, but rather the prediction that the number of transistors that can be packed on a chip will double every two years while the price decreases by half

motherboard The main circuit board inside a personal computer to which other circuit boards can be connected. It contains electrical pathways, called traces, etched onto it that allows data to move from one component to another.

mouse An input device that, when moved about on a flat surface, causes a pointer on the screen to move in the same direction

mouse pad A rubberized pad with a smooth fabric surface that facilitates use of a mouse

mouse pointer A type of cursor resembling a small on-screen arrow, movements of which correspond to movements made with a mouse

multiplexer An electronic device that increases the efficiency of a network system by allowing eight, 16, 32, or more low-speed devices to share simultaneously a single high-speed communications medium

multitasking The ability of an operating system to run more than one software program at a time

multiuser OS An operating system designed for use with large computer systems and capable of handling several users at the same time

narrowband medium A communications medium capable of carrying a smaller amount of data at slow speeds

National ISP A large Internet service provider that provides telephone numbers in most major cities. Their larger size than local ISPs often allows them to provide more services and technical support for users than local ISPs.

National Science Foundation Network (NSFnet) A wide area network developed to assume the civilian functions of the U.S. Department of Defense's ARPANet in case of nuclear attack

natural-language processing (NLP) A type of speech recognition software being developed that will, when perfected, enable a computer system to understand any person's language

network A group of two or more computers, software, and other devices that are connected by means of one or more communications media

network architecture The way a network is designed and built, just as an architect might design a new building or other facility

network topology The way computers and peripherals are configured to form networks

neural network An artificial intelligence technology that mimics the way nerve cells are connected in the human brain. Information is supplied to the neural network to train it to recognize certain patterns, resulting in a program capable of making predictions, such as weather forecasts and fluctuations of stock values.

nonimpact printer A printer that uses electricity, heat, laser technology, or photographic techniques to produce output

nonvolatile memory A type of computer memory specifically designed to hold information, even when the power is switched off

notebook computer A lightweight portable computer that can fit inside a briefcase

object linking and embedding (OLE) A feature of Windows operating systems and applications that allows material from one application to be ported into a document created in another application and linked in such a way that when the material is updated in the originating application, it is automatically updated in the application into which it has been ported

online Connected to a network such as the Internet

online course A course of study, such as English or psychology, offered over the Internet by some colleges and textbook publishers

online service A business that provides users with Internet access, and also offers special features such as online news, weather reports, financial news, and sporting news

on-screen desktop An on-screen work area on which graphical elements such as icons, buttons, windows, links, and dialog boxes are displayed. Using a desktop containing these elements is easier for many users because it allows them to easily make selections and to interact with the computer.

Open Systems Interconnection (ISO) model A set of communications protocols defined by the International Standards Organization based in Geneva, Switzerland, and adopted by the United Nation

open-source software system Sets of rules and standards for developing application programs that will run on any type of computer

operating system A type of software that creates a user interface and supports the workings of computer devices and software programs that perform specific jobs

optical character recognition (OCR) Software that allows a captured image to be manipulated (edited or altered) with a word processor or other application program

optical disk A secondary storage medium on which data is recorded and read by two lasers: a high-density laser that records data by burning tiny indentations, or pits, onto the disk surface, and a low-intensity laser that reads stored data from the disk into the computer. An optical disk can store several gigabytes of data.

optical mouse A type of mouse that contains no mouse ball and instead uses a light-based sensor to track movement. This mouse can be moved around on nearly any smooth surface, except glass, and thus no mouse pad is required.

optical scanner (scanner) A light-sensing electronic device that can read and capture printed text and images, such as photographs and drawings, and convert them into a digital form a computer can understand. Once scanned, the text or image can be displayed on the screen, edited, printed, stored on a disk, inserted into another document, or sent as an attachment to an e-mail message.

option button A type of button used with a graphical user interface and resembling buttons on a standard radio that enables you to choose from among a set of options

output Information that is written or displayed as a result of computer processing or the act of writing or displaying such data

packet Data that has been divided into small blocks and sent over the Internet to a specific destination where the blocks are reassembled

page scanner A type of scanner, resembling a table-top copy machine, on which pages being scanned (copied) are either laid face down on the scanner's glass surface or fed through the scanner by means of a side-feed device

Palm OS An operating system produced by Palm, Incorporated for use with the company's handheld personal digital assistants (PDAs)

palmtop computer A computer small enough to fit into a pocket

parallel port A slot (opening) for connecting printers, scanners, and other devices. A parallel port can transmit data eight bits at a time

parallel transmission A transmission method in which a group of 8 bits representing a single byte (plus one bit called a *parity bit*) are transmitted at the same time over separate paths

parity bit An extra bit added to a byte, character, or word to ensure that there is always either a predetermined even number of bits or an odd number of bits. If data should be lost, errors can be identified by checking the number of bits.

PC Card A type of expansion board developed specifically for the smaller PCs. A PC card plugs into the side of a notebook or portable computer. Most are about the size of a credit card, only thicker, and can be unplugged and removed when no longer needed.

peer-to-peer architecture A network design in which each PC or workstation comprising the network has equivalent capabilities and responsibilities

pen computer A computer equipped with pattern recognition circuitry so that it can recognize human handwriting as a form of data input

performance monitor A set of operating system instructions that monitor the computer system's overall performance

peripheral device A device, such as a printer or disk drive, connected to and controlled by a computer but external to the computer's central processing unit (CPU)

personal computer A single-user computer capable of performing its own input, processing, output, and storage

personal digital assistant (PDA) A handheld, wireless computer, also known as a handheld PC or HPC, used for such purposes as storing schedules, calendars, and telephone numbers and for sending e-mail or connecting to the Internet

pixel The smallest picture element that a computer monitor or other device can display and from which graphic images are built

platform Compatible computers from one or more manufacturers; the two popular platforms for personal computers are PCs and Macintoshes

plotter A hard-copy output device used to output special kinds of hard copy, including architectural drawings, charts, maps, diagrams, and other images

polling protocol A network protocol that continually polls all workstations to determine if there are messages to be sent or received by each workstation

POP server A special type of server that holds e-mail messages until they are accessed and read by recipients of the messages

port A plug-in slot on a computer to which you can connect a device, such as a printer or, in the case of accessing the Internet, a telephone line

Post Office Protocol (POP) A protocol in the recipient's communications software that allows a recipient to retrieve an e-mail message.

power-on self test (POST) A chip containing instructions that check the physical components of the computer system to make certain they are working properly when the computer is turned on

presentation graphics software An application program that allows you to create a computerized presentation that includes a series of documents called slides

print server A type of server that allows multiple users to share the same printer

print spooler A program within an operating system that increases a computer's efficiency by placing a document to be printed in memory buffers where they reside until a printer is ready to print it

print spooling A printing technique in which a document to be printed is placed in a buffer instead of being sent to the printer. The document is held in the buffer until the printer is ready to print it, thereby enabling the printer to print at its own speed. When a document is placed in a buffer, the CPU is free to begin executing the next instruction or carry out the next command by the user.

printer The most common type of hard-copy output device that produces output in a permanent form

printing The action of producing a document or file in hard-copy form on paper or plastic film

processor The brain of the computer, consisting of the arithmetic logic unit and the control unit

productivity (application) software A term that refers to programs that allow users to perform specific tasks, such as creating documents, preparing income tax returns, managing finances, sending and receiving messages over the Internet, and designing new products. Productivity software enables a user to be "more productive."

program A set of instructions to be executed by a computer; types of programs include applications and operating systems

prompt A symbol, character or phrase that appears on-screen to inform the user that the computer is ready to accept input

proprietary software Software owned by an individual or business that cannot be used or copied without permission

protocol A set of rules and procedures for exchanging information between network devices and computers

Public access network (PAN) A wide-area network operated and maintained by a large company, such as AT&T, MCI, and US Sprint that provides voice and data communications capabilities to customers for a fee

pull-down menu (submenu) A menu containing various lower-level options associated with main menu options

query A request for information from a database management system

Query by Example (QBE) A standard for querying, or asking for particular information from, a database management

random-access memory (RAM) A computer chip or group of chips containing the temporary, or volatile, memory in which programs and data are stored while being used by a computer

read-only memory (ROM) A computer chip on the motherboard of a computer containing permanent, or nonvolatile, memory that stores instructions

record In a table created by a database management system application, a row providing information about one entity, such as an individual or organization

recordable Capable of having files of information stored on, or written to

regional ISP An Internet service provider that serves one or more states

register A component of the ALU that temporarily holds instructions and data

relational database A type of database in which various tables can be linked (or related) in a way that allows you to retrieve data from more than one table. Linking tables is accomplished by designing tables so that they have a common data field, such as a product number.

repeater A specially designed electronic device that receives signals along a network, amplify the signals, and send the amplified signals along the network. Thus, a repeater works similarly to an amplifier in a home stereo system.

resolution A measurement of the sharpness of an image displayed on a computer monitor or other output device; resolution is measured in dots per inch (dpi), both vertically and horizontally, with higher resolution achieved by more dots per inch

rewritable Capable of having files of information stored on and overwritten, or restored

ring topology A network topology in which there is no host computer and each computer or workstation is connected to two other computers. Communications are passed in one direction from the source computer to the destination. If one computer isn't working, that computer is bypassed.

router An electronic device typically used in large networks, including the Internet, to assure that messages are sent to their intended destinations. When a router along a message's destination receives a message, it sends the message along the route to the next router, and so on, until the message reaches its final destination.

run-time version A limited version of a supporting program that's bundled with an application program.

An example is an early version of Microsoft's Excel that included a version of Microsoft Windows for those users who didn't yet have Windows.

saving The process of storing a copy of the displayed document to a secondary storage medium such as a floppy disk or hard disk. Once saved, a document (or portion of a document) can be retrieved and reused. Saving a document requires specifying the drive and assigning the document a file name.

scroll bar Rectangular bars at the side or bottom of a window that enable a user to see and work with other portions of the document. Small arrows at the tips of a scroll bar can be used to move horizontally or vertically to display other portions of a document. A small box between the two arrows can also be used to scroll through a document or application by dragging the box until the desired part of a document is displayed in the window.

search engine A software program that enables you to search for, locate, and retrieve specific information on the Internet about any topic

secondary storage (auxiliary storage or external storage) Hardware devices and media that enable the permanent storage of important information such as computer programs, files, and data and that allow the stored data to be reentered and reused

secondary storage External, nonvolatile storage, such as disk storage, that stores program instructions and data even after the user switches off the power

sector A numbered section or portion of a disk similar to a slice of pie on which programs, data, and information is stored

sequential access A storage technology whereby stored data can be retrieved only in the order in which it is physically stored, just as musical selections on a cassette tape are recorded and accessed one after the other

serial port (communications [COM] port) A port (opening) for connecting devices such as the keyboard, mouse, and modem to a computer. Serial ports transmit data one bit at a time.

serial transmission A data transmission method in which all the bits (0s and 1s) that comprise the data are transmitted one bit after another in a continuous line

server A computer and its associated storage devices that are accessed remotely over a network by users

Simple Mail Transfer Protocol (SMTP) A communications protocol installed on the ISPs or online service's mail server that determines how each message is to be routed through the Internet and then sends the message

simplex transmission A directional protocol that allows transmissions to flow in only one direction; that is, messages can be either sent or received but not both

site license A contract that allows an organization to load or use copies of a piece of software on a specified maximum number of machines

slide A document created using presentation graphics software that may contain text, graphics, images, sound, and other elements that can help capture and hold an audience's attention.

slide show A group of slides comprise a presentation. A slide show may include any number of individual slides.

smart card A plastic card resembling a credit card embedded with a computer chip onto which owner information is permanently encoded

soft copy A temporary version of output, typically the display of data on a computer screen

software engineer Person whose profession is to design and build computer programs

software piracy The act of copying or using a piece of software without the legal right to do so

software Programs containing instructions that direct the operation of the computer system and the written documentation that explains how to use the programs. Two main types of software are system software and application software.

software suite A combination of applications programs bundled as a single package. A software suite may contain applications such as word processing, spreadsheet, database, and possibly other programs.

sort A feature of many application programs, such as word processing programs and database management systems, that enables the user to organize selected information in a particular way, as, for example, alphabetically or by date

speaker-dependent program A particular speech recognition program whereby the computer captures and stores your own voice as you speak words slowly and clearly into the microphone

speaker-independent program A particular speech recognition program that contains a built-in vocabulary of prerecorded word patterns. The computer can recognize only spoken words that match a word contained in the built-in list of vocabulary words

speakers Computer devices that produce warning sounds to alert the user to errors or other matters that require attention and, with a computer equipped a powerful sound card like Creative Labs' Sound Blaster Pro can output high-quality sound from CD-ROMs, MIDI keyboards, or the Internet. Applications for which speakers are particularly important include computer games, multimedia distance learning programs, audio e-mail, and videoconferencing.

special-function keyboard A type of keyboard designed for specific applications involving simplified, rapid data input. For example, cash registers in most fast-food restaurants are equipped with special-function keyboards.

speech recognition (voice recognition) A computer system's capability to recognize and capture spoken words using a speech recognition program

spelling checker A part of a program or a standalone application that automatically searches for spelling errors and suggests correctly spelled alternatives

spreadsheet An application program used primarily for financial analyses and record keeping, resembling on the screen the paper with rows and columns used by accountants

star topology A network topology in which multiple computers and peripheral devices are linked to a central computer, called a *host*, in a point-to-point configuration

storage device A hardware component that houses a secondary storage medium

storage medium A medium, such as magnetic disk or magnetic tape, on which data is recorded (stored), similar to the way a VCR is used for recording a television program on the tape inside a cassette

storage register Special areas of main memory used to store program instructions being executed and data being processed

storing The activity of permanently saving instructions and data for future use

Structured Query Language (SQL) A standard for querying, or asking for particular information from, a database management system

style sheet A predefined set of formats, such as right-justified, 10-point Helvetica bold italic with 12-point leading, that can be automatically applied to selected text

stylus A sharp, pointed instrument used for writing or marking

supercomputer Fastest, most powerful, and most expensive type of computer designed for multiple users

SuperDisk drive A high-capacity storage device manufactured by Iomega Corporation

synchronous transmission A transmission method that provides a fast and efficient way of sending data in which blocks of bytes are wrapped in start and stop bytes called synch bytes

system clock A small electronic chip inside a computer that synchronizes or controls the timing of all computer operations. The clock generates evenly spaced pulses that synchronize the flow of information through the computer's internal communications channels.

system software A type of software that consists of a set of programs that control the operations of a computer system, including the computer itself and all components and devices that comprise the computer system. System software performs a number of functions including starting the computer, processing applications, formatting disks, copying files, and enabling the program you are using, such as a word processor program, to work smoothly with your computer. System software serves as the interface between the user, the user's application software, and the computer's hardware.

system unit The main part of a personal computer system that contains the motherboard and other components necessary for processing information

systems analyst Person whose profession is to study and evaluate computer operations and procedures used to accomplish specific goals

Systems Network Architecture (SNA) A networking program that uses a polling protocol for transmitting data. Workstations are asked one by one if they have a message to transmit. A "yes" response allows the message to be sent, and then the next workstation is polled.

T line A permanent connection between two points set up by a telephone company and typically leased by a business to connect geographically distant offices. A leased "T" line is always active and dedicated for use only by the leasing business that pays a monthly fee for use of the line.

T1 line A high speed telephone line that allows for both voice and data transmission and can carry data at a speed of 1.544 megabits per second
T3 line A high speed telephone line capable of carrying data at speeds of up to 44.7 megabits per second

tab A subset of options, each of which is labeled as if it were a manila folder within a file drawer. The name of the subset of options is displayed in a tab at the top of the "folder." Clicking on the tab brings the particular group of options to the front of the dialog box.

tape cartridge A secondary storage technology used with personal computers mainly for backing up the contents of a hard drive. The tape is housed in a small plastic container (the cartridge) that also contains a tape reel and a take-up reel.

tape drive A device that records and reads data to and from a reel of magnetic tape. Many large businesses and organizations use this sequential-access storage medium for backing up important programs and data.

telecommunications The combined use of computer hardware and communications software for sending and receiving information over communications media, including phone lines and other types of media

telecommuting An Internet application that enables workers to perform their work activities at home instead of at the workplace by using their computers, communications software, and a telephone line

template A previously created and stored form

terabyte A unit of memory measurement equal to approximately 1 trillion bytes

terminal An input/output device, consisting of a keyboard and monitor, typically used with multi-user computer systems

text box A type of dialog box used for typing information that will allow the computer to continue or complete a task

time-sharing A system by means of which several users are allowed to access and work with a computer system by rationing time to users who are connected simultaneously

title bar A rectangular area at the top of a window in which the window's name is displayed

token ring protocol A type of protocol that sends an electronic signal, called a *token*, carrying both an address and a message around a token ring network quickly

toolbar A type of menu on which sets of icons are displayed that represent actions unique to the software and ones frequently employed by users. The number and kinds of icons often vary among programs and among different versions of the same program.

touch pad An input device available with many portable computers that enables a user to enter data and make selections by moving a finger across the pad. A touch pad has two parts: one part acts as a button, while the other functions like the smooth surface of a mouse pad on which the user traces in the direction he wants the cursor to move on the screen.

touch screen An input device that allows the user to choose options by pressing a finger (or fingers) on the appropriate part of the screen. Touch screens are widely used in bank ATMs and in kiosks at retail outlets.

trace Electrical pathway etched onto a motherboard that connects internal computer components

track A numbered concentric circle on a magnetic disk, or groups of lines along the length of magnetic tape, along which programs and data are stored

trackball An input device consisting of a plastic sphere sitting on rollers, inset in a small external case, or in many portable computers, in the same unit as the keyboard. The user moves the ball with her fingers or palm to position an on-screen cursor.

Transmission Control Protocol/Internet Protocol (TCP/IP) A communications protocol used to define the technique of packet switching on the Internet. The *TCP* portion divides the information into packets and then numbers each packet so that the message can be reconstructed at the receiving end. The IP portion sends each packet on its way by specifying the *IP* address of both the sending and receiving computers so that the packets can be routed to the correct computer.

Turing test An experiment proposed by Alan Turing and originally called The Imitation Game whereby a human being interacts with an entity in a closed room, asking questions and receiving responses, and must determine whether the entity is human or a computer

twisted-pair cable A communications medium consisting of two independently insulated wires twisted around one another. One of the wires carries the information while the other wire is grounded and absorbs any interference that may be present on the line.

Uniform Resource Locator (URL) An Internet address

Uniform Resource Locator (URL) An Internet address for the site a user wants to visit

Universal Product Code (UPC) A type of code printed on products and packages consisting of lines and spaces that a computer translates into a number.

The computer then uses this number to find information about the product or package, such as its name and price, in a computerized database.

Universal Serial Bus (USB) port A type of port that is widely used for connecting high-speed modems, scanners, and digital cameras to a computer. A single USB port can accommodate several peripheral devices connected together in sequence.

UNIX An operating system developed by programmers at Bell Laboratories originally designed for large computer systems including minicomputers, mainframes, and supercomputers

user interface A set of instructions that allow the software to communicate with the user and, in turn, the user to communicate with the software. The manner in which the user enters data and commands and in which information and processing options are presented is controlled by the program's interface.

utility program A type of program that performs a specific and helpful task, such as checking for viruses, uninstalling programs, and deleting data no longer needed

utility software Programs that perform specific tasks, such as managing a monitor, disk drives, printers, and other devices. In addition to utility software that is included with the operating system, a separate utility program, such as an antivirus program, can be installed in a computer.

value Data, such as a number, entered into a specific cell in a spreadsheet program

value added network (VAN) A network in which a business uses the facilities of large communications companies to provide subscribers with additional services, such as providing subscribers with access to various network databases, electronic mail, and online advertising and shopping.

video capture card An add-on card which, when inserted in an expansion slot, converts an analog video signal into a digital signal

video input An input technology that occurs by using a special type of video camera attached to the computer and plugged into a video capture card in an expansion slot, which converts analog video signals into digital signals

video port A port (connection) for connecting a monitor to the system unit. The port may be built into the computer's system unit or provided by a video card placed in an expansion slot

virtual age A term applied to the present era in which computers and their ability to simulate reality are the dominant economic force

Virtual private network (VPN) A special type of wide area network (WAN) whereby a company has each branch office set up a local Internet connection through which company networking traffic is routed

vision-input system A type of input technology that enables users to see, and avoid, obstacles that may be in their pathway

volatile memory A type of computer memory whereby stored instructions and data are lost if the power is switched off

warm boot Process of restarting a computer while power is on; clears the memory and reloads the operating system

Web appliance A simplified computer device that connects the user to the Internet, where programs and other applications are available at Web site; Web appliances do not store and run programs themselves

Web page An electronic document stored at a location of the Web. The document can contain text, images, sound and video and may provide links to other Web pages.

Webtop Technology that allows individuals and businesses to lease and access software through a Web browser

wide area network (WAN) A network that spans a large geographical area

Windows 2000 Professional A Microsoft operating system designed for use with business desktop and notebook computers and containing the power as well as many of the features of the earlier Windows NT

Windows 2000 Server A Windows-based operating system specifically designed to be used on a network server

Windows 3.x The first versions of Microsoft's Windows operating systems, including Windows 3.0, 3.2, and 3.11

Windows 95 The release of the Microsoft Windows operating system that followed Windows 3.11, and offered Internet access and a new interface

Windows 98 An upgrade of the earlier Windows 95 operating system that offered improved Internet access

Windows CE An operating system, similar in appearance to the Windows 98 operating system, used for personal digital assistants or handheld PCs

Windows Millenium Edition (ME) A 1999 version of Microsoft Windows designed for users of less powerful PCs, such as those found in homes and small businesses.

Windows NT A powerful operating system, released in 1993, and designed for executing large applications in networked environments

Wireless Application Protocol (WAP) A protocol commonly used with low-bandwidth, wireless systems, such as cell phone networks

Wireless Markup Language A standardized language included in the Wireless Application Protocol (WAP) that converts an HTML-coded page to Wireless Markup Language (WML), removes the graphics, and then sends the text to the wireless device, such as a PDA, where it is displayed on the device's screen.

wizard An application or part of an application that guides the user, step-by-step, through the completion of a task or that anticipates what a user might want to do and performs all or part of a task automatically

word processing A productivity that refers to the use of a computer and a word processing program to create, edit, manipulate, format, store, and print a variety of documents, including letters, memos, announcements, and brochures.

World Wide Web (the Web) A global system of linked computer networks that allows users to jump from one place on the Web to another place on the Web. It is a retrieval system based on technologies that organize information into Web pages that can be accessed and displayed on a computer screen.

WORM (write once, read many) disk A type of optical laser disk that provides very high capacity storage that is often used by companies to store huge amounts of data, particularly images

Zip® drive A high-capacity floppy disk manufactured by Iomega Corporation

INDEX

A

Abilene backbone, D-51
Active Desktop, C-20
Add-in boards, B-9
Add-on boards, B-9
Addresses, A-25, B-32
Adobe, C-27
Advanced Research Projects Agency (ARPA), A-8
Africa ONE, A-26
Age of Empires II, D-38
AIBO (electronic dog), C-4
Allen, Paul, C-12
Alta Vista, C-45, D-46
America Online (AOL), D-20, D-24, D-42
Americans with Disabilities Act, A-15
Amplifiers, D-27
Analog, B-20
Analog signal, D-6
Ananova, C-49
AND, A-22
Antarctica, meteor hunting in, B-15
Apple Computer, B-28
  iMac computers, B-28
  Lisa, C-9. *See also* Macintosh
Applets, C-29
Application service providers (ASPs), C-49
Application software. *See* Productivity software
Aqua (interface), C-27
Arithmetic/logic unit (ALU), A-22–23
ARPANet, A-7–8
Artificial intelligence, A-19, A-28–29, C-49
ASCII (American Standard Code for Information Interchange), A-20
Asynchronous transmission, D-32
Atkinson, Bill, C-24
AT&T, D-20
Audio input, B-18
Auxiliary storage, B-29

B

Backgammon, D-38
Backward compatibility, B-37
Bandwidth, D-5–6, D-47
Bangalore (India), C-22

Banking
  and smart cards, B-41
  and video-input applications, B-20
Bar code readers, B-18
Bar codes. *See* Universal Product
  Codes
Baseband (coaxial cable), D-10
BASIC, C-12
Bejeweled, D-38
Bell Laboratories, C-27
Berners-Lee, Tim, A-6, A-9
Beta, C-27
Binary digits. *See* Bits
Binary number system, A-19–20
Biometric authentication devices,
  B-41
BIOS (basic input/output system),
  B-8
Biotechnology, A-5
Bitmap, B-17
Bits, A-19–20
Bits per second (bps), D-5
Bluetooth, Harald, C-45
Bluetooth wireless technology,
  C-45, D-23
Boeing Company, A-12
Book publishers, video-input appli-
  cations, B-20
Booting, C-5
Brandeis University, A-29
Bridges, D-28
Broadband (coaxial cable), D-10
Broadband medium, D-6
Browsers, A-9, C-45, D-30, D-43
  metabrowsers, D-45–46
Buffers, C-5–6
Bus, B-6, B-10, D-23
Bus bandwidth, B-10
Bus topology, D-23, D-25
Buttons, C-14
Bytes, A-20, A-25

C

Cable modem, D-10, D-43
Cache memory, B-8
Carnegie Mellon University, B-15
Carpal tunnel syndrome, B-14,
  B-15

Casio, C-26
CAVE (computer automatic virtual
  environment), D-4
CD-DVD, A-26
CD-R (compact disk, recordable),
  A-26, B-36
CD-ROM (compact disk, read-only
  memory), A-26, B-35–36
CD-ROM drives, B-36, C-25
CD-RW (compact disk, rewritable),
  A-26, B-37
CD-RW drives, B-37
CD writers, B-36
Cell, C-38, D-14
Cellular communications technol-
  ogy, D-14–15
Cellular phones, C-29
Central processing unit (CPU), A-
  21–23
  CPU chip, B-6
CERN, A-6
Charts/charting, C-38
Chat rooms, A-11, D-38
Check boxes, C-17
Client, D-17
Client/server architecture, D-17
Clip art, C-43
Clock cycle, A-23
Clock speed, B-7
Cluster, B-30
Coaxial cable, D-10
COBOL, C-31
Cold boot, C-5
Command-line interfaces, C-8,
  C-28
Communications (COM) ports, B-9
Communications hardware,
  D-27–29
Communications media
  wire media, D-9–11
  wire vs. wireless, D-8–9
  wireless media, D-11, D-13–16
Communications medium, D-8
Communications protocols
  asynchronous vs. synchronous
  transmission,
    D-32–33
  directional, D-31–32
  e-mail, D-34

Internet and Web, D-33–34
LANs, D-33
standards, concerns regarding, D-47
WANs, D-33
wireless application, D-34
Communications satellite, D-13. *See also* Satellite communications systems
Communications software, C-44–45, D-29–34
Compaq, C-26, C-45
Compilers, C-32
Computer network technicians, D-49
Computer programmers, A-7
Computer security engineers, C-47
Computer viruses. *See* Viruses
Computers, A-14
    categories of, A-16
    central processing unit, A-20–23
    computer systems, A-14
    data representation, A-19–20
    future of, A-28–29
    how computers work, A-19–23
    information processing cycle, A-13
    and the Internet, A-7, A-12–13. *See also* Personal computers; Storage; Viruses
Concentrators, D-29
Context sensitive, C-18
Continuous waves, D-6
Control unit, A-21–22
Conversation speech biometrics, C-48
Coprocessor, B-37
Copyright, D-48
Copyright infringement on the Internet, D-48
Corel, C-28
    Paradox, C-38
    Presentations, C-43
    Quattro Pro, C-37
    WordPerfect, C-34
    WordPerfect Office, C-46
CP/M (Control Program for Microcomputers), C-8
CPU. *See* Central processing unit
Creating text, C-34
Creative Labs Sound Blaster Pro, B-29

Credit records and embedded computers, A-28
Cross-platform OS, C-28
CRT (cathode ray tube) monitors, B-22

D

Data, A-13
Data register, A-23
Data transmission
    analog vs. digital, D-6–7
    bandwidth, D-5–6
    serial vs. parallel, D-8
Database, B-18, C-39
Database management software, C-38–42
Database management system (DBMS), C-40–41
Dataquest, B-40
Decoding, A-22
Default option, C-11
Dell, Michael, B-12
Dell Computer Corporation, B-12, C-45
Desktop, C-14
Desktop computers, A-17
Desktop publishing (DTP), C-45
Dial-up access, D-42
Dialog boxes, C-14–18
DigiScents, B-41
Digital, B-20
Digital cameras, B-20–21
Digital Millennium Copyright Act of 1998, D-48
Digitizing pens, B-16
Direct access, B-29
Disk, B-30
Disk drive, A-15
Disk packs, B-37
Disk server, D-18
Diskette, B-30
Display, A-16
Display goggles, B-23
Display screens, B-22
Display windows, C-14
Distance learning via Internet, A-11, A-29, D-39–40
DNA sequence, A-19

Docking stations, B-9
Document formatting, C-36
Domain name, D-44
Domain suffixes, D-44–45
DOS (Disk Operating System), C-8
  and OS/2 Warp, C-27
  and Windows NT, C-22
  and Windows 3.x, C-19
  and Windows 95, C-20
Dot-matrix printers, B-23, B-25
Dots per inch (dpi), B-17
Download, A-11
Dragon *Naturally Speaking*, B-19
Draper Laboratory, A-23
Drawing tablets, B-16
Drivers, C-7
Driving records
  and embedded computers, A-28
  and smart cards, B-41
DSL (Digital Subscriber Line)
  modems, D-43
Dumb scanners, B-17
Dumb terminals, A-18
DVD-ROM (digital video disk-
  ROM), B-37
DVD-ROM drives or players, B-
  37, C-20–21, C-25

E

e-commerce
  and the Internet, A-11, D-40
  privacy issues, D-47
  security issues, D-47–48
e-mail, A-5, A-11, D-37
  communications protocols, D-34
  corporate communications and
    censorship, D-13
  privacy issues, D-47
  software, D-30
Earth stations, D-13
Eastman Kodak, B-21
EBCDIC (Extended Binary Coded
  Decimal Interchange Code), A-20
Editing text, C-34
Electromagnetic, D-11
Electronic bulletin board system
  (BBS), D-40

Electronic commerce. *See* e-com-
  merce
Electronic Data Systems
  Corporation, D-21
Electronic devices, A-19
Electronic mail. *See* e-mail
Electronic spreadsheets. *See*
  Spreadsheets
Ellison, Larry, D-12
Embedded computers, A-28, B-4
Embedded files, C-46
Employment
  computer network technicians,
    D-49
  computer-related job statistics,
    A-7, A-27
  computer security engineers,
    C-47
  India's Silicon Valley, C-22
  information technology industry,
    career clusters, A-5
  online job searches, B-39
  Webmasters, D-15
Encyclopedia Britannica 2001, B-36
Enquire, A-6
Entertainment via Internet, A-11,
  D-38
Ericsson, C-45
eRoom Technology Inc., D-4
eRoom 5.0, D-4
Ethernet, D-33
Ethics
  cyberwarfare, C-46
  digital divide in U.S. society, D-9
  e-mail corporate communications
    and censorship, D-13
  elections and vote buying on the
    Web, B-10
  telecommunications equipment
    locations, A-26
  the Web and access for disabled
    people, A-15
Excite, C-45, D-46
Executing, A-22
Execution time (E-time), A-22
Expansion boards, B-9
Expansion slots, B-5, B-9

eXtensible Markup Language
(XML), D-44
External storage, B-29
Extranets, D-22–23

F

Face recognition hardware, B-41
Federal Express, B-18
Fetching, A-22
Fiber Distributed Data Interface
(FDDI), D-33
Fiber-optic cable, D-10
Fields, C-39
File compression program, C-31
File manager, C-7
File server, D-18
File specification, D-45
File Transfer Protocol (FTP), D-38
File transfers and the Internet,
D-38
Find, C-42
Fingerprint recognition hardware,
B-41
Firewall, D-21
Flat-panel displays, B-23
Floppy disks and drives, A-24, A-26
comparison to hard disks, B-34
formatting, B-32
handling and storing, B-33
HiFD disk drive, B-31
storage capacities, B-31
SuperDisk drive, B-31
uses, B-32
Zip disks and drive, A-26, B-31
Food and embedded computers,
A-28
Foot mouse, B-14
Footer, C-35
Form, C-39
Formatting
disks, B-32
text, C-35–36
Formulas, C-37, C-38
Freeware, C-47
Frequency range, D-6
Full-duplex transmission, D-31–32
Fuzzy logic, C-49

G

Gates, Melinda, C-12
Gates, William (Bill) H., A-12,
C-12
Gateways, D-28
Geosynchronous orbit, D-13
Gigabytes (GB), A-25
Gigahertz (GHz), A-23
Girl Tech, A-27
Global communications
Africa ONE, A-26
Mongolia, B-9
The People's Republic of China,
A-17
Global community and the
Internet, A-4
Global Crossing, A-26
Google, C-45, D-46
Grammar checker, C-34
Graphical user interfaces (GUIs),
A-9, C-9
dialog boxes, C-14–18
display windows, C-14
how they work, C-10
menus of options for key features,
C-10–11, C-13
on-screen desktop, C-14
online help, C-18
Graphics, A-15
Graphics cards, B-9
Graphics tablets, B-16
Grid, C-38
Grid computing, D-6
Groupware, D-30

H

Half-duplex transmission, D-31
Handheld computers, A-17, C-29
Handheld scanners, B-16
Handouts, C-43
Handspring Visor, B-16, C-26
Hard copy, B-22
Hard disks and drives, A-24, A-26,
B-33–34
Hardware, A-15, B-4
communications hardware and
networks,
D-27–29

future developments and trends, B-40–41

large computer hardware, B-37–39

storage devices, B-4, B-29

system unit devices, B-5–10

types of devices, B-4. *See also* Input devices; Output devices

Hasselblad, B-21

Header, C-35

Help (online), C-18

Hertz (Hz), A-23

Hewlett-Packard, C-26, C-27, C-28

HiFD (High-Capacity FD) disk drive, B-31

High-level languages, C-31

Higher-capacity floppy disks, B-31

Hodlee.com, D-46

Home page, D-43

Host, D-25

HotBot, D-46

HTML (Hypertext Markup Language), A-6, A-9, D-43–44

HTTP (Hypertext Transfer Protocol), A-6, A-10, D-34

Hubs, D-27

Hybrid topologies, D-26–27

Hypercard, C-24

HyperTalk scripting language, C-24

Hypertext, C-24

Hypertext documents, A-9

I

"I Love You" virus, D-49

IBM

DB2 Intelligent Miner for Data, C-49

OS/2, C-19, C-27

Via Voice, B-19

IBM Corporation, C-27, C-28, C-45, C-48

Icons, B-13, C-10

IDC (computer industry research firm), D-37

iMac computers, B-28

Impact printers, B-23

India's Silicon Valley, C-22

Information, A-13

Information processing cycle, A-13

Information retrieval via Internet, A-11, D-38

Information technology industry, career clusters, A-5

Informedia Digital Video Library (IDVL) project, D-51

Infoseek, C-45, D-46

InfoWorld magazine, D-38

Infrared, A-5, D-16

Infrared communications technology, D-16

Ink-jet printers, B-25–26

Input, A-13

Input devices, A-13, B-4, B-10

audio input devices, B-18–19

bar code readers, B-18

digital cameras, B-20–21

graphics tablets, B-16

joysticks, B-15

keyboards, B-11

mouse, B-13–14

optical scanners, B-16–17

pens and tablets, B-16

point-and-click devices, B-13–16

speech recognition, B-19

touch pads, B-14–15

touch screens, B-15

trackballs, B-14

video input devices, B-19–21

voice recognition, B-19

Instant messaging, D-24

Instruction register, A-22–23

Instruction time (I-time), A-22

Insurance records and smart cards, B-41

Integrated circuits, B-24

Intel Corporation, C-45

Celeron processor, B-7

cofounder, A-28

and Linux, C-28

Pentium 4 processor, B-7

500 MHz Celeron processor, B-7

80286 processor, B-7

Intelligent scanners, B-17

Interface, B-13

Interference, D-9

International Standards Organization (ISO), D-31

Internet Corporation for Assigned Names and Numbers (ICANN), D-45

Internet Explorer, C-20, C-25, C-26, C-45, D-44

Internet service provider (ISP), D-41–42

Internet (the Net), A-7, D-34–49
  access, via Windows software, C-20, C-25
  biometric authentication devices, B-41
  communications protocols, D-33–34
  and computers, A-7, A-12–13
  connecting to, D-41–46
  copyright infringement, D-48
  cyberwarfare, C-46
  and daily life, A-5
  digital divide in U.S. society, D-9
  future of, A-29, D-50–51
  global community of, A-4
  history of, A-7–9
  information transmission procedures, A-10–11
  instant access, A-29
  instant messaging, D-24
  and Mongolia, B-9
  and Native Americans, D-19
  navigational skills and employment requirements, A-7
  networking, D-4
  networking concerns, D-47–49
  and The People's Republic of China, A-17
  productivity applications, renting or leasing, C-49
  satellite network and high-speed access, A-12
  size of, A-5
  skeletal framework, A-12
  and smart cards, B-40–41
  and supercomputing, D-6
  and UNIX, C-28
  using the Net, A-5, A-11, D-37
  virus transmission, D-49. *See also* World Wide Web (the Web)

Internet2, D-50–51

Interpreters, C-32

Intranets, D-21–22

Iomega Corporation, B-33

ISDN (Internet services digital network) lines, D-11, D-43

iSmell, B-41

J

Java, C-29, C-31

Java Jacket, B-7

Java technology, C-29

Java virtual machine, C-29

Jaz® cartridge, B-33

Jobs, Steven, B-28

Joysticks, B-15

K

Kerning, C-35

Keyboards, A-13, A-15, B-11, C-7

Kilby, Jack, B-24

Kilobytes (K), A-25

L

Labor Department (U.S.)
  computer-related job statistics, A-7, A-27

Language translators, C-31–32

Laptop computers, A-17

Large computer systems, B-37–39, C-27

Laser printers, B-26–27

Leading, C-35

Links, A-9
  Active Desktop, C-20
  database programs, C-42
  OLE, C-46

Linux, C-28

Local area networks (LANs), D-18, D-33

Local ISP, D-42

Los Angeles bus system, signal-timing technology, C-19

Lotus
  Approach, C-38
  1-2-3, C-37
  SmartSuite, C-46

Lucent Technologies, A-26, B-39, C-45
Lycos, C-45, D-46

M

Machine cycle, A-21–22
Machine language, C-31
Macintosh
  and applets, C-29
  graphical user interfaces, A-9, C-9
  and Linux, C-28
  Mac OS, A-16, C-9, C-19, C-26–27
  Mac OS X, C-27
  Mac OS 9, C-27
  operating system, A-16, C-19
  video input devices, B-20
MacPaint, C-24
Macros, C-38
Magnetic storage devices, B-29, B-40
Magnetic tape storage, B-38–39
Mail server, D-34
Main memory. *See* Random-access memory
Mainframe computers, A-8, A-16, A-18
Manufacturers and video-input applications, B-20
Marine Corps (U.S.), D-21
Massachusetts Institute of Technology (MIT), C-19
Math coprocessor, B-37
Matrix, B-25
Matsushita Electric Industrial Company, B-4
MA4-TC wearable computer, D-23
McAfee VirusScan, C-30
McCaw, Craig, A-12, C-12
MCI, D-20
Medical records
  and embedded computers, A-28
  and smart cards, B-41
Medium, D-4
Megabytes (MB), A-25
Megahertz (MHz), A-23
Memory, A-16

Memory chips, A-28
Menu bar, C-10
Menus, C-10
Metabrowser, D-45–46
Meteor hunting in Antarctica, B-15
Metropolitan area networks (MANs), D-20
Microprocessor, A-16
  component of motherboard, B-5
  future of, A-28
  speeds and capabilities, B-6–7
  using to grow organs for transplants, A-23
Microsoft
  Access, C-38
  Excel, C-37
  Office, C-45, C-46, C-47
  Outlook, D-37
  PowerPoint, C-43
  Publisher, C-45
  Word, C-11, C-13, C-17, C-34, C-45. *See also* Internet Explorer; Windows
Microsoft Corporation, C-12, C-27
Microsoft Network (MSN), D-24, D-42
Microwave transmission systems, D-11
MIDI (Musical Instrument Digital Interface) keyboards, B-29
Military
  records and embedded computers, A-28
  and video-input applications, B-20
Minicomputers, A-16, A-18
MITS Altair, C-12
Modems, A-14, D-6
  alternatives to telephone/modem connection, D-42–43
  cable modems, D-10, D-43
  and communications software, C-44
  DSL modems, D-43
  ISDN modems, D-11, D-43
Molecular storage, A-28, C-49
Mongolia and Internet access, B-9
Monitors, A-15, A-18
  CRTs (cathode ray tubes), B-22

display goggles, B-23
drivers, C-7
flat-panel displays, B-23
future of, B-40
Moore, Gordon, A-28
Moore's Law, A-28
Motherboards, B-5
 buses, B-10
 components, B-5–6
 expansion slots, B-9
 and microprocessor (*See* Microprocessor)
 ports, B-9
 and RAM (*See* Random-access memory)
 and ROM (*See* Read-only memory)
Motorola, C-45
Mouse, A-9, A-13, B-13–14
Mouse pad, B-14
Mouse pointer, B-13
Multimedia devices
 presentation software programs, C-43
 Windows ME, C-25
 Windows 98, C-20–21
Multiplexers, D-29
Multitasking, C-6
 display windows, C-14
 Windows CE, C-26
 Windows NT, C-22
 Windows 2000 Server, C-25
Multiuser OS, C-28

N

Nanorobots, A-29
Napster, D-38
Narrowband medium, D-6
NASA, B-15
National ISP, D-42
National Labor Relations Act (NLRA), 1935, D-13
National Science Foundation Network, A-8
National Tribal Telecommunications Association, D-19
Native Americans, phone service and Internet access, D-19

Natural-language processing (NLP), C-48
Navy (U.S.), D-21
Netscape Navigator, C-26, C-45, D-44
Network servers, A-18, C-25, C-29, D-17
Networks, A-5, A-12
 architecture, D-17–18
 classifications, D-16–23
 and communications hardware, D-27–29
 components, D-4
 computer network technicians, D-49
 coverage, D-18–23
 extranets, D-22–23
 Internet concerns, D-47–49
 intranets, D-21–22
 local area networks (LANs), D-18
 optical networks, D-50
 topologies, D-23, D-25–27
 users, D-20–23
 wide area networks (WANs), D-19–20
 and Windows 2000 Professional, C-23
Neural networks, C-49
NeXT Step operating system, A-6
Node, D-23
Nokia, C-45
Nomad and meteor hunting in Antarctica, B-15
Nonimpact printers, B-23
Nonvolatile memory, A-24
Norton
 Anti-Virus, C-30
 Utilities, C-30
NOT, A-22
Notebook computers, A-17, B-10
NSFnet, A-8
Number formatting, C-38

O

Object linking and embedding (OLE), C-46
Object-oriented programming, C-24
Octopus.com, D-46

Odigo, D-24
On-screen desktop, C-14
OnePage, D-46
Online, A-11
 courses, D-39
 discussions, A-11
 games, D-38
 job searches, B-39
 music, D-38
 service, D-42
 shopping, A-11, A-29, B-40–41,
  D-38
Open-source software, C-28
Open System Interconnection
 (OSI) model, D-31
Operating environments, C-19
Operating systems, A-9, A-15,
 C-4–5
 commonly used operating
  systems, C-6, C-19–23,
  C-25–29
 CP/M, C-8
 DOS, C-8
 PCs and Macintosh, A-16
Optical character recognition
 (OCR) software, B-17
Optical disks and drives, A-26,
 B-34
 advantages, B-35
 CD-R, A-26, B-36
 CD-ROM, A-26, B-35–36
 CD-RW, A-26, B-37
 DVD-ROM, B-37
 storage capacities, B-36
 WORM disks, B-39
Optical mouse, B-14
Optical networks, D-50
Optical scanners, B-16–17
Option buttons, C-17
OR, A-22
Oracle Corporation, D-12
Organ transplants and microchips,
 A-23
OS/2, C-19, C-27
OS/2 Warp, C-27
OSs. See Operating systems
Output, A-13, B-22
Output devices, B-4, B-22–23, B-
 25–27, B-29

P

Packets, A-10
Page scanners, B-16
PageMaker, C-45
Palm, Inc., C-26
Palm OS, C-26
PalmPilot, B-16, C-26
Palmtop computers, A-17
Paragraph formatting, C-35–36
Parallel ports, B-9
Parallel transmission, D-8
Parity bit, D-7, D-8, D-32
Pathname, D-45
Pattern recognition software,
 C-48–49
PC cards, B-10
PCs. See Personal computers
Peer-to-peer architecture, D-18
Pen computers, A-18
Pens and tablets, B-16
The People's Republic of China
 and Internet access, A-17
Performance monitor, C-8
Peripheral devices, A-15, A-24,
 B-9. See also Secondary (external)
 storage
Personal computer systems, A-14
Personal computers (PCs), A-7,
 A-16–18, B-4
 and applets, C-29
 hardware configurations, B-5
 storage capacity measurements,
  A-25
 video input devices, B-19–20.
  See also Operating systems
Personal digital assistants (PDAs),
 A-17–18, B-16, C-26
Pitch, D-6
Pixar, B-28
Pixels, B-17, B-21, B-22
Platform, C-19
 cross-platform OS, C-28
Platform for Privacy Preference
 (P3P), D-47
Plotters, B-27
Pocket calculators, B-24
Point-and-click devices, B-13–16
Pointers, B-15
Pointing levers, B-15
Polling protocol, D-33

POP server, D-34
Portable computers, A-17
Ports, B-5, B-9
Post Office Protocol (POP), D-34
Power interruptions
   and RAM, A-25, A-26
   and ROM, A-24
Power-on self test (POST), B-8
Power supply, B-6
Presentation graphics software,
   C-42–44
Print server, D-18
Print spooler/spooling, C-7
Printers, A-13
   dot-matrix printers, B-23, B-25
   ink-jet printers, B-25–26
   laser printers, B-26–27
Printing documents, C-37
Privacy issues, D-47
Processors, A-16, B-6
Proctor & Gamble, B-41
Productivity, D-41
Productivity software, A-15,
   C-32–47
   categories of, C-33
   communications, C-44–45
   database management, C-38–42
   desktop publishing (DTP), C-45
   presentation graphics, C-42–44
   renting or leasing, C-49
   spreadsheets, C-37–38
   word processors, C-33–37
   16-bit applications, C-19
   32-bit applications, C-19, C-20,
     C-22, C-26
   64-bit applications, C-19
Programs, A-13, C-4
Prompt, C-8
Proprietary software, C-47
Protocols. *See* Communications
   protocols
Public access networks (PANs), D-20
Pull-down menus, C-10–11, C-13

Q

QBE (Query by Example), C-42
QuarkXPress, C-45
Query, A-22, C-42
Quickbrowse, D-46

R

Radio buttons, C-17
Rainbow Six, D-38
RAM. *See* Random-access memory
Random access, A-25
Random-access memory (RAM),
   A-24–25, B-7
   and cache memory, B-8
   connecting sockets on mother-
     board, B-5
   managing, C-5–6, C-22
   measuring storage capacities, A-25
   and operating systems, C-5
Read-only memory (ROM), A-24,
   B-5, B-8, B-35
Readable, A-25
Real time, D-38
Recordable, B-36
Records, C-39
Red Hat, C-28
Regional ISP, D-42
Registers, A-22–23
Relational database, C-41
Repeaters, D-27
Reports, C-42
Resolution, B-17
Rewritable, B-36
Ring topology, D-25
Robots
   and daily life, A-28–29
   designing and building other
     robots, A-29
   Nomad and meteor hunting in
     Antarctica, B-15
ROM. *See* Read-only memory
Ronen, Avner, D-24
Ronen, Maskit, D-24
Routers, D-27–28
Run-time version, C-29

S

Satellite communications systems,
   A-12, D-13–14, D-43
Saving documents, C-37
Scandisk, C-29
Scanners, B-16–17
Scent-producing software, B-41
Scroll bars, C-14
Search engines, C-45, D-46

Secondary (external) storage, A-24, A-26, B-29. *See also* Storage
Sector, B-30
Security issues
  computer security engineers, C-47
  e-commerce, D-47–48
  security encryption systems, D-48
  smart cards, B-40–41
  video-input applications, B-20
Sequential access, B-29
Serial ports, B-9
Serial transmission, D-8
Servers. *See* Network servers
SETA (Search for Extraterrestrial Intelligence), D-6
Shareware, C-47
Silicon Alley (New York), D-24
Simplex transmission, D-31
Site license, C-47
Slides, C-43
Slideshows, C-42
Smart cards, B-40–41, C-29
SMTP (Simple Mail Transfer Protocol), D-34
Social security records and smart cards, B-41
Soft copy, B-22
Software, A-15, C-4–8
  native to platform, C-19
  proprietary vs. freeware/shareware, C-47
  user interfaces, C-8–11, C-13–18. *See also* Productivity software; System software
Software engineer, A-7, A-15
Software piracy, C-47
Software reviews, C-33
Software suites, C-46
Sony AIBO, C-4
Sort, C-41–42
Sort routine, C-30
Speaker-dependent programs, B-19
Speaker-independent programs, B-19
Speakers, B-29
Special-function keyboards, B-11
Speech recognition software, B-19, C-48
Spelling checker, C-34
Spreadsheets, A-13, C-37–38

SQL (Structured Query Language), C-42
Stacks, C-24
Star topology, D-25
Start bit, D-32
Stop bit, D-32
Storage, A-13
  devices, B-4, B-29
  disk packs, B-37
  floppy disks and drives, A-24, A-26, B-30–33
  hard disks and drives, A-24, A-26, B-33–34
  large computer systems, B-37–39
  magnetic storage devices, B-29, B-40
  magnetic storage media, B-29–34
  magnetic tape storage, B-38–39
  medium, B-29
  memory, A-24–25
  molecular storage, A-28
  optical disks and drives, B-34–37
  RAM, A-24–25
  registers, A-23
  ROM, A-24
  tape cartridges and drives, B-34
  WORM disks, B-39
Storing, A-22
Stuffit, C-31
Style sheet, C-36
Stylus, A-18
Submenu, C-10
Sun Microsystems, B-7, B-39, C-27
Supercomputers, A-8, A-16, A-19, C-29
Supercomputing, via the Internet, D-6
SuperDisk drive, B-31
Sutherland, Donald, B-7
Swanson, Janese, A-27
Synch bytes, D-33
Synchronous transmission, D-33
System clock, A-23, B-6
System software, A-15, C-4. *See also* Language translators; Operating systems
System unit devices, B-4, B-5–10
Systems analyst, A-7
Systems Network Architecture (SNA), D-33

T

T lines, D-11
T1 lines, D-11
T3 lines, D-11
Tabs, C-16
Tape cartridges and drives, B-34
TCP/IP (Transmission Control Protocol/Internet Protocol), A-10, D-34
Technical support, C-38
Telecommunications, D-4
Telecommunications equipment locations, A-26
Telecommuting, D-41
Teledesic, A-12, C-12
Telephone service and Native Americans, D-19
Templates, C-34, C-43
Terabytes (TB), A-19, A-25
Terminals, A-18
Texas Instruments, B-24
Text boxes, C-18
Text formatting, C-35
Time-sharing, C-28
Title bar, C-14
Token, D-33
Token ring protocol, D-33
Toolbars, B-13
Torvalds, Linus, C-28
Toshiba, C-45
Touch pads, B-14–15
Touch screens, B-15
Toy Story, B-28
Traces, B-5
Track, B-30
Trackballs, B-14
Traffic management
  and embedded computers, A-28
  Los Angeles bus system, signal-timing technology, C-19
Transceiver, D-23
Transponders, D-13
Turing, Alan, C-49
Turing Test, C-49
Twisted-pair cable, D-9

U

Uniform Resource Locators (URLs), A-6, A-10, D-44

United Nations, D-31
United Parcel Service (UPS), B-18
Universal Product Codes (UPCs), B-18
Universal Serial Bus (USB) ports, B-9, C-20–21
UNIX, C-27–28
UNIX X-Windows, C-19
US Sprint, D-20
User interfaces, C-8–11, C-13–18
Utility program, C-29
Utility software, A-15, C-29–31

V

Value added networks (VANs), D-20
Values, C-37
Video capture card, B-19
Video input devices, B-19–21
Video ports, B-9
Virtual age, A-9
Virtual private networks (VPNs), D-20
Viruses, A-15, C-30, D-49
Vision-input system, B-20
Visual BASIC, C-31
Voice commands, A-28
Voice recognition hardware, B-41
Voice recognition software, B-19
Volatile memory, A-24, A-25

W

Warm boot, C-5
Wearable computers, B-7, D-23
Web addresses, D-44–45
Web appliance, C-49
Web languages, D-43–44
Web pages, A-9, A-29, D-43
Web sites
  Ananova, C-49
  Internet2, D-51
  Java technology, C-29
  job searches, B-39
  Mac OS, C-9
  Northwest Center for Emerging Technologies, A-5
  shareware offerings, C-47
  software piracy, C-47
  software reviews, C-33
  technical support, C-38

Windows, C-21
Webmasters, D-15
Webtops, C-49
What-if calculations, C-37
What You See Is What You Get (WYSIWYG), A-6
Wide area networks (WANs), D-19–20, D-33
Windows
    and BASIC, C-31
    graphical user interfaces, A-9
    and Linux, C-28
    multitasking, C-6
    operating system for PCs, A-16
    and OS/2 Warp, C-27
    performance monitor, C-8
    Sound Recorder, B-18
    Start button, C-14
    Web site, C-21
Windows CE, C-26
Windows Explorer, C-7
Windows Millennium Edition (ME), C-25
Windows NT, C-22
Windows 3.x, C-19
Windows 95, C-20
Windows 98, C-20–21
Windows 2000 Professional, C-23, C-25
Windows 2000 Server, C-25
WinZip, C-31
Wire media
    coaxial cable, D-10
    fiber-optic cable, D-10
    ISDN lines, D-11, D-43
    T lines, D-11
    twisted-pair cable, D-9
Wireless Application Protocol (WAP), D-34, D-47
Wireless communications devices, C-26
Wireless communications media
    cellular technology, D-14–15
    infrared technology, D-16
    microwave transmission systems, D-11
    satellite systems, D-13–14, D-43
Wireless transmitting technology
    Bluetooth, C-45
    communications protocols, D-34
    future of, B-40

and personal digital assistants, A-18
Wizards, C-20, C-34, C-43
WML (Wireless Markup Language), D-34
Word processing, C-34
Word processors, C-33
    creating text, C-34
    editing text, C-34
    formatting text, C-35–36
    printing documents, C-36
    saving documents, C-36
World Wide Web Consortium (W3C), A-6, D-47
World Wide Web (the Web)
    addresses, D-44–45
    communications protocols, D-33–34
    cyberwarfare, C-46
    disabled people, access to, A-15
    elections and vote buying, B-10
    founder of, A-6, A-9
    future of, D-50–51
    history of, A-6, A-7–9
    instant access, A-29
    languages, D-43–44
    path of Web site request, D-45
    privacy issues, D-47
    search engines, D-46
    security protections, D-47.
        See also Browsers;
        Internet (the Net)
WORM (write once, read many) disks, B-39
Wozniak, Steve, B-28
Writable, A-25

X

Xerox Corporation, C-9
XML (eXtensible Markup Language), D-44
Xybernaut Corporation, D-23

Y

Yahoo!, C-45, D-24, D-46

Z

Zip disks and drive, A-26, B-31

CREDITS

CHAPTER 1

Page

A-3   Lee White/CORBIS
        Ronnen Eshel/ CORBIS
A-4   *(Clockwise)*
        Jim Sugar/ CORBIS
        Eye Ubiquitous/ CORBIS
        Layne Kennedy/ CORBIS
        Kevin Fleming/ CORBIS
        Ed Kashi/ CORBIS
A-6   Courtesy of A/P Wide World Photos
A-8   CORBIS
A-11   *(Left to right)*
        Dave G. Houser/ CORBIS
        Mark Gibson/ CORBIS
        Richard T. Nowitz/ CORBIS
A-12   PhotoDisc
A-14   Fig. 1-10 Brad Knefelkamp/Encore
A-15   *(Top to bottom)*
        AFP/CORBIS
        Bob Rowan/CORBIS
A-17   Fig. 1-11Courtesy of Hewlett Packard
        Fig. 1-12 Jose Pelaez/The Stock Market
        Fig. 1-13 CORBIS
        Donofrio Studios
A-18   Fig. 1-14 PocketScript™ Wireless Pad courtesy of
        PocketScript, Inc.
        Fig. 1-15 HP Netserver 1h 6000 courtesy of Hewlett Packard
        Fig. 1-16 CORBIS
        PhotoDisc
A-19   Cray SV1 courtesy of Cray, Inc.
A-22   Pentium 4 courtesy of Intel, Inc.
A-29   Roger Ressmayer/CORBIS
A-34   PhotoDisc

CHAPTER 2

Page

B-3   *(Top to bottom)*
        Alvin Henry/The Stock Market
        Dennis Degnan/CORBIS
B-4   SuperStock
B-5   Fig. 2-1 Brad Knefelkamp/Encore
B-6   Fig. 2-2A Brad Knefelkamp/Encore
        Fig. 2-2B Brad Knefelkamp/Encore

B-7   Fig. 2-3 Pentium 4 courtesy of Intel
B-8   Cray SV1 courtesy of Cray, Inc.
B-9   Fig. 2-4 Brad Knefelkamp/Encore
B-10   Fig. 2-5 56K Global GSM and Celluar
       Modem PC Card and the 56K Modem
       PC Card courtesy of U.S. Robotics
B-11   Fig. 2-6 Brad Knefelkamp/Encore
       Fig. 2-7 Bob Rowan/CORBIS
B-12   Reuters NewMedia Inc./CORBIS
B-13   Fig. 2-8 Brad Knefelkamp/Encore
B-14   Fig. 2-10 IntelliMouse® by permission
       of Microsoft Corporation
       Fig. 2-11 Expert Mouse® courtesy of
       Kensington Technology Group
       Fig. 2-12 n5195 courtesy of Hewlett
       Packard
B-15   Fig. 2-13 William Whitehurst/The Stock
       Market
       Fig. 2-14 Charles Gupton/The Stock
       Market
B-16   Fig. 2-15 Visor Delux courtesy of
       Handspring™
       Fig. 2-16 Intuos 12x18 courtesy of
       Wacom Technology
       Fig. 2-17 David Young Wolff/Tony Stone
       and Brad Knefelkamp/Encore
B-18   Fig. 2-19 Johnny Stockshooter/Index
       Stock Imagery
       Fig. 2-20 Brad Knefelkamp/Encore
B-19   Fig. 2-21 QuickCam® courtesy of
       Logitech
B-20   Fig. 2-23 Photo PC 3002 courtesy of
       Epson America
B-22   Fig. 2-25 Brad Knefelkamp/Encore
B-23   Jose Pelaez/The Stock Market
B-24   Roger Ressmeyer/CORBIS
B-25   Fig. 2-28 ML 591 courtesy of Okidata
B-26   Fig. 2-29 DeskJet 1220C courtesy of
       Hewlett Packard
B-27   Fig. 2-30 Phaser 750 courtesy of Xerox
       Fig. 2-31 Designjet 500PS courtesy of
       Hewlett Packard
B-28   Kashi/CORBIS
B-29   Fig. 2-32 Brad Knefelkamp/Encore
B-30   Fig. 2-33 Brad Knefelkamp/Encore
B-32   Fig. 2-35 Brad Knefelkamp/Encore
B-33   Fig. 2-38 Brad Knefelkamp/Encore
B-34   Fig. 2-39 Brad Knefelkamp/Encore

B-36   Fig. 2-41 Brad Knefelkamp/Encore
B-37   Fig. 2-42 SuperStock
B-41   (Top to bottom)
       PictureQuest/CORBIS
       Don Mason/The Stock Market

CHAPTER 3
Page
C-3   Cameron/The Stock Market
C-9   Courtesy of Apple Computers, Inc.
C-10   Brad Knefelkamp/Encore
C-12   Peter Tunley/CORBIS
C-24   Courtesy of Apple Computers, Inc.
C-26   (Top: left to right)
       Fig. 3-26 PhotoDisc
       PhotoDisc
       CORBIS
C-27   Fig. 3-29 Netserver 1h 6000 courtesy of
       Hewlett Packard
C-28   Oracle Enterprise Manager courtesy of
       Oracle
C-32   Rob Levine/The Stock Market, Inc.
C-45   Archivo Incono Grafico, SA/CORBIS
C-48   The Stock Market
C-49   Fig. 3-46 Audrey™ courtesy of 3Com
       Corporation

CHAPTER 4
Page
D-3   (Top to bottom)
       PhotoDisc
       CORBIS
D-12   Reuters NewMedia, Inc./CORBIS
D-23   Eyewire
D-27   Fig. 4-21 56K External Voice Faxmodem
       courtesy of U.S. Robotics
       600 675 Residential adsl Router (NS)
       courtesy of Cisco Systems
       1500 Hub courtesy of Cisco Systems
       Fig. 4-22 Cisco Catalyst 2900 X1 Switch
       courtesy of Cisco Systems
D-29   Fig. 4-24 Cisco 6920 RateMox
       Multiplexer courtesy of Cisco Systems
D-30   Eyewire
D-39   Paul Barton/The Stock Market
D-50   D. Boone/CORBIS